D0090311

A MINISTERING CHURCH

A MINISTERING CHURCH

Gaines S. Dobbins

BROADMAN PRESS
Nashville, Tennessee

To

ELLIS ADAMS FULLER

who exemplified in high measure
the qualities of a good minister of Jesus Christ

Library of Congress catalog card number: 60–9530
Printed in the United States of America
5.N59K.S.P.

Preface

TODAY'S CHURCH PRESENTS a puzzling picture to many ministers and members. What is the church, and what is it for? History records the long and often painful evolution of the church from its primitive beginnings in the apostolic age to its present complexity. Theology undertakes to present the many-sided doctrinal aspects of the church. Ecclesiology deals with the science of church organization and management. Sociology takes account of the church as a significant social institution. Psychology recognizes the church as an important factor in the study of human behavior. Education includes the church as an institution of learning. Economics recognizes the church as a potent influence in business, industry, and politics.

The word "church" employed thus is used in the generic sense, as the family, the school, the state. The immediate, everyday concern of most ministers and church members is not for the abstraction, however, but for the concrete reality, a church as a local body of baptized believers. What shall be its pattern? To what extent shall it be shaped by New Testament teaching and example and to what extent by tradition and expediency? Granting that its organization and methods must respond to the pressure of need and opportunity and that conditions today are vastly different from those of past eras, what ministries must a church perform and through the services of what kind of ministers?

The new order calls for a rethinking of the qualifications and functions of Christian ministers. What shall be said about the apparent clash of demands on the minister as preacher, pastor, teacher, counselor, administrator? With church membership in America at an

v

all-time high and churches inevitably growing numerically larger, a multiple ministry becomes an increasing necessity. Specialization raises many problems concerning the church staff. These problems must be faced in the light of New Testament principles and tested administrative practice. A new world is opened up in the study of the administrative process as worthy of the best thought of which ministers and members are capable. Leadership is no longer to be thought of as limited to the church staff and church-elected officers, but as the total church membership implementing the ideal of servantship. The business of the church staff—or of the minister aided by trained volunteers—is to develop a serving church in which every member has a place of usefulness. Admittedly this is a tremendous undertaking, but it recovers the meaningfulness of the church as an institution of primary importance in a culture in which the individual is in danger of being lost.

The picture of the active minister preaching on Sunday morning to a passive congregation gives way to that of an active congregation inspired and led by the preacher-administrator and his fellow ministers and co-workers serving together to carry out the full commission of Jesus Christ through a dynamic church related to other like-minded churches in a program of world Christianization. Such a church will not get lost in the clouds but with practical idealism will teach and train, worship and work, serve and sacrifice, comfort and counsel, motivated in all it does by Christian love and with the winning of others to Christ as its supreme objective. In a world growing almost overwhelmingly large with increasing numbers of people and their problems, such a church must not be little and cannot live in isolation but must recognize itself as having inescapable relationships with other bodies and institutions which it can claim as allies and with which it can co-operate without compromise.

Grateful acknowledgment is made of permission to use quoted materials from copyrighted sources. Unless otherwise indicated, Scripture quotations are *from the Revised Standard Version of the Bible;* copyrighted 1946 and 1952. Gratitude is expressed also to colleagues and students who through the years have enriched the author's life with their companionship and stimulation. My appreciation is very great for the privilege of teaching in Southern Baptist Theological Seminary for more than three decades and for the present privilege of teaching in Golden Gate Seminary.

Contents

Chapter I

What a Church Is For

OURS IS AN INQUIRING age. We are interested in the exploration of the atom and the planets. We observe with fascination the successive inventions of scientists as they seek to travel faster and farther into space. But the disquieting question arises, "What for?"

This question is being raised not only concerning cyclotrons and rockets but also concerning institutions. We are asking, "What are they for?" about the state, the school, the press, radio, television, jet-propulsion, automation, atomic energy, and the innumerable things that claim our attention and support.

The church cannot escape this inquiry. A generation has arisen that does not take the church for granted. Called on to attend its services and finance its activities, men are asking, "What for?" They may listen to endless discussion as to the origin and nature of the church and to much confusing controversy as to which is the "true church," but this does not answer their question as to what the church is for.

Back of function is being. What a thing is for depends on what it is. Search for knowledge of being may take a negative or a positive direction. We may arrive at knowledge of an object or an institution through a process of elimination as we seek to discover what it is not. In the study of the church and its functions, more than any other institution, it is important to examine the negative aspect. What is not a church and what is it not for?

What the Church Is Not

A *saving institution.*—To be saved has many meanings. Health may be saved, life may be saved, wealth may be saved, happiness

1

may be saved, the soul may be saved. Hospitals are institutions for the saving of health, insurance companies make provision for the eventuality of death, banks safeguard wealth, the family seeks happiness, the school saves from ignorance, the church stands primarily for the salvation of the soul.

An accepted measure of value is durability. Precious gems and metals are those that resist the ravages of time. Buildings are worth most when constructed of materials that do not decay. Institutions are valuable in proportion to the enduring service which they render. Since the soul survives bodily death and continues an infinite existence, and the church is designed primarily to safeguard the soul, the church has long been conceived as the institution of greatest value among men.

The elevation of the church to this high position raises the question, Is the church a saving institution or an institution of the saved? Early in Christian history the church began to be conceived as a saving institution. It could not save its adherents from persecution and death, but it made them unconquerable because they believed that within its fold they were saved to eternal life. Soon the dogma arose, *extra ecclesiam, nulla salus*—outside the church, no salvation. This teaching raised and answered some basic questions. How does the church save? By the power of Christ mediated by the church through its sacraments. When does the church save? Whenever the sacrament of baptism is received—the earlier the better. How does the church keep the soul safe? By its worship and discipline, which extends to the whole of life and into and beyond purgatory. Who are the agents of this salvation? The priests of the church, who are the successors of the apostles and to whom is continued the promise made by Christ to Peter of "the keys of the kingdom."

The New Testament emphatically denies that the church is such a saving institution. Sacramental salvation is clearly repudiated by Christ and his New Testament interpreters. Christ's controversy with the religious leaders of his day centered largely in the belief and teaching that salvation came through inheritance and ritualistic observance of the Law. Paul and those who sided with him fought the issue out with the Judaizers in the Jerusalem Conference. Nothing is more certain in the total teaching of the New Testament than that the church is not a saving institution.

"The ministry."—When Jesus announced, "I will build my church,"

he spoke to a group of convinced, confessing believers. The words were directly addressed to Simon Peter. In the lists of apostles Peter's name invariably appears first. The promise of "the keys" apparently was made specifically to Peter. What more natural than that tradition should give to Peter the primacy, thus making him "the prince of the church," the vicar of Christ on earth? About Peter were gathered the apostles, appointed by Christ himself and endowed by Christ with special authority and power. To have been baptized by one of the apostles gave special distinction to the Christian convert. When in the course of time the apostles passed away, baptism at the hands of those who were baptized by the apostles conferred special honor and position. Evidently Christ did not refer to a building or an organization when he said, "I will build my church." Did not his church therefore consist of the men to whom he addressed these words? And would not his church continue to be their successors?

Many factors contributed to this changed concept of the church as the hierarchy. Pastors of strong city churches achieved pre-eminence. Persecution both called for and called out capable and courageous leaders whose prestige was recognized. As the churches increased in number, they felt the need of unity and catholicity, and this brought to the forefront men of exceptional intellectual and spiritual power. Pastors of mother churches became the overseers of the smaller related missions or churches. These men eventually became more concerned with their administrative and priestly offices than with their prophetic calling. More and more they claimed for themselves exclusive rights—the power of "binding and loosing," that is, of excommunication and of restoration of the lapsed; approval of baptism and confirmation; authority of ordination; and control of finances. Identification of the church with the bishop became a dogma with Cyprian (ca. 200–15), who declared: ". . . they are the Church who are a people united to the priest, and the flock which adheres to their pastor . . . the bishop is in the Church, and the Church in the bishop." [1] Thus was laid the foundation for the hierarchy, which came to signify not only the rule of the church by the priest but also the inseparableness of the church from the priest.

The church as identified with "the ministry" is a misconception that has been carried over to some extent in Protestant and evangelical thought. The churches that emerged in the Reformation came to be known as Lutheran, Zwinglian, Calvinist, Wesleyan, etc. Independents who magnify local autonomy sometimes betray the influence of hierarchical and episcopal thinking when they refer to "the Reverend John Doe's church," meaning the First Baptist Church of Bigville. It is not easy to break away from this conception of the church as the hierarchy, the episcopacy, the ministry.

"*An ark of safety.*"—Noah and his family were saved from destruction by their faith in God. While they were in the ark, they were safe. The swelling waters carried to their death the scoffing, unbelieving neighbors. Noah and his wife, their sons and their wives had only to stay in the ark to escape death. The record does not indicate any effort on their part to rescue those who were perishing about them. Noah and his family were saved *from* drowning, but they were not saved *to* the rescuing of others.

The church has been likened to the ark. Those who have entered it are both saved and safe, according to this concept. What they are saved from is of paramount importance; what they are saved to is often looked on as uncertain and incidental. Those in the church, like Noah and his family in the ark, are saved by grace through faith, and once saved are always saved, "kept by the power of God through faith unto salvation ready to be revealed in the last time" (1 Peter 1:5, AV).

The security of the believer is guaranteed, but not by the church. Not from the church, but from Christ comes the promise, "I give them eternal life, and they shall never perish, and no one shall snatch them out of my hand" (John 10:28). This assurance he gives to those who hear his voice, who know and follow him.

The safety of the Christian is not the safety of the ark. It is the security of the believer who is losing his life to save it and who is identified with Jesus Christ in his redemptive sacrifice and service.

The word translated church which Jesus said, "I will build . . . ," literally means "the called out." Called out from what to what? The implied picture is that of a doomed city out of which have been called those saved from death to life. Having been thus called, what are the saved called to do? They are to re-enter the doomed city and call out others, and they in their turn are to call out others, with invincible determination. The "gates" will be opened not by battering rams, but by the use of "the keys," the saving truth of the gospel. There may be suffering and even physical death, but there can be no defeat! The church is not an ark of safety but an army with banners, not guaranteed against loss of battles but assured against ultimate defeat.

A political agency.—The business of the state is to safeguard the welfare of its citizens. To this end it enacts and enforces regulatory and punitive laws. Its officers are vested with power over the liberty and lives of the people. To insure "life, liberty, and the pursuit of happiness" for the many, the state may deny these privileges to those who violate its laws.

The argument for the use of force in religion can be made to seem plausible. There are two categories of value—the material and the spiritual. Government assumes the right to use force in upholding the rights of material possessions, including the human body. Crimes against property and persons are punishable by law. Since spiritual values are greater than material values, should not crimes against the church and the soul be even more the concern of the state than crimes against property and the body? Religious heresy and rebellion, it is argued, should therefore be punishable by the law of the land.

Persecution of Christians in the early centuries took two main forms—social and legal. Pagans looked on Christians as social undesirables and therefore to be shunned and discriminated against. This is the kind of persecution to which Peter refers in his first epistle. Legal persecution was first directed against the Christians because they were considered bad citizens—disloyal to the emperor, disturbers of the peace, violators of the law. When later the Roman Church achieved ascendancy over the Roman state, persecution by the Church was justified on the ground that heresy was spiritual crime. Catholic historians have contended that the Church itself did not persecute; it turned spiritual criminals over to the state for punishment. The Reformation corrected many Catholic abuses but stopped short of dissolution of union of church and state. On the theory of the supremacy of the spiritual over the material, state churches, both Roman Catholic and Protestant, maintained their right to exercise a measure of political control.

Free churches hold as a Christian axiom the doctrine of "a free church in a free state." Bryce, in *The American Commonwealth*, says: "Of all the differences between the Old World and the New this is perhaps the most salient. Half the wars of Europe, half the internal troubles that have vexed European States . . . have risen from the-

ological differences or from the rival claims of Church and State."
Mr. Bryce then concludes: "It is accepted as an axiom by all Americans that the civil power ought to be not only neutral and impartial as between entirely different forms of faith, but ought to leave these matters entirely on one side, regarding them no more than they regard the artistic or literary pursuits of the citizens." [2] To Baptists is accorded the distinction of having established in America the first churches standing for complete separation of church and state, for absolute religious liberty, and for renunciation of all religious persecution. E. Y. Mullins thus sums up the matter: "The State has no ecclesiastical and the Church has no civic function." [3]

An instrument of social reform.—Jesus, in his prayer for the disciples, said: "I do not pray that thou shouldst take them out of the world, but that thou shouldst keep them from the evil one. They are not of the world, even as I am not of the world" (John 17:15–16). Evidently he was not thinking of the world in terms of the world of humanity, but of the world sinful and unredeemed. He came to wrest this evil world from the kingship of Satan. His concern was for the individual but also for the whole of society. His "good news" is that all areas of human living can and ought to be under the sovereignty of God.

The problem is not whether the church is concerned with the social order; it cannot be otherwise and be the church of Jesus Christ. The question is that of strategy of attack. Shall society be saved so that within a Christian environment individuals may be more surely saved? Or shall individuals be saved who in turn will constitute a saved society?

The church as inclusive of all who can be brought into its membership became an early Christian concept. To bring this about, baptism was invested with saving power. In the course of time, every child born within a "Christian state" likewise was born by baptism into the church. Thus was realized the ideal of "one king, one law, one faith." In theory the church could thus determine the moral character of society by virtue of its spiritual dominance over the people.

The breakdown of this theory and the separation of church and state led to an opposite emphasis on individual salvation. Carried to an extreme, this view separated religion from life, isolated the Christian from worldly affairs, and disavowed the church's responsibility for society and the state. Revolt from this untenable position led to the social gospel, with its "good news" of equality of privilege, economic prosperity, social justice, abundant living as the right of all. According to the preachers of this gospel, the church should conceive of itself as an instrument of social reform and convert and commit its members to social righteousness.

The New Testament is reinforced by history in its clear teaching that the church is not just an instrumentality of social reform. The Christian gospel is the good news of salvation of persons; but these saved persons constitute a society which becomes Christian inasmuch as it is dominated by Christians who live according to their faith. S. L. Greenslade, in *The Church and the Social Order*, states the case well:

Two things are vital. Socially, Christians will promote not so much the old-fashioned charity, though that will always be necessary, as community, genuine partnership in every walk of life, in family, school, factory, government, in the house of God. Spiritually, the Church must preserve its other-worldliness. The very tension which has often perplexed the noblest Christians and hindered social progress is nevertheless essential. For the only answer to the all-devouring State, if it is an evil one, is that its ends are contrary to God's and must be resisted; if it is a "welfare" State, that it is only a means to an end, and that the divine purpose to which it must subordinate itself is not to be realized in a historical Utopia, but in the Kingdom of Heaven, in a divine society of individual persons beyond history.[4]

A receptive audience.—Mark reports that "Jesus came . . . preaching," that is, announcing the good news that "the kingdom of God is at hand" and calling on his hearers to "repent, and believe in the gospel" (Mark 1:14–15). The preaching of Jesus attracted great numbers of listeners, "and the great throng heard him gladly" (Mark 12:37). However, the preaching of Jesus was not to passive audiences. While some heard him gladly, others were incensed to the point of attempted murder. In his home town the preaching of Jesus incited such rage that the listeners "rose up and put him out of the city, and led him to the brow of the hill on which their city was built, that they might throw him down headlong" (Luke 4:29). A church may properly provide a place of rest and worship, but its greater function is to stimulate thought, to stir emotion, to move the will to action.

Communism charges that the religion preached and taught by the Christian church is an "opiate of the people." Must we not admit that there may be truth in the charge? Going to church to listen to a comforting sermon may ease the guilty conscience, dull the sense of responsibility for human ills, and provide a brief escape from reality. Christianity and passivity have little affinity for each other. The church must ring out the call to repentance and summon to active faith in Christ's revolutionary purpose.

The kingdom of God.—Jesus said very little about the church as such. The kingdom of God was uppermost in his speech and purpose. On just two occasions Jesus is recorded as having referred to the church. The terms "the kingdom of heaven" and "the kingdom of God" are found in the Gospels more than one hundred times.

A prevalent error is the confusion of the church with the kingdom. "The kingdom of God" means very simply the reign of God in the hearts and lives of men. Jesus came that this reign might be actualized. When he, the King of heaven, came, the kingdom of heaven came with him. It is not the business of his disciples to bring in the kingdom; it is already here. It is the business of the church to bring the kingdom to men and to show them how to enter it. The concept of "the universal church," consisting of the saved everywhere and of all times, represents the error of confusing the church with the kingdom. The church is the agent of the kingdom, but it is not the kingdom. Many grave errors arise when the church is equated with the kingdom. Its character as a local congregation of baptized believers is obscured, and thus the way is paved for the concept of the catholic church or the church of the current ecumenical ideal. Relation of the church to the kingdom is that of flesh to spirit, of body to personality, of means to end. The church is indispensable to the kingdom, but it is not the kingdom.

Having cleared away certain misconceptions, let us now inquire, What is the church? The history of the church indicates two contrasting errors: on the one hand, to regard the church too highly; and on the other, to regard it too lightly. Prior to the Reformation the tendency was to exalt the church; more recently the tendency has been to decry the church. Obviously, there is needed a better understanding of the church as it seeks to follow the New Testament pattern, fulfilling its mission in today's changed and changing world.

From abstractions concerning "the church" we turn to concrete considerations of "a church" functioning in life situations.

What the Church Is

Christ's idealism in action.—Jesus Christ combined in perfect proportion the practical and the ideal. His idealism, both in his example and in his teaching, embodies perfection. The flawlessness of his character and of his ethics has stood the test of criticism and trial. At the same time, his practicality has produced results that have vindicated his idealism.

How to put his principles into practice is the problem of the idealist. The church is Jesus' answer. Made up of disciples or learners whose lives have been transformed by Jesus Christ, a church represents Christ's idealism in action. To the question of the outsider, "Will Christianity work?" the confident answer of those within the church should be, "Come and see!" No claim will be made to attainment of the perfection of Christ's ideals, but commitment to them will be affirmed and honest effort at attainment will be found.

In an atmosphere conducive to Christian growth, character will be in process of development. In a spiritual democracy, equality of rights and privileges will be practiced. In relationships that are often strained, forgiveness will be exercised. In situations of need, help will be given. In an atmosphere of love, solutions to problems of antagonism will be found. With self asserting its claims, sacrificial giving of service and substance will abound. Toward the sinful and erring, compassion will be shown; and to the lost, witness of the saving power of Christ will be given. With all their imperfections, those who constitute a body of Christ's baptized believers join with Paul in the longing that they "may know him and the power of his resurrection, and may share his sufferings, becoming like him in his death," and that they may "attain the resurrection from the dead." With Paul they confess that they have not already obtained this nor are they already perfect, but they press on to make it their own, because Christ Jesus has made them his own (Phil. 3:10–12). Through a church made up of such aspiring persons Christ's idealism is practically demonstrated.

A dynamic Christian group.—A church is more than, and other than, an aggregate number of members. A church as "the body of Christ" connotes an organism, comparable to the human body.

A church is more than an organization. An organization consists of related parts that work together for a given end; an organism consists of living parts, each of which is necessary to the complete life and functioning of the whole. Persons thus related to one another form a dynamic group. Within such a group, powers are developed and released that would not be possible apart from their integration. We observe that this kind of dynamic group was in operation at Pentecost.

A New Testament church represents "togetherness" at its best. The individual is not absorbed into the group; his identity and worth as an individual are heightened. Yet he becomes more than just an individual by virtue of the "we-ness" of the group to which he belongs. Personality is strengthened at its weak points, and its strong points are enhanced by such group identification, underlying which is identification with the living Christ.

Herein we find the true power of a church. Jesus likens it to the life cell in the mustard seed, which though very small has the power of growth out of all proportion to its original size. Or, again, the power of the church is like that of yeast, whose microscopic organisms can change the whole lump of dough. History records the growth and transforming power of a church in an unfavorable environment—a power wholly disproportionate to size and wealth.

A beloved community.—The modern city has been described as "suburbs in search of community." Centrifugal forces in society tend to move people away from one another. Independence may be stressed more than interdependence. Suspicions and fears bring separation, and separation easily flares into antagonism and aggression. Cliques develop, even in churches; national and racial barriers arise; social classes isolate themselves from other classes. Yet deep within the heart of men is the longing for harmony. The social sciences support the truth that man is basically co-operative.

Just as there are centrifugal forces that pull men apart, so there are centripetal forces that bind them together. The very word "community" indicates common interest, linkage, co-operative activity. The more of these voluntary associations there are, the closer knit people become in true community. The future of civilization largely depends on which of these forces will ultimately win—the centrifugal or the centripetal. The threat of destruction to the point of practical annihilation comes from masses of men drawn together by a common ideology into opposing sectors, each of which then moves against the other.

A Christian church offers the solution in its concept of regenerate men forming a beloved community. A New Testament church is the best expression of community known to man. The history of division should not obscure the true genius of the church. The church of the intention of Jesus has not failed to produce and maintain community; divisive churchmen have failed to practice the community inherent in the church. Such community is not to be recovered through the organization and pronouncements of "councils," but by return to him as center who said, "And I, when I am lifted up from the earth, will draw all men to myself" (John 12:32). "Community is achieved by atoning reconciliation with God the Father," concludes George Laird Hunt in *Rediscovering the Church*.[5] Professions of community on the part of those "communions" that have put something other than Christ and his atoning death at the center are hollow. Community that gathers about Christ and obedience to him will produce ecumenicity, rather than proposed ecumenicity creating community.

As Emil Brunner has well pointed out, the basic misunderstanding of the church grows out of the conception of it as institution rather than as fellowship. "No true *Ecclesia* can be made out of twenty ecclesiastical institutions; Christian fellowship can spring only from spiritual knowledge of Christ . . . For in Christ recognition of the truth and the will to fellowship with men are one. Only faith which proves its reality by love is true faith." [6] A church takes institutional form in order to carry out its purposes, but the structure is not the church itself. Churches working together may create and support institutions, but these institutions are not the church. A church is truly the *ecclesia* of Christ when its members are in vital union with him as the branches with the vine and are in fellowship with one another as members of the household of faith. A church as community does not exist for its own sake, but as a means of bringing others into the Christian community.

A church is a steward of the gospel. A steward is one entrusted with that which belongs to another. A church is not entrusted with the gospel as something to be treasured and kept for itself. Indeed, the surest way for a church to lose the gospel is to refuse to share it. An antimissionary church is a contradiction in terms. For a church to refuse or neglect to have some part in taking the gospel from its own doors to the uttermost parts of the earth would be to forfeit its charter as a church.

The gospel with which a church is entrusted is an exclusive way of salvation and life. It admits no rival. It does not claim to be a superior way of salvation among other ways. Rather, a church stands with Peter to say boldly, "And there is salvation in no one else, for there is no other name under heaven given among men by which we must be saved" (Acts 4:12). A church is guilty of malfeasance if it offers to lost men a synthetic gospel or a gospel that represents compromise of this essential and daring claim. A church dares not offer itself or the example of its members as having power to save. It offers what has been entrusted to it—the good news of salvation by Christ on the simple terms of repentance and faith.

A servant of humanity.—When Peter sought to picture Jesus Christ to Cornelius, the Roman officer, he described him as one anointed of God with the Holy Spirit and with power, who "went about doing good and healing all that were oppressed by the devil, for God was with him" (Acts 10:38). Peter thus compressed into a sentence what the Gospels took many pages to relate and what countless volumes have been written to expand. Could any better description of a church be asked—that, anointed of God with the Holy Spirit and with power, it goes about doing good, healing and delivering the sin-sick, by reason of divine indwelling?

A church that does not minister to human need has abandoned the New Testament pattern. A church may well be grateful for, and give its support to, social service agencies, but it should beware of assuming that these agencies leave it without responsibility. The trained personnel of service organizations may well be depended on to render first aid, to provide material assistance, and even to counsel those in trouble, but they cannot take the place of a church with its compassionate ministries rendered in the name of Christ. A church should seek to infuse this spirit into the services of such institutions as hospitals, orphanages, homes for the aged, charitable and penal institutions, and all other such agencies that serve needy humanity. A church should realize that Jesus had its members especially in mind when he said, "As you did it to one of the least of these my brethren, you did it to me" (Matt. 25:40).

A school of Christ.—"Jesus went about . . . teaching" (Matt.

9:35). Everything that he did and said had teaching value. At times he taught formally; more often he taught informally. He taught by who he was, by what he said, by what he did. It is noteworthy that he called his followers "disciples"—learners. It is consistent with his total teaching ministry that he commissioned his disciples to go and make disciples. The Christian religion is a teaching religion, and the Christian church is a teaching church.

Teaching may be of two main kinds—formal and transmissive, and informal and experiential. Each type of teaching possesses value. The teacher or preacher may confront a listening group and teach them by telling. It is contrary to fact to say that telling is not teaching, for much of what people know comes through this process. Learning may result from such formal procedures as asking and answering questions, conducting a recitation, guiding a discussion, supervising a project, utilizing visual aids, telling and dramatizing stories, and the like. A church is at its best and will produce its richest fruitage when it carries on a program of teaching and training in well-organized fashion under competent and consecrated leadership.

A church functions as a school when it makes use of life situations for teaching and learning purposes. When Jesus came down from the mountainside where he had taught the Sermon on the Mount, he brought with him his class, surrounded by a great multitude. A loathsome leper halted him with a plea to be healed. What Jesus did constituted a lesson in compassion never to be forgotten by his disciples. A little later a Roman soldier, a Gentile, pleaded with Jesus on behalf of a sick servant. The conversation of Jesus with this man and the consequent healing of the servant taught the disciples a lesson that they needed to learn. While the disciples were crossing the lake of Galilee and Jesus lay asleep in the boat, a storm arose. His calming of the waters taught them an unforgettable lesson in faith. When they landed on the other shore, they were met by two violently insane men. How he dealt with these men and the owners of the swine who put property above persons taught an impressive lesson on the value which Jesus puts on human beings. When Jesus defied rabbinical tradition and openly ate with publicans and sinners, he was teaching a lesson designed to change the whole narrow Jewish outlook of the disciples.

The healing miracles of Jesus had a twofold purpose: to relieve suffering and to reveal his Father as the God of love. Matthew, recounting these instances, sums it up by saying that "Jesus went about all the cities and villages, teaching in their synagogues and preaching the gospel of the kingdom, and healing every disease and every infirmity" (Matt. 9:35). Matthew saw in all that Jesus was doing the curriculum of the Master Teacher.

A church is a school in this deeper experiential, creative sense. Continually situations arise that can be dealt with redemptively. There is distress to be relieved; there are barriers to be broken down; there are heart hungers to be satisfied; there are sins to be forgiven; there are latent possibilities to be realized; there are doubts to be resolved and faith to be strengthened; there are children to be protected, young people to be guided, mature people to be directed, and old people to be comforted. There are homes to be established through Christian marriage; there are babies to be welcomed into the world; there is death to be met and conquered. Sometimes strife and division develop in the church itself as in the case of the quarrel among the twelve. Life presents the problems, and a church is the school where the answers are to be found.

Chapter II

A Church Needs Many Ministers

Servants of religion through the ages have been given many designations. Men of no other calling possess such varied titles. The letters of the alphabet are almost exhausted by these appellations—apostle, bishop, clergyman, deacon, divine, elder, evangelist, friar, gospeler, herald, interpreter, Jesuit, leader, minister, neophyte, officer, priest, pastor, prophet, preacher, parson, rabbi, rector, shepherd, teacher, wise man. The listing of these varied designations indicates something of the multiplicity of functions of the religionist.

The two words most widely used to designate the religious leader are "priest" and "minister." "Priest" refers to office; "minister," to function. "Priest" is derived from *presbuteros*, elder. In primitive religions worship was conducted by the head of the family or the patriarch of the tribe or the king of the nation. Thus the word "priest" denotes official position, eldership. "Minister" (literally, servant) emphasizes the function of the religious leader—as one who serves at the altar, or who performs priestly duties, or who is the chief servant of a congregation, or who serves as pastor of a church, or who gives direction to teaching and other specialized activities. From ancient times until now, as ritual grew more elaborate and needs of service multiplied, specialists have been required whose aptitudes and training fitted them for division of responsibility. The priesthood and the ministry today call for specialization.

Israel Had Its God-Appointed Guides

Early in the Old Testament narrative is introduced abruptly the somewhat shadowy figure of Melchizedek, king of Salem, who "brought out bread and wine; he was priest of God Most High" (Gen.

15

14:18). Having bestowed a priestly blessing on Abraham, Melchizedek received from him an offering of tithes. This combination of king and priest was afterward viewed as the ideal ruler of Israel, representing both the kingly and the priestly order "after the order of Melchizedek" (Psalm 110:4). In the New Testament this ideal is fulfilled in Christ (Heb. 5:6–7).

There are references to priests before Aaron, but these relate usually to priests of the Egyptians and the Midianites. With Aaron, brother of Moses, the Israelitish priestly line begins, although priestly prerogatives were not confined exclusively to the Aaronic priesthood. The tribe of Levi, unable to obtain land of its own, was given priestly status and privileges, its members receiving their living from the other tribes. It is supposed that Moses was of the tribe of Levi and that he gave his priestly functions to his brother Aaron. Eventually the priestly functions came to be monopolized by the Levites. Under this conception of the priesthood as hereditary and professional, worship was corrupted and religious life deteriorated.

In strong contrast to the priests were the prophets. Theirs was not the ministry of the altar but of the word. They were "speakers for God," seeking to call Israel back to its divinely given mission and interpreting the covenant relationship in terms of ethical content. They spoke with the voice of authority, saying, "Thus saith the Lord." They warned, rebuked, exhorted to repentance, foretold disaster for disobedience, and pleaded for faithfulness to Jehovah as the one true God. To them it was given to foresee the coming of Messiah, whose reign would bring in "the day of the Lord." At times they were prophets of doom, and again they were prophets of hope. Through all their preaching ran the redemptive note. God in his good time would save his people and establish his reign.

Between the priest and the prophet were two other servants of God and of Israel—the seer and the sage. The priest mediated between God and the people, presenting to him their sacrifice and supplications; the prophet represented God to the people, serving as a medium of communication between the Creator and his human creation. The seer was more a foreteller and was often depended on to predict the future. Such men as Gad, Iddo, Jehu, Asaph, Jeduthun were given the power of insight and were often divinely commissioned to disclose the purpose of God to David and others in high position. The seer was a prophet in a sense but lacked the moral force of such prophets as Elijah, Isaiah, Jeremiah, Ezekiel, Daniel, Hosea, Joel, Amos, and others.

The sage or wise man differed from priest, prophet, and seer. Wise men possessed the gift of literary artistry combined with practical wisdom. Their sayings are marked by concentrated force, vigor of thought and style, quintessence of wisdom. The wise men did not deal with contemporary issues as did the prophets, but spoke timeless truth in timely language. Their accumulated writings served to give counsel concerning almost all the problems and affairs of life. They sought to induce reverence for God and to uphold respect and justice for men. The Psalms, the Proverbs, and Ecclesiastes are usually classified as "wisdom literature." For the most part, the counsel given is intensely personal and provides divine wisdom for right living.

Another class of servants of religion in Israel were the *sopherim*, or scribes. The first mention of the scribe is found in the time of David (2 Sam. 8:17). Later, scribes are mentioned along with priests or Levites. Scribe, both in Hebrew and in Greek, simply means writer. However, the scribe in Israel was more than a copyist; he came to be accepted and honored as an interpreter. The scribes were authors, collators, and editors of a vast amount of Hebrew literature—the Midrash, expositions of the Old Testament text; the Halakah, commentaries on the oral law; the Mishnah, a digest of Jewish traditions and explanations of the Scriptures, forming the texts of the Talmud. Rabbis were scribes whose specialty was teaching. The rabbis gained prominence following the restoration and the establishment of synagogues as the public schools of the Jews. Their sayings were collected in the Pirke Aboth, or sayings of the fathers, and often were considered more authoritative than the Scriptures themselves. The scribes were meticulous scholars as well as interpreters and teachers, learned in the law and in the traditions of Israel. The rabbis did much to preserve and enforce the doctrines and practices of Judaism.

Paganism Had Its Many Priests

A sharp distinction is observed at once between the religionists of Israel and of the heathen cults. The religious leaders of Israel were spiritual guides, seeking to bring the people under the control of the will of God. The heathen priests were magicians, seeking to control the gods for the sake of the people. They assumed that this control could be exercised chiefly through sacrifices and ceremonies. The priest was supposed to have special access to divinity and to possess special knowledge and skills in reaching and influencing the gods. Evidence of communion with the deity was the experience of ecstasy or trance which enabled the seer to foretell the future. At first the priest's presence only was thought to be necessary when sacrifices were made or rituals performed. When these services became more elaborate, the priests became the performers of the sacrifices and rituals until at length the conduct of worship became their monopoly.

The history of the priesthood in paganism discloses the tendency toward specialization of priestly functions. There were chief priests, servant priests, "reciter" priests, diviners, soothsayers, oracles, magi, holy men, dervishes, shamans, lamas, on and on in almost endless designations.

In modern ethnic religions the influence of education and scientific thought has tended to put the priest more in the role of teacher and conductor of worship in contrast to the older concept of him as magician. Even the medicine man of the animistic religions is inclined to be more utilitarian and to depend more on his crude home remedies than on voodoo or the exercising of evil spirits by the practice of superstitious rites. Modern Buddhist priests are often teachers of the philosophy of Buddhism by educational means in imitation of Christian churches. The pagan priesthood today, still powerful in many parts of the world, exhibits a great variety of functions performed by a multiplicity of religious specialists.

Jesus Revolutionized the Concept of the Ministry

At no point was Jesus more revolutionary than in his concept of the priest, rabbi, scribe. He was rejected by these "blind guides" of the people and in turn denounced them. In his selection of the inner circle of disciples, no one from the official religious group was included. He deliberately ignored, and sometimes openly violated, ceremonial laws which they regarded as sacred. In words that sound strange from the lips of the gentle Jesus he pronounced bitter woe on these religionists, calling them hypocrites, children of hell, blind guides, whited sepulchres, generation of vipers! He disavowed the whole priestly business and set himself to overthrow the priestly system. No wonder the priests hated him and would be satisfied with nothing less than his death.

Those whom Jesus gathered about him were not of the priestly order. They were men of the people—laymen. When Peter and John were referred to as "unlearned and ignorant men" (Acts 4:13, AV), it does not mean that they were illiterate or of low mentality but that they were not trained in the rabbinical schools. They and their fellow apostles were disqualified in the eyes of their Jewish neighbors because they had no professional religious training.

Jesus chose these men with much care and after intimate acquaintance. He called them first to faith in him and in his messianic claim (John 1:15 ff.). After an interval, in which the first four believers had gone back to their usual occupation, Jesus called them again to give up their jobs and follow him as learners (Matt. 4:17–22). And still later, after further study of these men and following a night of prayer, Jesus called his growing group of disciples about him and from them chose twelve, whom he called apostles or missionaries (Luke 6:13–16). Mark records that he appointed the twelve "to be with him, and to be sent out to preach and have authority to cast out demons" (Mark 3:14–15). Later, following his death and resurrection, Jesus called these and his other disciples a fourth time to go "into all the world and preach the gospel to the whole creation" (Mark 16:15).

The two words used by Jesus to describe these called men are "disciple" and "apostle"—never "priest," "rabbi," or "scribe." The word translated disciple means, literally, a learner, but connotes more than a student. To Jesus a disciple is a convinced learner, a follower, an adherent. Literally, an apostle is one sent, a missionary, a person commissioned to represent another. To Jesus the apostles were those who constituted the inner circle of the disciples, chosen by him to be fully taught and to become his special representatives in teaching and winning others. They belonged to no priestly order, and they were given no sacerdotal rights or privileges.

The quarrel among the twelve points up Jesus' remarkable teaching concerning pre-eminence. James and John, with their mother, sought from Jesus the promise of an undisclosed favor. When it came to light, the favor was that of appointment to the two highest positions in the coming kingdom. Jesus, pained by this display of selfish ambition, replied that it was not within his power to confer such special favors. When the ten heard of the incident, they were angry —probably because each one wanted the same thing! In the process of healing the breach and restoring the broken fellowship, Jesus described the structure of secular society—heathen rulers lording it over those beneath them and these in turn tyrannizing those subject to them, in descending order from highest to lowest. "It shall not be so among you; but whoever would be great among you must be your servant." Making himself an example, he concluded, ". . . even as the Son of man came not to be served but to serve, and to give his life as a ransom for many" (Matt. 20:26-28).

Here is the revolutionary principle: Humility is the measure of importance, and service is the measure of greatness. Jesus took the ignoble word "servant" and made it a symbol of highest honor. Thereafter his called men would bear the title of minister—servant —as a badge of honor and not of shame. By whatever other titles they may be known, Christ's men are never to forget that their characteristic mark is that of a servant. Here is the remedy for ministerial self-seeking and self-importance.

The Early Christians Had a Multiplicity of Ministers

After his death and resurrection Jesus called his followers again. He had called them to faith, to fellowship, to discipleship; now he called them to partnership in the furtherance of his purpose of world redemption. In the Great Commission as recorded by Matthew he told them—and us—what to do. Going, they are to make disciples, baptize them, and teach and train them so that they will go, make more disciples, teach and train them so that they will go—on and on, in ever widening circles, until the saving message has been given to the whole creation. In the commission in Acts he told his disciples —and us—how to do it. In the power of the Holy Spirit they will bear witness to the good news of salvation through Christ, beginning at home and extending the witness ever farther unto the ends of the earth (Matt. 28:19-20).

The Commission in Matthew's Gospel was probably given to the more than five hundred to whom he appeared (1 Cor. 15:6); the commission in Acts, to the one hundred and twenty who later assembled in the upper room at Jerusalem (Acts 1:15). While the leadership of certain of the apostles is recognized, there seems to have been no distinction between them and the other disciples as to responsibility for carrying out Christ's commission. When the day of Pentecost came, "they were all with one accord in one place," and the power of the Holy Spirit came upon all alike. Preceding Peter's sermon all bore witness, both men and women, to the multitude attracted by the noise and by the cloven tongues resting upon each of the disciples.

The picture in Acts is that of a witnessing, growing, self-governing church. From one hundred and twenty the membership increased to more than three thousand, then to about five thousand men (Acts 4:4). A little later additions to the church ceased to be reported in numbers but are spoken of as "multitudes both of men and women" (Acts 5:14). If the number of women equaled the number of men in the five thousand figure and if "multitudes" more represents conservatively a doubling of the previous figure, may we not reasonably estimate that the Jerusalem church had about twenty thousand members?

To minister to this great city church there was a group made up of the twelve (Judas' place having been filled by Matthias), with seven "helpers" (deacons), giving the church a staff of nineteen specially appointed servants. When the disciples were scattered abroad by the persecution of Saul, they "went about preaching the word" (Acts 8:4), "except the apostles" (Acts 8:1), who remained in Jerusalem to care for the needs of the church. That the apostles had no monopoly on preaching is evidenced by the fact that Philip became the evangelist in Samaria, later winning and baptizing the Ethiopian eunuch—a clear example of freedom from clericalism. While the apostles were honored and respected because of their relation to Christ, they possessed no authority over other servants of Christ and performed no service that could not have been done by any authorized deacon or layman. The concept of superiority and subordination in the Christian ministry is not found in this period of beginnings.

Ordination Gives Rise to "Orders of the Ministry"

Fundamental in the teaching of Jesus is the doctrine of the equality of all believers. This truth, however, does not imply a dead level of status. From his followers Jesus chose twelve men and set them apart for special training and service. Of the twelve, Peter is always named first in the list, and James and John became more prominent than their fellows. Leadership, Jesus pointed out, was not his to give as a special favor, "but it is for those for whom it has been prepared" (Matt. 20:23). In almost any group there are a few among the many who by reason of natural and acquired abilities rise to places of leadership. Jesus says concerning these places that they are "prepared by my Father" (Matt. 20:23). Personally, these individuals are no more important than others; functionally, they are called to positions of greater responsibility.

The church at Corinth was disturbed by factions, some favoring the leadership of Paul, some of Apollos, others of Peter. Paul rebukes this factionalism, asking, "What then is Apollos? What is Paul? Servants through whom you believed, as the Lord assigned to each" (1 Cor. 3:5). Later in the letter Paul calls attention to "varieties of service," "varieties of gifts," "varieties of working," by which he means that there are varieties of ministries due to personal endowments and abilities. Writing to the Ephesians, he says that when Christ ascended he led into captivity a host of captives and gave gifts to his churches: some men as apostles (missionaries), some as prophets (preachers), some as evangelists (tellers of the good news), and some as pastors and teachers (shepherds and instructors).

Obviously, these are not separate offices but types of functions, some men having more ability and responsibility in one activity than the other, but none of them possessed as exclusive prerogatives. These gifts are to be exercised "for the equipment of the saints, for the work of ministry, for building up the body of Christ" (Eph. 4:12). Thus each member will be related to every other member, and all will be in union with Christ, the head. Thus the church will build itself up through love (Eph. 4:15–16). A church needs leaders but is not dependent on them; Christ is the head and each member is a minister.

In this original New Testament sense "ministry" simply meant service. The word most often used is *diakonia*, servant, which in Acts is used to describe the ministry of the apostles (Acts 1:17). In this sense the apostles were deacons. When Paul thanks God for putting him into the ministry, he uses the word which literally means "deaconship." Following Old Testament terminology, the New Testament speaks of the appointed religious leader as *presbuteros* or elder. Originally denoting age, the term "elder" came to be associated with headship of the family or tribe and so with leadership regardless of age. When Paul and Barnabas on their journey revisited the churches and "appointed elders for them in every church" (Acts 14:23), the word translated "appoint" means literally "to elect by stretching out the hand" and refers to the action of the congregation. Luke speaks of "apostles and elders" (Acts 15:22, AV), and again of "apostles and elders and brethren" (Acts 15:23, AV). Paul's instruction to Titus to "appoint elders in every town" (Titus 1:5) obviously refers to his service in helping the churches to select their spiritual leaders.

In New Testament practice a distinction is made between the bishop and the deacon. The word translated "bishop" is *episkopos*, overseer, superintendent, administrator. This is Paul's inclusive word for the pastorship. The Greek word is defined by Thayer as "an overseer, a man charged with the duty of seeing that things to be done by others are done rightly." In the New Testament sense, the bishop is the superintendent, or overseer of any Christian church, that is, the pastor. Associated with him are *diakonoi*, servants of the church. The qualifications given for the bishop and the deacon are almost identical (1 Tim. 3). Were the elders pastors or deacons? Evidently they may have been either. There is little New Testament evidence for the later distinction of the pastor as belonging to the clergy and the deacon as belonging to the laity. The pastor's priority is that of responsibility for the whole of the church and its administrative work. Deacons seem to have had less general and more specialized responsibilities.

Ordination in New Testament practice was a meaningful but simple affair. It had little of the later ecclesiastical meaning which came to be attached to the ceremony. When it is said that Jesus "ordained twelve," the word used signifies "to make," "to constitute"; that is, he made men apostles, with apparently no public ceremony. The other word translated "ordained" means to set, put, place, and is properly translated "appoint." The appointment of one to serve as a religious leader of a church was usually accompanied by the ceremony of laying on of hands. In token of their approval and confidence, members of the congregation placed their hands of blessing on the one thus being set apart. This laying on of hands conferred no priestly authority, it gave no special privileges, it made no change in the character of the one thus approved. Paul and Barnabas had been

active in service long before their ordination to be missionaries by
the Antioch church. They were among the prophets and teachers
and were equally "set apart" to their divinely called ministry as missionaries.

When we turn from the New Testament, we soon find the bishop
drawing apart from the elder and the elder drawing apart from the
deacon. Priority was claimed by and for those who could trace their
baptism and ordination in unbroken succession back to Christ. Special authority inhered in the man who could say, "I was baptized by
a man who was baptized by a man who was baptized by an apostle
who was baptized by Christ himself."

Gradually the prophetic ministry gave way to the ecclesiastical
ministry. Bishops of the city churches began to claim authority over
the smaller neighboring churches. Ministers of these churches laid
claim to superiority over their subordinates, the deacons. Thus by the
close of the fifth century "orders of the ministry" were established,
which in the course of time became the hierarchy with its pope,
cardinals, archbishops, bishops, priests, deacons, acolytes, and so on,
in descending order.

By the middle of the third century Cyprian (*ca.* 200–58), one of
the most vigorous and influential of the early church fathers, declared, ". . . they are the Church who are a people united to the
priest, and the flock which adheres to its pastor." [1] Again Cyprian declares that they only who are set over the church can remit sins. [2]
Bishops thus become a special and higher order of priesthood, and
later one of them, the bishop of Rome, was to become the head of the
Church. The control of the bishops was made secure when they delegated to themselves the sole right of ordination. Holy orders eventually became one of the seven sacraments. Ordination thus confers
on bishops, priests, and other ministers of the church "the power and
grace to perform their sacred duties," and "imprints on the soul a
character or mark which endures forever." [3] The one ordained receives the power to (1) offer the holy sacrifice of the Mass; (2) bless
anyone or anything; (3) rule a portion of God's flock; (4) administer
the sacraments of baptism, penance, the holy Eucharist, and extreme
unction, and to unite in matrimony.

In all of this we see a radical departure from the simplicity of the
New Testament concept of the ministry and of ordination. To an
extent of which many are probably unaware, the concepts and

practices that gather about ordination and the ministry have been influenced by Catholic tradition and doctrine. These heresies concerning the ministry constitute the root of evil from which most of the corruptions associated with the Roman Catholic Church have sprung.

The Reformation Partially Recovered the New Testament Pattern

There were reformers before the Reformation, but so powerful was the hierarchy that they were crushed. Luther attacked the Church at two of its most vulnerable points—its false doctrines and its corrupt priesthood. "Salvation by faith" and "the priesthood of believers" became the war cry of Luther and his fellow reformers. Luther's rupture with the church and its control over the priesthood was dramatized by his marriage. Yet Luther dared not go all the way in his break with Rome. He retained infant baptism, sacramental salvation, union of church and state, ordination as conferring special grace and powers, the priesthood as separate from the laity.

The Anabaptists proposed to go all the way, seeking to restore the church to its original form as a congregation of baptized believers and the ministry to its function of preaching, teaching, and pastoral care. These "rebaptizers" were misunderstood, feared, hated, and bitterly persecuted. Yet they did much to lay foundations on which other "dissenters" built—Mennonites, Hutterites, Brethren, Quakers, Congregationalists, Baptists. Common to all these bodies were their congregationalism and anticlericalism. They sought to restore the church to the people and the people to the church and to bring back the New Testament concept of the ministry as men called of God, approved of their brethren, and selected by the people to serve them. Ordination was retained as having New Testament precedent and historical warrant, but not as "holy orders" giving men special status and prerogatives.

The Minister Becomes the Preacher-Pastor

The Reformation movement magnified preaching. Men must be won from Catholicism to Lutheranism or Zwinglianism or Calvinism. When the older methods of coercion and persecution were at length abandoned, how could men be made adherents of the church? The chief means was persuasion—and this is the function of preaching. During the early period of the Reformation the objective of preaching was not so much to win men to Christ as to the cause of the reformers. There was a considerable political element in the Reformation movement. Its success promised relief from Rome's burdensome taxation, its ecclesiastical political domination, and its suppression of nationalism. It encouraged the political aspirations of princes and citizens alike, who gave their support to the Reformation preachers for not altogether unselfish reasons. The art of preaching was revived, and preachers were given new standing and respect.

As more and more free churches came into being, they felt the need of a minister who would be pastor as well as preacher. One man had to combine the function of preacher, teacher, and pastor, due in large measure to the scarcity of ministers and the inability of congregations to support more than one man. The simplicity of organization of these early free churches made no heavy demands on the preacher-pastor, so that one man could serve several churches with reasonable acceptability. Thus there developed the part-time church and the circuit-riding preacher. When a man felt the call of God to the Christian ministry, he interpreted it in terms of the "call to preach." Sometimes, as a neophyte, he was "licensed" or given liberty to exercise his preaching gifts on a probationary basis. His ordination was "to preach the gospel" and to "shepherd the flock of God." Often the examination for the ordination was brief and perfunctory, it being generally agreed that any man who felt he was called to preach should be recognized and approved. The quality and effectiveness of his preaching were left to God, who would put the words in the preacher's mouth if he opened it in faith. His pastoral service consisted of visiting the sick, burying the dead, and marrying all who were duly licensed. So his duties were not extensive.

The relatively untrained men of this earlier period rendered valuable service to the cause of Christ and the churches. Many of them farmed or worked at other vocations to make a living and preached without pay. Some received small compensation, but it was not looked upon as salary; this was too suggestive of a "hireling ministry." In spite of their limitations, these men were often eloquent and persuasive preachers, winning multitudes to Christ through their sermons. The annual revival was their time of reaping, when two weeks of special evangelistic meetings would often bring in a harvest of souls. American evangelical Christianity was shaped in large measure by these earnest preachers.

Modern Demands Restore the Multiple Ministry

At the turn of the present century vast changes began to occur in America as well as in the rest of the world. Machinery began to replace manpower, the scientific method replaced trial and error, rapid transportation and swift communication brought changed ways of living, and an economy of plenty began to take the place of the old economy of scarcity. Two world wars changed the face of the world and then confronted it with its destruction should there be a third world war. "Boom" was followed by "bust" and by "boom" again. Population increased explosively, making it difficult for supply to keep up with demand. Social revolution kept pace with political and economic revolution, bringing recognition to minority groups and unprecedented power to labor. Mobility took the place of stability, and the nation on wheels and in the air brought about unparalleled transiency accompanied by increased incidence of divorce, family disorganization, delinquency, crime. The speed with which change takes place accelerates with each passing decade.

Churches have been compelled to meet change with change. Unchanged churches in a changed and changing environment would meet the fate of any other organism—they would perish. The problem is that of maintaining the original church pattern established by the New Testament and yet changing the methods of its operation to meet new conditions. The basic functions of the church are constant —worship, preaching, teaching, training, evangelizing, giving, serving, healing. Yet each of these activities must be carried on in ways appropriate to changed conditions.

Worship, a church's life center, has always used music as a major instrumentality. In an age made music conscious by radio, television, films, and records as never before in history, the music of a church calls for skilled direction. Out of this need has come the minister of music, dedicated and trained, giving his full time to direction of the music ministries of the church. To supply the teaching and training ministries of the church, organizations have been developed with increased complexity, designed to meet the needs of every age group, from the youngest to the oldest, and demanding an ever increasing staff of paid specialists. These educational ministries require a minister of education, often with age-group aides, called and consecrated to this service. With increased membership and complexity of organization comes increased responsibility for supervision and business management. The ministry of church administration - thus becomes a full-time vocation, calling for specialized ability and dedication to the office as being God-assigned. A missionary-minded church will foster branch Sunday schools and missions and seek continually to extend its outreach from its Jerusalem to the uttermost parts. Pastors of these missions must be found and called and made a part of the staff of the mother church.

What status shall these servants of the church be given, and how shall they be related to one another? The problem is not new. With variations, as we have seen, this multiple ministry is found in the New Testament churches. Jesus trained a dozen men who became the *diakonoi* or servants of the church at Jerusalem. This church then added seven other servants with specialized responsibility. In the church at Antioch there were prophets and teachers, among them Paul and Barnabas, who were ordained and sent out as missionaries. Apostles were distinguished from elders, but whether the elders were prophets or deacons is not clear; they perhaps could be either. Deacons preached and baptized, and pastors served the congregation. The bishop was the minister in his administrative capacity.

Does this lack of clear distinction among apostles, prophets, elders, pastors, bishops, deacons, and teachers present a confused picture? No, it is in accordance with the basic principle laid down by Jesus that there should be no distinction of rank among his followers and the servants of the churches. According to the plain teaching of the New Testament, ordination does not make a man a minister. It is a simple ceremony of recognition that God has called him to the gospel ministry and of commendation of him to churches of like faith and order. It avoids the disaster which befell Christianity in its Catholic development—that of "orders of the ministry," resulting eventually in the hierarchy.

According to this concept, the ministers of the church are not set apart and employed to perform the varied functions of the church, but rather to enlist and direct and inspire the members to share effectively in every activity. Members of the church thus will be stimulated and guided to be missionaries, to preach on occasion, to teach or be taught, to train or be trained, to worship through music, to give and serve, to win the lost to Christ, to bear witness in all of life's relationships. Thus will be fulfilled the ideal of the church and its members as "built upon the foundation of the apostles and prophets, Christ Jesus himself being the chief cornerstone, in whom the whole structure is joined together and grows into a holy temple in the Lord; in whom you also are built into it for a dwelling place of God in the Spirit" (Eph. 2:20-22).

Chapter III

Ministers Must Be Administrators

A MEETING OF ONE OF the state medical associations was in progress. On the agenda was a full-length discussion of "The Doctor as Administrator." A curious reporter inquired of the chairman: "Does this mean that you doctors are executives? Do you have to practice business as well as medicine?" The president of the association, an eminent physician, previewed the proposed discussion, which included the operation of the doctor's office, purchase of supplies and equipment, patients' records, medical accounting, fee collecting, staff relationships, hospital connections, interoffice consultations, referrals, medical society obligations, public health responsibilities, legal liabilities, protection against malpractice suits, assurance of good public relations, investments, insurance, taxes— the list grew with comments from bystanders.

Ministers are confronted with similar complexity of duties. Must ministers be administrators? Yes, of necessity and by choice. To minister and to administer are cognates. Serving calls for ways and means of serving; ministering requires administering. The minister, like the physician, is a professional specialist and must combine the skills of his specialty with the accompanying skills of the executive. There is no escape in any profession from administrative responsibility.

All professional men feel the pull of this division of demand on their time and energy. No matter how much he would prefer to do so, the doctor cannot devote himself exclusively to medicine, nor the attorney to law, nor the teacher to education, nor the architect to designing, nor the artist to sculpture or painting, nor the composer to music or writing, nor the scientist to experimentation. Should the minister at times feel like rebelling against the calls that take him from study and personal service, let him be reminded that his predicament is that of all his fellow workers in specialized fields. The answer is neither rebellion nor resignation, but administrative competency.

Administration Is Not "Practical" Versus "Spiritual"

Christian ministers are peculiarly liable to the temptation to resent demands made on their time and energy for administrative duties. They may feel that their calling is distinguished by its concentration of concern for unseen and eternal values. They are aware that their Master said: "Do not lay up for yourselves treasures on earth . . . but lay up for yourselves treasures in heaven. . . . For where your treasure is, there will your heart be also"; and again, "No one can serve two masters; for either he will hate the one and love the other, or he will be devoted to the one and despise the other. You cannot serve God and mammon" (Matt. 6:19–21, 24). They are reminded that Paul, their great predecessor in the ministry, admonished: "Walk by the Spirit, and do not gratify the desires of the flesh. For the desires of the flesh are against the Spirit, and the desires of the Spirit are against the flesh; for these are opposed to each other, to prevent you from doing what you would. . . . If we live by the Spirit, let us also walk by the Spirit" (Gal. 5:16–17, 25). To Timothy Paul wrote, "No soldier on service gets entangled in civilian pursuits, since his aim is to satisfy the one who enlisted him" (2 Tim. 2:4). Are not these divine warnings to the minister not to engage too seriously in the administrative affairs of the church?

Should the minister reason thus, he might well pause to ask himself whether these words were addressed to ministers alone or to all Christians. The world's work demands that the majority of Christians devote themselves during most of their waking hours to the practical affairs of life. Must they give up their jobs in order to obey Christ? Do the warnings of Paul concerning the flesh and the Spirit require disassociation from business and professional duties in order to be "spiritual"? Are there two categories of spirituality—one for the minister, who must keep himself aloof from the contamination of practical affairs, and another for a businessman, who can hardly be expected to maintain true spirituality under the pressure of his occupation? The alternative is all too widely assumed. The minister's prayer for himself as well as for his Christian brothers in business must be Christ's: "I do not pray that thou shouldst take them out of the world, but that thou shouldst keep them from the evil one" (John 17:15).

A true picture of spirituality is that of Jesus at work in Joseph's carpenter shop, and in later years almost certainly the head of a large household, the dependence of his widowed mother and the guide and guardian of his brothers and sisters. The Jesus of the Gospels is not a remote figure, apart from the busy life of his time, but rather a man among men, prodigiously active, organizing and training his helpers, defending himself against attacks of his enemies, responding to the clamorous calls for his healing and help on the part of individuals and multitudes, building his church on rocklike foundations. A similar picture of the deeply spiritual Paul is that of a man of restless energy, going from place to place teaching and preaching, constituting churches and enlisting and training their leaders, winning souls and sending them out to win others, even in prison busily writing letters to the churches whom he could not visit in person. The minister who would withdraw into his study and spend most of his time preparing sermons has forsaken the example of Jesus and Paul.

Administration Concerns the Minister's Total Task

That administration is a detached fragment of the minister's total calling is a mistaken idea. Administration constitutes the circle of which other duties are related parts. Everything that the minister does of consequence is associated with the administrative function. This is made clear by Paul's choice of the word "bishop" to designate the man of God. It is not accidental that *episkopos*—bishop—should have been used in the only detailed description of the qualifications and duties of the man elsewhere called minister, pastor, elder, teacher, preacher, missionary, evangelist. It is customary to say that "bishop" is just another word for pastor and that every pastor is a bishop. But is there not a deeper reason for the use of the term? If we believe that Paul's words here as elsewhere carry the authority of inspiration, must we not believe that his use of *episcopos* is purposeful and significant?

The bishop's qualifications, both private and public, must be such as to fit him to "care for God's church" (1 Tim. 3:5). Everything that he is and does should be to the end that he may thus exercise this care. His personal character must be above approach, his conduct must be stainless, his habits must be such as to set a good example, his family life must be a model for the community, he must be mature in judgment and wisdom, and he must maintain a good reputation in the sight of all men if he is to fill well the office of pastoral director.

Quality of character is basic to the minister's success in every aspect of his calling and is his underlying qualification as bishop or administrator. Not every man can at once be an eloquent preacher, a skilful pastor, a brilliant teacher, an outstanding evangelist, a notable scholar; but every man called of God can faithfully "care for God's church." He will be doing this in his preaching, in his pastoral care, in his teaching, in his evangelizing, in his enrichment of himself through study—indeed, in every aspect of his ministry. If this is not true, and the church suffers from neglect, whatever he does will be ultimately of little avail.

The history of the cure of souls bears testimony to the preeminence of ministers whose over-all concern was the care of the church of God. Richard Baxter, whose *The Reformed Pastor* is still an unexhausted mine of wisdom, insisted that the pastoral office is much more than "those men have taken it to be, who think it consisteth in preaching and ministering sacraments only." [1] Baxter made much of "plain preaching"—preaching that came out of contacts with people in everyday living. "Why do you not speak so as to be understood?" he inquires, and insists that "he that would be understood must speak to the capacity of his hearers and make it his business to be understood." [2] To this end the preacher must live with his people, understand and speak their language, and be closely associated with them in the life and work of the church. George Herbert, whose *Country Parson* was widely read a century ago, took much the same position, insisting that the preacher include "tillage and pasturage" in his knowledge and that he illustrate difficult doctrines from farming even as Jesus had done.

Giants of the pulpit in more recent years, such as Henry Ward Beecher, Phillips Brooks, and Theodore L. Cuyler, uniformly insisted that preaching can never be separated from pastoral work. Cuyler, in *How To Be a Pastor*, wrote near the turn of the last century: "The humblest minister may become a faithful and successful

pastor. God never intended that this world should be saved by pulpit geniuses or else He would have created more of them. . . .
Every herald of the gospel who loves his Master, loves his Bible,
loves his fellow-men, and who hungers to win souls to the Saviour,
can be a good pastor, if he honestly aims to become one." [3]

George A. Buttrick, for many years one of New York City's outstanding pulpit figures, addressing a group of pastors, said: " 'You
can never build up a strong congregation solely by preaching. You
must go to the people yourself. You build up a spiritual church by
wearing out shoe leather and automobile tires. You can hold it together by worthy preaching.' " [4] Jowett, in the Yale Lectures on
Preaching, answered the question, "What, then, shall be our sovereign purpose in moving among men in common affairs?" He replies:

It will surely be to relate the common to the divine, and to bring the
vision of the sanctuary into the street and the market and the home. We
are to go among men helping them to see the halo on the commonplace,
to discern the sacred fire in the familiar bush. . . . It must be our ministry to help them to recover their lost inheritance, and to retain the sense
of heavenly fellowship while they earn their daily bread.[5]

Arthur Hewitt goes so far as to say: "Pastoral work is not to be asked
whether it is more important than this or that. It is our only business!" [6] To be sure, pastoral work is not wholly administrative, but it
cannot be done effectively apart from the processes involved in administration.

Administration Affords a Field of Scholarly Study

Usually, the minister's complaint is that pastoral work and administrative duties interfere with his study. The answer is twofold:
By its very nature, administration conserves time which otherwise
might be consumed to little purpose, thereby providing more time
which the minister can spend in his study; and administration is
itself a rich field of study.

What is study? Ordinarily, we think of study as related to books.
To study is to read, to retrace the thinking of others, to investigate by
the use of literary tools. Such study as this is, of course, highly important. Ideas are the minister's stock in trade, and if he runs out of
ideas, he faces spiritual bankruptcy. With the Bible at the center,
the minister must surround himself with books and must continue to

be a student as long as he lives. A Britisher, visiting the United States, was asked to state his chief impression of American ministers. He replied, "The thing that has impressed me most is the splendor of their automobiles and the poverty of their libraries." When this becomes the minister's distinctive, he is on the way to forfeiting his right to be called a good minister of Jesus Christ.

All study, however, is not carried on in a secluded room filled with books. A pastor pointed to a window high up in the tower of the church building. "Don't give my secret away," he explained, "but that is where I study. It can be reached only by means of a vertical ladder which few would be willing to climb. Here I escape from the demands made on me by administrative duties in order that I may study." Unquestionably, there is value in privacy for this kind of study. But what was this pastor doing when with the staff he planned the week's work, met with committees to deal with church problems, helped the Sunday school officers and teachers to do a better job, gave attention to membership training and the recruitment of needed officers and leaders, talked with the treasurer and finance committee about the stewardship program of the church, advised with the committee about starting a new mission, arranged for a funeral and a wedding, counseled with a couple on the verge of divorce, sat in with a group responsible for the approaching community chest drive, gathered materials for reports to the next annual meetings of district association and state convention? Does not all this require study of the first order?

Perhaps the minister's difficulty is just at this point. He has learned how to study in preparation for teaching and preaching, but he has not considered study of these practical matters as coming within the scope of scholarship. He may therefore make an unstudied approach to these time-consuming responsibilities. He learned in seminary the technique of the exegesis of a difficult Old Testament or New Testament passage. He learned the principles of homiletics and can apply them with reasonable skill in the construction of a sermon. He studied religious education and is confident of his ability to teach as he stands before a Sunday school class or leads the officers and teachers in their preparation to teach. His study of theology enables him to state clearly the doctrines of the Christian faith and to interpret their significance for present life. But for more than half of every working day he is confronted with situations to which his study of Greek and Hebrew, of exegesis and interpretation, of principles of preaching and teaching, and his other methods of theological inquiry simply do not directly apply. If the minister is not to blunder through in this field of his responsibility, as he certainly would in his preaching and teaching without skilful methodology, he must be a student of administration.

Confronting this need, the minister will discover that administration is a subject fully as respectable academically as theology and philosophy. The literature of various aspects of administration is vast and expanding. Looking about him, the minister discovers that the new and fascinating world of business and industry, with its amazing progress in supplying human needs, has been made possible largely by the application of sound principles of administration. Examining the catalog of a university, he will note the multiplicity of courses in administration related to almost all fields of human endeavor. Looking past business and industry, he will see that the social sciences depend on administrative processes for their successful operation. The whole realm of political science brings to its service trained administrators and would be overwhelmed by its complexity if experts in administration were not available. Education has many unsolved problems, but its situation would be chaotic if it did not employ the science of administration in the operation of educational institutions.

Strangely enough, theological schools have until recently thought of administration as a subject outside the curriculum. A course in pastoral duties was traditional, and sometimes the subject was lifted to the level of academic respectability by labeling it "pastoral theology." More recently, theological institutions have begun to respond to the pressure of need and have included courses in church administration as essential to the preparation of the modern minister. A whole new world of helpfulness is thus opened up to the minister as he begins to learn to deal with the increasing administrative demands made on him by the same sort of mastery of principles and methods that he has been disciplined to exercise in his function as preacher and teacher.

Administration Is an Art to Be Practiced

Elizabeth Barrett Browning is credited with having said, "The art way is the only way to tell truth." Certainly the distinguished poet and wife of Robert Browning, the still more distinguished poet, did not mean to say that one must be an artist in order to tell the truth. Rather, she meant that all effective communication of truth must possess elements of artistry. For what is art but just that—the communication of truth with such insight and skill as to evoke involuntary appreciation? A child may strike random and discordant notes on a piano; an artist will translate these meaningless sounds into music. Anyone can daub a mixture of clashing colors on a canvas; an artist can take the same colors and canvas and paint an exquisite sunset. In the course of a week each of us probably will have used most of the basic words in the vocabulary; an artist will take these words and write or speak them in such fashion that what he says will be read or heard with delight and remembered with growing appreciation.

Ministers well may think of themselves as artists. They are seeking to communicate truth with insight and skill so as to affect human life. They have two principal media of communication—words and behavior. The minister knows that there must be elements of artistry in his preaching if it is to be effective.

"But," the minister objects, "administration makes me a mechanic, not an artist." Jesus was an artist with words, but there is another side of his artistry. Observe him in life situations and note the skill and insight with which he discovered and developed disciples, answered his critics, turned skeptics into believers, planned and carried out practical projects, relieved sufferers and comforted mourners, built his church and established his kingdom. It is astonishing how often Jesus was interrupted, how difficult it was for him to be alone even for prayer, yet observe with what patience he welcomed these demands on his time and energy. To portray him, the great artists have seized not so much on what Jesus said as what he did.

Ordway Tead says in *The Art of Administration:*

"Administration is . . . a fine art because it summons an imposing body of special talents on behalf of a collaborative creation which is integral to the conduct of civilized living today. This creation is comprised of the ongoing operation of numerous organizations through which human individuals are hopefully gaining many of their necessary and rightful satisfactions." [7] Mr. Tead points out that the administrator as artist should be in command both of general principles and ways of applying them. He insists that the administrator, thus conceived, is primarily concerned with persons rather than with processes. Administration is of course concerned with organization and management, with efficiency and profits, with conservation and economy, but underlying all this is administration's basic concern for persons. There may be many immediate and instrumental aims, but the ultimate aim is enriched and growing personalities. According to this viewpoint, "The measure of the soundness of whatever features the management may desire to provide is the *enhancement of the selfhood of all participants.* They have to be helped to grow toward a condition where a sharing of partnership attitudes and cooperative practices will progressively become the fact." [8]

This viewpoint may well revolutionize the attitude of the minister toward his administrative duties. A card on the pulpit stand, placed so that the preacher could not avoid seeing it, bore these words: "What are you trying to do to these people?" This question is equally pertinent in all administrative matters. The details of church life, the management of its affairs, the direction of its leaders, the cooperative solving of its problems are not machinery; they are the gospel on its behavioral side. In these ordinary affairs the minister sees human nature in action, he observes a democratic society given demonstration, he watches men and women grow under difficulties, he observes the impact of personality on personality, he studies the sources of conflict and their resolution. He finds out why and how persons can best work together. He realizes that in all these situations there are opportunities for communication of Christian truth fully as effective as preaching from the pulpit.

In every situation the minister sees himself in the role of teacher and the interpersonal relationships involved as the curriculum. He learns, as Ordway Tead has said, that "nothing less than the cultivation of whole men is what our kind of society is dedicated to. Nothing less than this, therefore, has to be shared as a responsibility by administrators who have themselves become wholesome enough to know how their labors combine the creative demands both of self and society." [9] Is it not clear that the minister is no less an artist as administrator than he is as preacher and teacher?

Administration Involves Orderly Processes

Administration is both an art and a science. This aspect of artistry, as we have seen, calls for insights, intuitions, interpretations, inspirations, especially as the artist seeks to communicate to persons his feeling, thinking, and willing. The artist, even though a genius, is not freed from the demands of exactness. There are laws which apply to the fine arts just as really as to physics and chemistry. When the minister considers methods of administration, he is dealing with his job on its scientific side.

At the outset, it should be understood that administration is means, not end. When confusion occurs at this point, the minister is justified in his rebellion against his role as administrator. The same thing may be said about preaching—it is never an end in itself. The beginning point of the administrative process is always the definition of aims. Always the question must be confronted, What is the Christian purpose of the administrative activity? Tested thus, some activities will be found out of line, as when the purpose is to advance personal prestige, or to gain control over others, or to take advantage of the unsuspecting, or even to increase the numbers and wealth of the church for its own sake.

Jesus taught his disciples to pray, "Thy kingdom come. Thy will be done in earth, as it is in heaven" (Matt. 6:10, AV). Again he said, "But seek first his kingdom and his righteousness, and all these things shall be yours as well" (Matt. 6:33). Paul makes Christ's lordship the test of purpose: "He is the head of the body, the church . . . that in everything he might be preëminent" (Col. 1:18). Correlative with the lordship of Christ is the supremacy of the worth of persons: "Why do you pass judgment on your brother? Or you, why do you despise your brother? For we shall all stand before the judgment seat of God. . . . It is right not to eat meat or drink wine or do anything that makes your brother stumble" (Rom. 14:10, 21). Failure to exalt Christ and to respect persons has been responsible for as many divisions in churches as failure to preach and receive sound doctrine.

Having defined the purpose of the activity, the next step in the administrative process is to locate the difficulties in the way of achievement. Good administrative procedure calls for an honest and objective evaluation of obstacles. The minister may tend to minimize the difficulties, since as a man of God he magnifies the resource of faith. Faith is not negated by fact but is exercised more intelligently when the opposing circumstances are known.

Alongside the liabilities should immediately be placed the assets. What are the favorable factors? What are the resources, personal and material? What are the intangibles, the supplies of the spirit?

How now do assets and liabilities compare? What will be necessary in order to make the opportunities outweigh the difficulties?

The next step calls for planning and organizing. Planning involves looking ahead, foreseeing obstacles, predicting outcomes. "Don't cross a bridge until you come to it," says an adage. This is bad advice; men who have accomplished most foresaw the need of a bridge and had it ready when the time for crossing came. Planning considers alternatives: if we take this or that or the other direction, what will be the consequences? Organizing means bringing together the resources needed to make the plan work. Person must be related to person, activity to activity, so as to achieve maximum effectiveness with minimum waste and friction. Planning and organizing a fruitful program of teaching and training, or of enlisting and evangelizing, or of giving and serving, or similar church enterprises requires fully as much spiritual awareness as planning and organizing a sermon in its setting of worship.

Plans having been made and organizations having been set up on paper, directing and co-ordinating the procedures will be necessary. Ministers are especially liable to the error of making plans without providing adequate direction. Who will be the director? Who will be associated with him? What will be the limits of their authority? What assistance will they need? How will their actions receive church approval? These questions having been answered, problems of co-ordination arise. How will those responsible for a church organization, for example, the Sunday school, relate themselves to pastor and staff, deacons and church officers, and other organizations of the church? Much confusion and sometimes friction may be avoided through careful co-ordination.

Always there is the administrative question of control. A New Testament church ideally is a spiritual democracy, but every activity cannot be under the direct control of the total congregation. Has the pastor, as chief officer of the church, executive control? Is control vested in the deacons, chosen representatives of the church? Are heads of the several church organizations, with their associates, in full control of these agencies? Good administration calls for a policy of correlation according to which authority will be translated into teamwork. The church council is an example of good administrative policy-making.

When it is said that all the affairs of a New Testament church are under church control, obviously it does not mean that its servants and leaders are deprived of initiative. What is required is obedience to Paul's injunction, "But all things should be done decently and in order" (1 Cor. 14:40). A church, under guidance of its minister, fulfils its mission as it carries on its work through orderly administrative processes.

Administration Prevents Conflict and Preserves Peace

At the birth of Jesus angels sang, "On earth peace among men with whom he is pleased" (Luke 2:14). Tragically, earth has known little of peace since the coming of the Prince of peace. Even more tragically, the peace of the world has been disturbed often by religious wars in which Christians have destroyed Christians. Despite all the teachings of the New Testament to the contrary, churches have not always obeyed the injunction, "Be at peace among yourselves" (1 Thess. 5:13). The history of almost any congregation will record the sad story of internal strife.

What occasions this disruption of church fellowship? Sometimes the contention is over doctrinal differences, but even when this is apparently true, often there are underlying causes that are personal in nature. Again and again the disturbance may be traced to faulty administration. Perhaps the pastor, consciously or unconsciously, showed favoritism toward certain members or slighted others. Perhaps unauthorized policies were pursued or activities carried on. Perhaps ill-advised plans were made and their attempted execution resulted disastrously. Perhaps the plans were good and church approved but the leadership was unfortunate. Perhaps those associated on a committee could not work together because of clash in temperament. Perhaps the false principle that "the end justifies the means" betrayed confidence and incited anger. Perhaps there was downright unworthiness and malfeasance. Almost always there was the element of hurt pride, bringing resentment and retaliation. Veteran pastors could document almost every one of these causes of church disruption.

Since preaching is not often the cause of these difficulties, it usually cannot be the cure. Almost every preacher has known the heartbreak of preaching a gospel of peace and love to loveless church members who are at strife with one another. Then he begins to learn that peace and love are not learned by listening. In the interpersonal

relations of working together in the church, Christians learn to put
into practice what they have been taught from the pulpit and the
classroom.

The minister is working at a supremely important matter when he
thus utilizes situations of experience to demonstrate the operation of
Jesus' great commandment "that you love one another as I have
loved you" (John 15:12). Just as earnestly as he prays for guidance
in proclaiming the gospel and interpreting its application from the
pulpit, so must the minister pray for wisdom in dealing with affairs
involving the relation of persons to persons in the church. The
study of the Bible will be more rewarding if he studies his people
with a view to teaching them how to get along together.

Karen Horney classifies persons as to their relations to one another
in three categories, those who move against others, those who move
away from others, and those who move toward others.[10] In the first
two groups are found those who constitute administrative problems.
The minister is familiar with the constitutional "aginner," the man
who habitually moves against others. He may be like the deacon who
voted against his own motion because he didn't like to see anything
passed unanimously! Usually such a person is deeply insecure and
needs reassurance. To him may come a sense of security and significance through selection for leadership of a project which otherwise he would have opposed. The wise pastor will break through
this barrier of contrariness by means of administrative procedure
that bolsters rather than shakes self-confidence.

More personality-warped than those who move against others are
those who move away from others. Church rolls often are loaded
with the names of such persons. They constitute a large percentage
of the inactive members who simply have dropped out of sight.
Often they have experienced no specific hurt; they simply have
come to feel themselves of no consequence in the church and conse-
quently have quit. Nobody seems to know or care what has become
of them. Sometimes they fall into worldliness and sin, but in many
cases they live inoffensive but useless lives. Their loss is often the result of faulty administration. In the planning and distribution of responsibilities they were left out.

These "aginners" and "quitters" join the troublemakers when
factionalism arises in the church. They may not know what it is all
about, but they come to the congregational business meeting pre-

pared to join one or the other of the factions seeking a majority vote. Thus the door may swing wide open to a disgraceful exposure to the public of unchristian conduct on the part of Christian people. In almost every case the difficulty might have been avoided by the practice of Christian principles of administration.

Administration is put to one of its severest tests when conflict has occurred and peace must be restored. Again preaching alone is not adequate. There must be planning, organizing, directing, co-ordinating, spiritual energizing, re-enlisting in service and giving, the co-operative shaping of policies based on Christian principles. It is of this kind of ministry that Paul writes to the disturbed church at Corinth: "Such is the confidence that we have through Christ toward God. Not that we are sufficient of ourselves to claim anything as coming from us; our sufficiency is from God, who has qualified us to be ministers of a new covenant, not in a written code but in the Spirit; for the written code kills, but the Spirit gives life" (2 Cor. 3:4–6).

Administration Supplies the Need of Fellowship

Henry Clay Lindgren raises the question, "Why are other people so important to us?" He calls attention to the troublesomeness of groups in modern society—how they block and frustrate attempts to meet needs and how they inhibit and frustrate thought and action. They isolate themselves from certain groups that particularly annoy and block them, but in so doing usually turn to other groups that promise more satisfaction. Some people feel that the fewer groups they belong to the better off they are; others feel that it pays to belong to as many groups as possible. Whether life is lived in association with few or many groups, it cannot escape the necessity of group relationship, for the sense of belonging is essential to the individual's well-being. Professor Lindgren concludes that "a satisfying group life is essential for personal happiness and emotional health, and it is actually in our relationships with mature groups that we find some of our best opportunities for freedom of thought and expression." [11]

Dwellers in the country may live miles apart and yet be close together. City dwellers may live close together and yet be total strangers. There is a saying that a city church is composed of people who do not know one another and wish they did; a country church is composed of people who know one another and wish they didn't! Geography does not necessarily make the difference. A city or a country church may have few bonds that bind its members together. To paraphrase Edgar Guest, "It takes a heap o' livin' in a church to make it home." Just to sit together in the Sunday worship service does not change an aggregation of unrelated Christians into "a gathered community." Robert C. Walton describes a church of the New Testament era as such a community:

There was an ideal of ordered corporate life. Individuals might break it by their quarrelsomeness, their heresies, or their relapse into paganism, but the Christians everywhere were a new brotherhood. The churches, separated from contemporary society, in the world yet not of it, were closely-knit communities in which the middle walls of partition were broken down, and men were increasingly conscious of the fellowship of the universal church.[12]

How does such community develop, and how is it maintained? The answer is contained in two words—regeneration and participation. The first step, without which no other step is possible, is a saving experience involving repentance toward God and faith in the Lord Jesus Christ. Those who have undergone this experience are bound together as a community of the redeemed, which transcends distinctions of class or nationality or race. This is the foundation on which realized community must be built through voluntary association in Christian activities—worshiping, teaching and learning, training for and in service, sharing through witnessing and giving, accepting and discharging responsibility. To fail to participate is to remove oneself from the "gathered community."

"But," the minister may object, "aside from worshiping and giving, are there enough places of active service in a church to go around? Is not this ideal of every-member service, especially in a large church, administratively unattainable?" No, not if the major function of administration is conceived as division of labor and delegation of responsibility. Within the framework of the church's organizations for teaching, training, missionary promotion, stewardship practice, witnessing, and service may be found a place of active participation for every member from the youngest to the oldest not physically or mentally incapacitated. Here is an answer to the minister's discouragement over the poor quality of work done in some of the church's organizations. The teaching and training, the witnessing and serving may not measure up to high standards; nevertheless, participation is building community and fellowship is growing Christian character.

One of the results of the increasing urbanization of life is the lonely person. Paul E. Johnson thus states the case:

No one can be a person in the mature sense unless he is free to assert his individuality. Yet to assert one's individuality is to separate oneself from the sustaining relationship and to endure the distress of standing alone. The price of independence is loneliness. The price of dependence is surrender of individuality. The cost of either alternative is too great to bear. If the dilemma is insoluble and inescapable, then we are left in despair.[13]

A church, seeking to realize this ideal of every-member involvement, has the answer to the dilemma, the cure for the despair. No one need ever suffer from the agony of loneliness who finds a place of usefulness and significance in the manifold activities of a community of Christians called a church.

Never let it be said that administration is a handicap to the minister's spiritual service or the church's spiritual functioning! One might as well say that hands and feet, heart and lungs, nerves and brain and the multiplex activities of other parts of the human organism are hindrances to the growth of personality. Through this ministry can be fulfilled the ideal: "For we are his workmanship, created in Christ Jesus for good works, which God prepared beforehand, that we should walk in them" (Eph. 2:10).

Chapter IV

Ministers Must Discover and Develop Leaders

WHY IS IT," asked the exasperated pastor at a church council meeting, "that the smartest people in this church will not accept places of leadership?" "That's easy," replied a deacon, "they are the smartest people in the church!" Their "smartness," he explained, was evidenced by the fact that they obtained the benefits of church membership without paying the price of leadership. Actually, were they not paying the high price of neglect? The problem of how to interest and enlist them is an administrative responsibility of primary importance.

Ask any group of ministers, "What is your most difficult administrative problem?" Almost invariably the reply will be, "Lack of responsible, competent, consecrated leaders." The lack can never be supplied once for all, for in our mobile society, places that are satisfactorily filled one year will have to be filled again the next year. Even when there is not a high incidence of transiency, leaders must be replaced for various reasons and new leaders discovered to take care of enlargement. Every minister and staff member knows that the quality and adequacy of leadership determines more than any other human factor the success of the church. Administration is functioning at its best when it provides a continuing supply of reasonably satisfactory leadership.

When capable Christian men and women turn aside from the call of their church to serve in places of responsibility and others equally capable are overlooked and never given the opportunity to

46

serve, there is something wrong with the church's concept and interpretation of leadership.

The idea may have arisen that a church, being a sacred institution, must draw its leadership from those who are ordained—a special brand of ministers and deacons who have received a divine call and who have been set apart to run the church. Or the concept of the leader may be that of the dominant person who enjoys notice and authority and to whom the right to run the church is readily surrendered. Or the idea may prevail that leadership should be in the hands of a select inner circle of especially devout people who haven't anything much else to do. Or leaders may be chosen haphazardly from the faithful few who attend the congregational business meetings. Wherever such false or inadequate views prevail, the blame usually can be laid at the door of faulty administration.

Leadership Is an Inescapable Responsibility of the Minister

A leader is one whom others follow. Jesus assumed his right of leadership when he said to his first disciples, "Follow me!" The picture of him given in the Gospels is that of the perfect leader. He won the confidence of those whom he called, he took them into partnership, he gave them vision and instruction, he communicated to them his sense of divine mission, he infused into them undefeatable faith and loyalty, he disclosed the difficulties as enormous but the rewards as glorious. From the mount of vision, where he taught the life-transforming truths recorded in the Sermon on the Mount, he went with the disciples into the valley of human need, and "great crowds followed him" (Matt. 8:1). Later, when the multitudes abandoned him and he knew that he was to be killed, he said to the little group gathered about him, "If any man would come after me, let him deny himself and take up his cross and follow me" (Matt. 16:24). Victorious over death, ascended and undefeatable, he continues to lead the spiritual forces of the universe.

Ministers called to follow this supreme Leader cannot escape responsibility for leadership. Acceptance of this leadership responsibility, however, may be fatally misinterpreted. The minister may see himself as seated on a white horse, his eyes as a flame of fire, on his head a crown, leading a victorious army! History, ancient and modern, is full of stories of ministers with this delusion of grandeur who mistook the picture of the conquering Christ for their own. The leadership of Christ which earthly ministers are to strive to copy is that of the teacher and servant who gathered about himself disciples whom he trained to be servants. What glories await the faithful minister when he is welcomed into heaven by the Master he may not fully know, but his supreme award this side of the grave will be in winning others to Christ and developing in them qualities of leadership translated into terms of servantship. By the very terms of his calling and of his response in following Christ, the minister must be a leader, and his leadership finds its highest expression in discovering and developing other leaders.

Leadership Needs a New Approach

A minister may look over the congregation or leaf through the membership register with a sense of near despair. "They just don't have leadership possibilities," he may conclude. He may eagerly watch for newcomers with leadership attributes who may be persuaded to join his church; or, in his worst moments, he may cast an envious eye on qualified persons who belong to a neighboring congregation. Perhaps he assumes, as is commonly done, that leaders are made from those who are born with certain innate traits—superior intelligence, winsome personality, instinctive initiative, native friendliness, spiritual sensitivity, inherited strength of character, exceptional powers of persuasion.

For centuries it was believed that such characteristics were due largely to heredity and would ordinarily be possessed by members of certain favored families. While it is undoubtedly true that more leaders come from some families than from others, the explanation is not biological inheritance. Careful studies have exploded the "trait theory" of leadership. An extensive review of studies made in this field led the researchers to conclude that the relatively slight differences in traits of personality between leaders and nonleaders "tends to negate the trait approach to leadership and suggests the utilization of other frames of reference in the study of leadership phenomena." [1] Of course, there are hereditary factors, such as intelligence level and physical stamina, but these factors are highly variable and are not confined to favored families. The truth seems to be evident that leaders are made rather than born and that the qualities of leadership are acquired rather than inherited.

Another finding is that leadership is not a generalized quality of personality. Leadership emerges as a specific reaction to a specific situation. A person may be a leader of children but could not lead adults; a leader of activity but not be a leader of thought; a leader in social affairs but could not lead a prayer meeting; a leader in business matters but could not lead a discussion; or the leader of a building campaign but could not lead an evangelistic crusade. Occasionally, an exceptional person is found who can lead in many directions, but as a rule leadership, especially in a church, is limited to certain specific areas. There are few normal individuals who are not qualified to lead in some ways.

Does the leader gather about himself a group of followers, or do the followers create the leader? Obviously, it works both ways, but more often the leader emerges from the situation created by those who become his followers. History is replete with instances of situations that called forth the leader rather than the leader's giving rise to the situation. Leading and following are interactive. This fact can be observed in almost any church, where a situation of need brought forth a person to meet the need. One may step into shoes too little for him and never be comfortable; but one may step into shoes too big for him and grow to fill them. There is justification for calling persons to church jobs beyond their abilities, if at the same time provision is made to guide their growth.

This interactional aspect of leadership is thus stated by Cecil Gibb:

Leadership is always relative to the situation—relative, that is, in two senses: (a) that leadership flourishes only in a problem situation and (b) that the nature of the leadership role is determined by the goal of the group; and this is, in fact, the second principle of leadership, that it is always toward some objective goal. The third principle is that leadership is a process of mutual stimulation—a social interactional phenomenon in which the attitudes, ideals and aspirations of the followers play as important a determining role as do the individuality and personality of the leader.[2]

This view of leadership relieves the minister of the thankless duty of seeking out people who seem to have leadership qualifications and appointing them to church tasks. His much more satisfying function is to aid groups in the church to recognize their need of leadership and then to produce it from their own ranks. This does not mean that a class or department or other unit of the church organization will find and select its own leaders; election to office is always the responsibility of the church. It does mean that every such group will be alert to its needs of leadership and to the leadership needs of other groups and count it high distinction to furnish such leadership from its own membership rather than having them imposed from without.

The distinction between the leader and the follower is in fact not a sharp one. The leader in one situation is a follower in another. In a sense, all members of a church truly identified with its fellowship are both leaders and followers, some in one capacity, others in another, leaders producing followers and followers producing leaders. In the midst stands the minister, not with appointive power, but with Spirit-filled ability to instruct, inspire, interpret, and guide.

Leadership Calls for Insight in Discovery and Recruitment

The minister may have sight without insight. He may look at his congregation and see a miscellaneous collection of mediocre individuals, prosaic and ordinary, with here and there an exceptionally bright and promising person. He may see in the children an average bunch of boys and girls and in the young people a typical lot of adolescents. "Not much promise of leadership in this crowd," he may conclude. Yet the chances are that within the membership of such an average church are as good prospects for leadership as Jesus had in the group that gathered about him. The difference is that Jesus added insight to sight—he saw what anyone could see in these plain men and women, but he saw more and more deeply.

What did these disciples of Jesus lack? Almost everything—formal education, social status, political prestige, skill as churchmen, fluency in speech and writing, theological training, material possessions. When it is recorded that they left all and followed Jesus, their "all" did not constitute a very impressive total! From these unpromising peasants Jesus chose twelve, with an insight that represents the highest mark of a leader. Only one of them disappointed him, and this not because of any fault of the insight of Jesus.

What did Jesus see in these men that justified his choice? They were unspoiled by the rabbinical education which unfitted the religious leaders for his use. They possessed the honesty and common sense characteristic of successful working men. Their minds were open, and they were hungry for truth. They were dissatisfied with themselves and the world in which they lived, hence were susceptible to Jesus' call for revolutionary change. They were capable of intense enthusiasm and loyalty and were willing to pay the price of sacrifice for the accomplishment of a great purpose. They saw in Jesus the fulfilment of their highest hopes and in his kingdom the realization of their messianic dream. In spite of all their handicaps, they had those essential qualities that Jesus recognized as fitting them for his purpose. His greatness as leader is indicated by the fact that he did the best he could with what he had. And how gloriously these men responded to his confidence and to his guidance!

It is noteworthy that Jesus lived with these men before he chose them. John, in apparent amazement, points out the keen discrimination of Jesus in his selection of followers. He did not commit himself to all alike, "because he knew all men and needed no one to bear witness of man; for he himself knew what was in man" (John 2:24-25). The minister must cultivate this quality of discriminating insight as he seeks to discover and recruit leadership. What shall we look for? Veteran administrators list such attributes as (1) physical and nervous energy, (2) purpose and direction, (3) enthusiasm, (4) friendliness, (5) decisiveness, (6) intelligence, (7) teaching ability, (8) technical mastery, (9) integrity, (10) faith.[3] Rarely will these qualities be found in one person, but some of them are obvious in the members of almost any congregation and others may be perceived as potential.

The pastor, together with staff members and a discreet personnel committee, should regularly canvass the total church membership, name by name, with a view to rating them as "available" and "unavailable" for places of responsible service in the church. The "unavailables" will be set aside as being too young or too old, physically or mentally incapacitated, nonresident or inactive, spiritually and morally disqualified. The "availables" may then be classified as actual or potential, ready for immediate enlistment or requiring some form of pretraining. Those now ready may be studied with a view to the specific type of service they may best be invited to consider. The most effectual approach designed to engage prospects should be sought with a view to enrolling them in an appropriate course of study. The discovery and enlistment of present or prospective church workers can never be wholesale or a one-man undertaking;

each person must be given individual attention by responsible co-operating persons under the guidance of the minister.

Finding the right people for church jobs is an unending activity. The personnel-nominating committee may facilitate its work by the use of a form to be checked by church members indicating their interests and attitudes. The following form has been found especially valuable because the inquiry discloses interests and abilities outside the church as well as within. Frequently the clue to a church member's leadership potential is not found in his present church activity, which may be quite limited, but in his vocation. This form is designed to obtain information along both lines.

The Fellowship of the Responsible

We believe that the obligations and privileges of service in our church are for *every* member. As a church member, you will recognize that you belong to one of the following groups:

1. Unable to serve actively because of age, health, work, or other conditions.
2. Unwilling to serve because of lack of experience or training.
3. Ready to serve now if given something to do within present ability.
4. Already serving but in need of further training and counsel.

Our church needs your service and you need to serve for your Christian growth and happiness. We want to provide you a place of service or of preparation. We would like to know (1) your previous experience in church work; (2) your experience in other activities that fit you for church work. Please check carefully the blank spaces in the form below and return to church right away.

Check any experience you have had in:

ADMINISTRATION

____deacon____treasurer____financial secy.____clerk____other;____ business manager____foreman____personnel director____other executive.

SUPERVISION

____Supt. C.R.____Nursery____Beg.____Pri.____Jr.____Int.____Y.P. ____Ext.____TU officer____WMU officer____Brotherhood officer____other;____public school supt.____public works supt.____ personnel supervisor____other.

MINISTERS MUST DISCOVER AND DEVELOP LEADERS 53

ACCOUNTING, OFFICE WORK

____SS secy.____TU secy.____WMU secy.____Brotherhood secy. ____other;____bookkeeper____public accountant____office accounting____business secy.____typing____mimeographing____filing____ mailing____librarian____other.

PUBLIC RELATIONS, PUBLICITY

____church visiting____class or dept. visiting____church publicity ____other;____radio, TV____selling____advertising____promotion ____newspaper____other.

TEACHING, TRAINING

____Nursery____Beg.____Pri.____Jr.____Int.____Y.P.____Adult____ other;____public school____private school____commercial____college____other.

MUSIC, WORSHIP

____choir member____choir director____inst. musician____soloist ____other;____public school music teacher____band or orchestra ____TV or radio____usher____other.

SERVICE

____church host or hostess____dining room, kitchen____building, grounds____other;____public service____hotel or restaurant____social work____health____other.

SPECIAL INTEREST IN

____administration____supervision____accounting____public relations____teaching, training____music, worship____service____other. ____Will consider immediate invitation to serve. ____Will consider enrolment for pretraining. ____Will serve on occasions but not regularly. ____Will study and pray—not available for active service now.

Leadership Demands Tact and Skill in Supervision

The most appropriate over-all scriptural designation of the minister is *episkopos,* bishop or supervisor. Supervision is a major function of the minister as leader and a major means of developing leadership. Tactful and skilled supervisors have come to be recognized as indispensable specialists in industry and education. On them more than on any other members of the personnel executive group depend the smooth operation of the enterprise, harmonious relations among the workers, good morale throughout the entire organization, and maximum productivity in line with high standards.

Minister and staff gather about them auxiliary supervisors— general superintendent of the Sunday school, director of the Training Union, presidents of Woman's Missionary Union and the Brotherhood, director of music ministries, director of stewardship and church finance, age-group specialists and superintendents, according to the size and complexity of the church. It is undesirable and usually impossible for the minister to give direct supervision to the many workers involved in the activities of the well-organized church. His responsibility is that of supervisor of the heads of departments and organizations, whom he will teach the art of supervision. They in turn will give direct supervision to the many workers.

The end result of supervision is to prevent failure and assure success. Prevention of failure is a highly important matter. The officer or teacher who is failing bears a heavy burden and is liable to become a menace to his fellow workers. Very few people are willing to admit that they are failing or, if so, that it is their fault. Thus they tend to compensate by criticizing and belittling others, seeking to save face through faultfinding. The supervisor who understands this will not retaliate, but will try quietly to find the cause of failure and to remedy it. Often this can be accomplished by means of a sympathetic interview in which the failing worker will be given full opportunity to express himself, after which he may be led to see his mistake and correct it. A book or pamphlet placed in the hands of a failing worker often will turn the tide from failure to success.

"Success" is a relative term. To the question, "Am I succeeding or failing?" the answer is rarely an unqualified yes or no. The tactful supervisor will not pass judgment. Rather, he will begin by finding something to commend and lead the worker to a self-revelation of unsatisfactory results. "Since you would like to make improvement," the supervisor says, "let us find ways of doing it." Improvement then becomes a co-operative quest by which the unsatisfactory worker, with the help of the supervisor, discovers better ways of working and in the discovery develops confidence.

Superintendents of Sunday school departments and leaders of Training Union groups need especially to be given this view of their responsibility. They have other incidental duties, but their main job is that of improving teaching and learning. To that end they should visit classes and observe Training Union programs. Such visits should be friendly, inconspicuous, care being taken never to embarrass the teacher or leader. Mental notes should be made which afterward will be transferred to notebook for use in the supervisory conference. The supervisor will be alert to note the degree of preparation, the use of helps, relation of teacher or leader to class or group, spontaneity of participation, utilization of previous assignments, commendation of good work, poise and tact in difficult situations, concern for individuals, definiteness of purpose, progress of procedure from beginning to conclusion, evidences of spiritual fruitfulness. Such points as these may then be taken up in the interview which follows, privately in some cases and with fellow teachers or leaders at times.

A veteran supervisor thus sums up the job:

The modern supervisor must learn that the price of good supervision is eternal vigilance and alertness to the problem of the humans working under his direction. He must become "people-orientated." This means that he must think of people first and of himself last. He must remain neutral. He must not get himself involved emotionally in any situation. He must be objective. He must attempt to understand all situations in terms of the person involved first, the organization he is serving second, and of himself last of all. The best supervisor is the one who makes it possible for other people to work at their highest and best level in the interest of the company for which they are all working.[4]

Leadership Is More Effectual When Group-Centered

In the Christian concept the leader is not one set apart, but one who is identified with the church or a group within the church and has been given responsibility for stimulation and guidance of thought and activity. The less attention he calls to himself, the better leader he is. The more credit the group derives for achievement, the more creditable is the leader. The Chinese philosopher Lao-tzu, who lived in the sixth century B.C., is credited with having said: "A leader is best when people barely know that he exists; not so good when people obey and acclaim him; worst when they despise him. Fail to honor people, they fail to honor you; but of a good leader, who talks little, when his work is finished, his aim fulfilled, they will say, We did this ourselves." [5]

Leadership Is Known by the Leaders Produced

The good leader knows that he is expendable, that he serves best when he prepares others to replace him. The measure of the minister is not "what we've done since I came," but "how well they have done after I left." John the Baptist said concerning Jesus, "He must increase, but I must decrease" (John 3:30). Blessed is the minister who in sincerity can say this concerning the leaders whom he discovers and develops!

Ministers, necessarily skilled in the art of public speech, tend to talk too much in the training of leaders. Those who listen may gain inspiration, but they are prone to go away from the speech-making session with a feeling of frustration and inadequacy. When a text in a study course is taught, all too often it is teacher-centered rather than class-centered. Excellent exposition of the contents of the book may be made, but there is usually little carry-over into actual practice. If participation is secured, it may be of the recitation type, with the teacher still at the center as he asks all the questions and comments on the answers. What is needed is not abandonment of the study of books under the guidance of teachers who make the subject matter come alive, but a supplementary method which shifts responsibility from teacher to learner. This supplemental teaching-learning experience for the development of leaders is popularly known as the "group workshop method."

According to Paul Douglass, "The church operated as a group workshop encourages the definition of purposeful goals, the involvement of people in participant roles, and the concern for individual and social change which results from effectual group performance." [6] Continuing, Mr. Douglass states the conditions which make for such a productive group: (1) clear purpose; (2) operational freedom; (3) clearly defined roles; (4) responsibility for clearly defined and worthwhile tasks wholeheartedly undertaken; (5) mutually constructive criticism; (6) skill in interchange, with respect for persons; (7) open-mindedness; (8) friendly, unanxious atmosphere; (9) confidence and co-operation in the spirit of love; (10) satisfaction of achievement through pooled effort; (11) ethically guided; (12) goal-oriented and God-related.

Take an actual situation. A church becomes dissatisfied with the quality of teaching in its Sunday school. Criticism has been expressed of the Sunday school as "the most wasted hour of the week." [7] There is just enough truth in the exaggerated criticism to disturb the pastor, the minister of education, and the group of thoughtful officers and teachers. Renewed emphasis may be placed on the study of books on better teaching and better Sunday schools. Supplementing such textbook study may be a workshop dealing with the actual local situation and its improvement.

Gathered about tables, with notebooks and pencils and source materials, officers and teachers under guidance of the minister may tackle the problem of actually improving the quality of teaching that goes on in their Sunday school. The purpose having been clearly defined, it will be agreed that entire freedom to express his opinion and contribute his experience and ideas may be felt by everyone. Each member of the group will state his or her role in the procedure —pastor, minister of education, general officers, department superintendents, secretaries, musicians, teachers. Each in turn is given opportunity to reply to the questions: Considering the teaching situation from my particular angle, what weakness do I see? What do I think I could do to bring about improvement? Each of these brief statements having been recorded and read back to the group, the questions become: What can we do together to effect the needed improvement? How can officers help teachers and how can teachers help officers, avoiding criticism of one another and maintaining mutual respect and regard? By this time certain desired changes will be evident. The question then must be confronted, Can we examine these proposed changes with open minds and without becoming defensive? A call to prayer at this crucial moment would be in order, as divine wisdom and Christian spirit are sought. In an atmosphere free from anxiety and self-interest, members of the group pool their resources, re-examine their materials and methods, restate their objectives, and recommit themselves to the teaching enterprise as a God-given responsibility.

The steps thus indicated cannot ordinarily be taken in one session. The workshop method calls for continued activity over a period of time. It may well be followed by a series of book studies, which will take on new life and meaning as giving guidance in developing the plans resulting from the workshop experience. Or, reversing the order, the book study may concentrate attention on the need of the workshop method in order that the ideas discussed in class may be given practical application. Douglass well says:

A productive group must provide role satisfaction to its members. Members find that role satisfaction only when they operate in situations which demand their mastery of new knowledge and their performance with improved new skills, and which provide opportunity for practice in the use for new power. . . . Practice in the skill of doing is essential to every step in character growth and role satisfaction.[8]

Leadership Maintains Good Public Relations

Ministers may think of the church in such exclusively local terms as to overlook its public relations. A church in the New Testament concept is primarily a specific body of baptized believers, independent and self-governed. Yet a church would be a feeble affair that did not recognize its interdependence and interrelatedness. A church is not a public institution in the same sense as a school or a post office or a civic center; yet it is a public institution in the sense that it lives for and by the community in which it is located. A church could not exist in a desert where there are no people. By the same token, residence in a community without a church would be undesirable to most Americans. The cultivation of right attitudes of the church toward its community and the community toward the church is termed "public relations."

A church is unfortunate if it has poor public relations. Many factors enter into this undesirable situation. The location of the church may have stirred resentment, some residents feeling that the church is an infringement on their privacy, with cars lining the street and sometimes blocking driveways and creating pedestrian hazards. The building may be an offense—poorly designed, unattractively built and kept, an architectural eyesore. The church may give the impression of inconsiderateness concerning public welfare—noisiness, a smoky furnace, paper-littered premises, disregard of health requirements. More frequently, the church's poor public relations are due to neglect—unfriendliness, lack of attractive publicity, disregard of its need of good will.

Good public relations depend on effective communication. Communication is concerned basically with meanings. Members of the community will ask: What meaning has this church for me and my family? What meaning has it for our neighbors? What meaning has it for the neighborhood as a whole? What meaning has it representatively as belonging to a denomination? What meaning has it for the nation and the world? "Probably the most important function of communication is to give meaning to life," observes Henry Clay Lindgren, social psychologist.

As long as the events which go on around us "make sense". . . to ourselves, we are able to cope with life as we see it. For purposes of our peace of mind, it does not matter whether our interpretations are correct, as viewed by the objective outsider; the important thing is that they must *seem reasonable* to us. When events occur which do not seem reasonable and in which we are very much personally involved, our anxiety is aroused. If we are emotionally mature, this anxiety will impel us to study and investigate the puzzling situation until it again "makes sense" to us, in other words, until learning occurs.[9]

The sort of communication that makes for good public relations is not just what appears on the church bulletin board or in the announcement page of the Saturday newspaper. Good public relations are the product of broad-minded, public-spirited leadership. A narrow, self-centered leadership inevitably will result in bad public relations. There may be no positive offense against the public welfare; the fault may be a negative lack of concern for the public good. There may be need for better public schools, better roads, better health facilities, better local government, better provision for recreation, better race relations, and similar improvements; but a church may go on its way apparently oblivious of these needs. The birth of babies may go unnoticed, children may be receiving no Christian education, families may be without church homes, the poor may not have the gospel preached to them, as the church continues in its narrow round of services, apparently unconcerned. Such a church, in the nature of things, has poor public relations and little community good will.

Good will is an intangible with high asset value. Corporations list their trade-marks among their resources, giving them monetary value along with physical properties. The United States Supreme

Court has defined good will as "the disposition of the customer to return to the place where he has been well served." Certainly, this is a matter of very great importance to a church. Since a church has no intangibles to sell or material services to render, whether or not people attend its meetings and support its program depends largely on their attitude toward it. This favorable attitude is determined in great measure by the church's leadership. Friendliness, kindness, courtesy, considerateness, concern for others, sacrifices for the common good, unfeigned love—these are the hallmarks of leadership that make for good public relations. The greatest exponent of this essential to the success of the Christian enterprise is Jesus Christ himself, who said, "I am among you as he that serveth" (Luke 22:27,AV), and who made himself the example of one who "came not to be ministered unto, but to minister, and to give his life a ransom for many" (Matt. 20:28,AV).

Chapter V

Ministries Must Be Shared by Members

T HE REFORMATION in large measure restored congregationalism. The very word "hierarchy"—government by the priesthood—had become an offense. It reversed the principle announced by Jesus, "The sabbath was made for man, not man for the sabbath" (Mark 2:27). The reformers insisted that the ministry was for the congregation, not the congregation for the ministry. The emphasis was more on the individual person.

This concept brought organizational revolution. In the hierarchical system the priesthood was highly organized, the congregation only loosely organized. Now the demand arose for a reversal of emphasis—the congregation began to be highly organized, under direction usually of a lone minister, who was identified not so much with a priestly or ministerial caste as with the congregation. Whereas in the previous centuries "the church" had connoted priesthood, in the reformed and dissenting bodies "the church" connoted congregation.

This changed concept led to rediscovery of the laity as having more significance in the work and management of the church than the clergy. The democratic concept of government "of the *people*, for the *people*, and by the *people*" was carried over into the polity of most of the non-Catholic bodies in America. There arose accordingly a demand for efficient congregational organization. Resultant types of organization have followed no uniform pattern. While there have been common salient features, variations have developed in line with the doctrinal views and traditions of the church and the ministry held by the several denominations.

Congregational Organization Is Determined by Authority

Neither lay authority nor clerical authority can be absolute. Back of any kind of authority is its source. Whether authority is vested primarily in the minister or in the layman, each exercises authority in some measure because of his office. More important than the authority of office is the prestige of the office holder. Of still greater force is the authority of common experience, according to which like-minded persons give their consent to control because it fits in with their background. Practically, there is the authority of inheritance by means of which a system of controls is passed on from generation to generation. Historically, there is the authority of the dominating personality, whose ipse dixit eventually becomes sacred and is translated into a body of discipline. Always there is the authority of the holy Scriptures, to which appeal is made in Christian circles for support of any other form of authority.

According to the view of authority accepted, congregations may be thus classified broadly:

A congregation may be viewed as subjects under authority. The power of "binding and loosing" may be interpreted as having been given exclusively to Christ's ministers, beginning with Peter. In unbroken succession, it may be held, this power has been transmitted from generation to generation and is now possessed by the priesthood in the same measure as at the beginning. A congregation therefore is a "flock of God" in the charge of the divinely appointed pastors of the church, just as sheep are in the charge of the shepherd. A congregation will need organization, but always with a view to securing obedience to their priestly superiors in carrying out the purposes of the church.

A congregation may be viewed as freemen under authority. The hierarchy represents monarchical government—the pope as supreme head of the Church, then in descending order the cardinals, the archbishops, the bishops, the priests, etc.

The episcopate represents more nearly constitutional government —bishops as heads of the church, with orders of the clergy according to rank, bishops and clergy exercising authority under the limitations of articles in the nature of a constitution acceptable to the people. Within the framework, clergy and laity possess a large measure of liberty.

For effective exercise of their functions, members of the congregation need organization. In the controlling body (synod or general assembly or conference) there is lay representation. Laymen have important responsibilities in the unit of organization known as the diocese. Within the local congregation is the vestry, made up of lay persons charged with the care of temporal affairs. In consultation with the bishop of the diocese, the vestry ordinarily will choose the rector. Organizations within the local church utilize the abilities and resources of members of the congregation as musicians, teachers, leaders of evangelistic and missionary groups, and in varied parish activities.

A congregation may be viewed as under delegated authority. Representative government is a variant of constitutional government. It tends to reverse the order, the direction being from the people to officials rather than from officials down to the people. The authority of a general assembly is recognized, its power derived "from the consent of the governed." The church is neither wholly free nor wholly bound. The elders of the church form a presbytery, and the affairs of a local church are in the hands of this body. The congregation does not surrender its authority, however, for it may reject the rule of the presbytery or it may at will replace an elder who is unsatisfactory. This form of government calls for still more careful and thorough organization of the congregation as having both ultimate control and immediate support of the church program.

A congregation may be viewed as a connectional body. In this view the church is made up of branches, each of which is originally related to the parent body. In general, the form of government is that of the episcopate, but with much greater emphasis on lay participation and responsibility and with larger freedom of the local congregation. The authority of the general conference is limited by the jurisdictional division; and both of these higher units of organization are limited by the authority of the local congregation. In one great connectional body (Methodist) the constitution provides that "the General Conference shall be composed of not less than six hundred nor more than eight hundred delegates, one-half of whom shall be ministers and one-half laymembers, to be elected by the annual conferences." According to this plan, the congregation, with its greatly increased responsibility, must have correspondingly increased organization for the performance of its functions.

A congregation may be viewed as autonomous believers. Moving toward complete separation of church and state and away from all controls by official persons or bodies, dissenting churches sought to lodge authority in the local congregation only. Realizing the necessity for fellowship and co-operation, they formed free associations or conventions, the authority of whose findings or actions would be binding only as they were voluntarily accepted by local congregations. That these associations and conventions possess considerable authority few would deny, but the authority is that of local, independent, autonomous congregations, and joins with other churches only as it sees fit, with no other than moral compulsion. Evidently such churches will need to major on organization if they are to function effectively.

Congregational Organization Is Conditioned by Function

Within these varied types of church polity, considered organizationally, there may be wide differences of concepts as to the function of the congregation. Within the same denominational body a church may be conceived functionally in a number of ways:

A congregation may function as a regiment. In military affairs a regiment consists of a number of companies of soldiers, which in turn are divided into smaller units, all under a common command. "To regiment" has come to mean the placing of persons under authority so as to secure a maximum of uniformity with a minimum of individuality. A regimented church, therefore, would be one in which heavy emphasis is placed on organization according to an exact pattern, with everybody keeping step and carrying out orders without question. The most important aspect of this type of regimented church will be the selection and training of leaders as officers in command. To break step will be interpreted as a serious offense, incurring psychological if not physical penalties.

A congregation may function as a body of worshipers. In such a church the matter of highest importance is the preparation and conduct of orderly, enriched, satisfying worship. To this end much stress will be laid on the sanctuary as a place of worship, music as a means of worship, liturgies and ceremonies as aids to worship, the sermon as the climax of worship. From such worship, it is held, will flow concomitant values. Much attention must be given accordingly to the organization and conduct of services of worship, together with training in worship.

A congregation may be viewed as an audience. Here the test of success is found in the number of persons who come to hear the preacher and attend responsively to his message. If the audiences are large and enthusiastic, the church congratulates itself on having an attractive and popular minister. The church usually finds to its satisfaction that when the crowd holds up well for the Sunday services, other things go well also—the church organizations, the growth in numbers, the finances, the support of the church program. It is not easy to maintain an audience at high level in these days of keen competition for listeners. To do so requires skilful organization of the congregation so that friend will invite friend, family will bring family, young people will attract other young people, in an ever widening circle. Publicity must be skilfully employed so that the church will be kept attractively before the public.

A congregation may function as an agency of social action. To pastor and people with social consciences none of the views indicated up to this point is adequate unless regimentation, worship, teaching, witnessing, and listening result in aggressive and constructive Christian service. The community and the world are seen as a battleground between the forces of good and evil, of justice and injustice, of education and ignorance, of health and disease, of light and darkness. "Be ye doers of the word and not hearers only!" is the slogan of this church. Good intentions are not enough. There must be planned organization of the resources of the church to meet human need in the name and for the sake of the Christ of action.

A congregation may function as a school in Christian living. Here much emphasis will be placed on the educational program of the church. As a rule, the most important single organization of such a church is its program of teaching and training, carried on by Sunday school and Training Union or similar agency. The worship services are viewed as having teaching values, and the sermon is at its best when it is expository. The test of effectiveness is the carry-over of religious education into conduct and character. The teaching church calls for elaborate organization of the congregation.

A congregation may be viewed as a community of witnesses. The church with dominant evangelistic and missionary spirit may be thus described. Such a church is more concerned with reaching the unreached, with winning converts, with extending the gospel and its fruits to the unevangelized at home and abroad, than with enjoyment or self-improvement. It is never satisfied unless there are continual additions to its membership and reportable results from its missionary undertakings and investments. This type of church obviously demands effective promotional organization.

Members of Congregations Should Know Themselves

Whatever the view of authority or function, efficient organization calls for classification of the church's constituency. A careful study of the membership records of a typical church will often reveal some startling facts. Since classification is an essential step in organization, it is necessary that the leadership of a church know the congregation as accurately as a business knows its customers. A well-ordered business does not take its customers for granted. All too often a church takes its membership for granted. While a church is not a business institution primarily, it may well learn from progressive business concerns the importance and the process of knowing its constituency.

A church should know its constituency. Willard A. Pleuthner points out that successful business firms have grown by finding out everything they could about such major matters as (1) present customers, (2) past customers, (3) why new customers are won, (4) potential customers, (5) statistics on increase or decrease in customers, (6) frequence of customer purchases, (7) what satisfied customers dislike about the company. Mr. Pleuthner insists that "this same type of information can help a church grow and become more successful in influencing its members and the community as a whole." [1]

At the heart of the life of almost every church is the blessed inner circle, the faithful few who attend all its services, contribute to all its causes, respond to all its calls for leaders and workers, put its welfare ahead of other interests. This group should be carefully listed and wholeheartedly appreciated. Beyond the inner circle are those not quite so devoted, whose attendance and giving are not so regular, who are not so responsive to the calls of the church for their loyalty. This group should be listed carefully, with recorded facts concerning their regularity and irregularity. Beyond this second circle is a third circle, made up of those who attend occasionally, give spasmodically, serve rarely if at all. Their names should constitute an exceedingly important list, and to them should be given careful and prayerful attention.

Beyond these three circles is a fourth, often overlooked and neglected—persons whose names are still on the membership rolls but who have ceased to be related to the church in any vital way. Some whose names are on this list may have removed to another community or they may have joined another church; sadly enough, some may have backslidden into worldliness and sin; others may be dead. In this group may be those who are overborne by ill health or misfortune or sorrow and who may have concluded that their church does not care. Those in this outer circle constitute a test of the genuineness of the care of minister and church and are a charge on their concern as no other members. A final group consists of those who are outside the fold of the church—nonmembers and unbelievers, "alienated from the commonwealth of Israel, and strangers to the covenants of promise," the "prospective customers" in the business firm's list. With utmost care these should be discovered and listed, for the future growth of the church will depend much upon reaching them.

An analysis of a church's constituency, present and prospective, in these several groups is not enough. The last two items in Mr. Pleuthner's list raise crucial questions for the church: What attracts and holds those who attend and support the church? What makes the church unattractive to others? Only when all the facts are in and when these two questions have been honestly answered is a church in position to organize the congregation more effectively for better results.

Congregational Organization Seeks Essential Values

To be attractive and effective the organization of a congregation must be simple and practical. While the organization may take many forms, the purpose in each case must be the learning of what Jesus Christ taught and the doing of what he commanded. Organization should never become an end in itself but always a means to Christian ends. Needless complexity should be avoided. All persons do not have the same gifts and interests and may not be expected to take part in all activities of the church alike. The whir of machinery must not be allowed to drown out the voice of the Spirit.

A congregation may be so highly organized that it resembles the tugboat equipped with a steamboat whistle; the blowing of the whistle so exhausted the steam in the boiler that there was no power left for navigation. How may a church organize for fellowship as well as for other purposes?

Organization is needed for cultivation of acquaintance. If we take seriously the ideal of a church as a family of believers, a household of faith, a beloved community, we should seek to make this ideal a reality in that each member of the congregation will be acquainted with every other member. As a congregation grows in numbers, the danger increases that more and more of its members will be strangers to one another, even to the minister and staff. Just to greet persons at the beginning or close of a service will not suffice. Occasions should be provided when definite opportunity will be given for members to be introduced and then to get together so that there will be easy recognition when they meet again.

At an all-church social, games may be played according to some of the familiar "icebreaker" schemes, so that each person present will become acquainted with every other person. For instance, those born during a certain month may form a group; then, successively, they may join other groups with other birth months. It is surprising how many will come thus to know fellow church members who were virtual strangers. On stated occasions, in regular church services members whose surnames begin with the same initials may be the guests of honor and introduced to the congregation. New members may be the invited guests of the church at the weekly family-night meal and be given a warm welcome. Acquaintanceship is a precious thing and should not be left to chance.

Organization is needed for deepening of Christian fellowship. Essentially, fellowship is partnership. Some friendships are formed because of mutual favors rendered, but the true basis of Christian friendship is common service in the cause of Christ and the church. Groups may be formed with the simple purpose of calling on one another in the cultivation of fellowship. These congenial groups may then be divided into pairs and the pairs sent out on missions of discovery, invitation, service. The pastor may discuss with these groups the elements of counseling and then guide them to persons who need Christian friends in whom they can place confidence as they disclose their troubles and heartaches. Pastors bear witness that divorce and family disorganization have been virtually eliminated from their churches by this plan of preventive fellowship.

Organization is needed for encouragement of participation in worship. Many who attend services of worship go away empty and disappointed because they did not join heartily in the services. Concern does not need to be ostentatious, but it should be real and should make itself felt. The stranger who is afraid that he may be embarrassed by doing the wrong thing in an unfamiliar service of worship may be made happy and comfortable by regular attendants who share bulletin and hymnbook and quietly prompt as to the next part in the service. Reverence begets reverence, and the well-organized congregation will insure dignified and worthy worship on the part of those who otherwise might be inattentive or irreverent. Family groups may be organized; groups of children may attend the worship services with their teachers; youth groups may be utilized in the conduct of the service. The ideal of a congregation organized for worship is that of total and fruitful participation.

Organization is needed for promotion of regular attendance. Many devoted Christians seem never to have had it occur to them that they are responsible for attendance on the services of their church. The exhortation that "everybody bring somebody" is a waste of breath. A congregation may be so organized that every area of the community is made the specific responsibility of certain members of the church to see that no unchurched family is unvisited, no need that the church can supply is neglected. To this end names and addresses should be given to members of the congregation with request that visits be made and information returned to the church. Occasionally, an all-church visitation day may be planned so that on specified Sunday afternoons every home in the community, legitimately a concern of the church, will be visited. No plan ever devised has been so effective in promoting attendance as that of regular and intelligent visitation on the part of an organized congregation.

Organization is needed for sharing in regular and generous giving. Many church members need to be convinced of their obligation to give according to Paul's proposal: "On the first day of every week, each of you is to put something aside and store it up, as he may prosper, so that contributions need not be made when I come" (1 Cor. 16:2). Here is the best plan of financing a church ever given—periodic, personal, proportionate, purposeful, preventive giving. That "the tithe is the Lord's" has never been abrogated. The every-member canvass often fails because the people canvassed have little or no conscience concerning their obligation to the church.

Tithers' enlistment visitation campaigns produce gratifying results. According to this plan, those members of the church who have experienced the joy of stewardship giving, with the tithe as the minimum, go personally to those members who have not yet entered this joy. Simply and unostentatiously they tell of the blessings which have come from systematic and proportionate giving, on the basis of the tithe, and seek to convince their fellow church member of the privilege and duty of sharing this experience. No effort will be made to collect dues or even to get a pledge. By Scripture reading and prayer the visitors seek signed commitment to follow the teachings of the Bible in the matter of giving to the support of the church which they love. Such an organized visitation with this purpose may produce spiritual results equivalent to a far-reaching revival.

In other ways a congregation may be organized and utilized to promote sharing in giving. Perhaps at no other single point is the careful and thorough organization of a congregation more fruitful than in this matter of securing adequate financial support that at the same time enriches the life of the giver.

Organization is needed for enlistment in fruitful Christian service. The spirit of service in and for one's church is caught more than it is taught. The offering of time and energy is often more difficult to secure than the offering of money. Willingness to serve is contagious. Refusal to serve is likewise contagious. An entire congregation may be awakened to the joy of service, or it may fall into a lethargy that kills the spirit of service.

It is often necessary to begin with a small group of devoted persons who are willing to undertake service projects for the church or on behalf of the church. Sometimes a beginning may be made with a group of boys and girls, or young people, or consecrated adults. Their example, without display, is brought to the attention of the congregation. This smaller group will add others to their number, the enlarged group will attract others, these will bring into the circle still others, so that the spirit of service grows somewhat as the concentric waves which follow the throwing of a stone into the center of a pool of water.

Not much Christian service is rendered as a matter of cold duty. Preaching may produce a feeling of aspiration or of guilt, but preaching alone rarely brings the response of actual service. The secret lies largely in definite undertaking of worthwhile projects, specific commitment of individuals and groups to the carrying out of these service projects, the sense of deep satisfaction that comes from unselfish giving of time and energy to the cause of Christ, and the quiet but effective reporting of results to the congregation. The service clubs are largely built on this principle. The seventy knew this joy when they returned from their mission and reported to Jesus, "Lord, even the demons are subject to us in your name!" With deep rejoicing Jesus received their report and promised them further victory and power; yet he warned them against self-centered exultation, saying, "Nevertheless do not rejoice in this, that the spirits are subject to you; but rejoice that your names are written in heaven" (Luke 10:17,20). The happiest of all congregations are those that know the joy of Christlike service, yet are not seeking credit for themselves.

Organization is needed for successful Christian living. A church is a means, not an end. Acquaintance, fellowship, worship, attendance, giving, service are means of grace for the development of the Christian life. There are no specific ways in which a congregation may be so organized as to guarantee Christlike conduct and character. Yet every organized activity should be subjected to this test: "that Christ may dwell in your hearts through faith; that you, being rooted and grounded in love, may have power to comprehend with all the saints what is the breadth and length and height and depth, and to know the love of Christ which surpasses knowledge, that you may be filled with all the fullness of God" (Eph. 3:17–19). No busy activity, no organizational efficiency can ever take the place of the reach of the congregation toward this high ideal. However, without organization, without ways and means, the ideal would be nebulous and ineffective, wishful thinking rather than practical achievement.

Congregational Organization Follows a Variety of Patterns

Ordway Tead defines collective co-operation as "a continuing, organized procedure which is centering the attention and the creative genius of those in the appropriate posts of management and those throughout the rank and file, on *the progressive improvement of any and all phases of operation looking to the increasing productivity of the entire enterprise.*" [2] There is no uniform way of achieving this result. Types of organization and methods of procedure will necessarily vary because of a number of factors. Among the determining conditions of types of organization will be the size of the congregation, its history and traditions, the kind of community in which the members live, the quality and amount of leadership, the educational level of the people, the personality and purposes of the pastor, the adequacy of employed staff, the willingness and capacity of the congregation to accept responsibility. Congregations in the main will be found to fall into the following patterns:

Organization may depend on the pastor. Many churches are accustomed to look to the minister for guidance as to the type of organization under which they operate. Usually the minister will follow more or less the denominationally established pattern. The congregation probably will follow his lead. If he is careless or impatient of organization, lazy members doubtless will breathe a sigh of relief that they are to be freed from responsibility. The well-organized, minister-led congregation usually will function through a series of committees. Generally the pastor is ex officio member of each of these committees, and often its functioning will depend largely on him. The congregation whose organization depends on the minister may have the appearance of smooth operation, and all may go well for a while, but eventually this breeds slackness with resultant inefficiency and dissatisfaction.

Organization may be directed by the staff. The larger church will require the services of more than one minister. The object of the staff is not to relieve lay members of duties and responsibilities but so to organize and direct them as to bring richer returns for the church and for their lives. Staff members will divide responsibility for the several age groups and the various church organizations and activities. Staff members best fulfil the duties of their respective offices when, individually and severally, they utilize the largest possible number of members of the congregation. Conceiving themselves as a team, they pray together, plan together, work together, keeping always before them the ideal of the priesthood of all believers, with concern for persons more than for the effective operation of organizations and for the kingdom of God more than local church interests.

Organization may gather about church-elected officers. "Official board" is not a happy designation, since the term may be interpreted to mean that the church-elected officers—deacons, elders, stewards, vestrymen—constitute a board of managers. New Testament precedent and long experience warrant the selection by the church of a responsible group of men and women to whom considerable authority and much responsibility are delegated. These lay office holders may well become leaders of the congregation in the several organized activities of the church.

Traditionally, the role of these lay leaders has been that of assistants to the pastor. As in the case of the overburdened apostles in the Jerusalem church, it is recognized as a mistake for the minister to "give up preaching the word of God to serve tables" (Acts 6:2). The official group of deacons and deaconesses (men and women servants of the church) therefore may be divided into subgroups, each subgroup or committee having responsibility for leadership of the congregation or a segment of the congregation in the achievement of such purposes as have been described. On paper this seems to be an ideal plan of congregational organization, but in practice it involves the obvious difficulty of discovering, training, and enlisting busy men and women for the difficult and detailed operation of the plan. Many churches have found it practicable to assign responsibility for oversight of the church organizations to committees of the deacons, and alert pastors have divided the labor of pastoral care among chosen lay men and women. The church council may be an effective link between the church-elected offices and the leaders of the church organizations, as they sit together on occasions for reports, planning, problem solving, and co-operative endeavor.

Organization may reside in the church agencies. Today's churches tend to function through their agencies—church school, training department, music department, youth fellowship, men's and women's missionary and service organizations. Once thought of as auxiliaries of the church, they now are better conceived of as agencies through which the church functions. The Sunday school is the church teaching, the Training Union is the church training its members, the music department is the church singing, the youth fellowship is the church at work with and through its young people, the men's and women's organizations are the church utilizing its adult resources for missions and service. These agencies, with their subdivisions, are all-inclusive and together provide places of usefulness for every member of the congregation. When these church agencies function effectively and unitedly, there is little need for any other congregational organization. Keeping these agencies at top-level efficiency is not easy and makes heavy demands on pastor, staff, general officers, division and department officers, teachers and leaders; yet such organization can be made to operate smoothly and fruitfully. Witness the many churches that have adopted this plan to their great satisfaction.

Organization may be of the congregation as a whole. This type of organization need not replace any other but becomes a supplement to other types. The plan calls for a carefully drawn map of the church community, which then is zoned according to concentration of the church's membership. The member families in each zone will be grouped together and furnished copy of the zoned map, with names of their fellow members indicated. At least one family in each district will be selected as monitor, whose duties will be kept simple and definite: to maintain kindly watchcare over the other members, noting illness or other need which should be the occasion of Christian concern, supplying the need personally or through other members of the group if possible, and informing pastor and church office; keeping watchful eye over the district to note the coming of new families to be visited or the arising of any situation of distress which the church might alleviate. Occasional meetings of these key families should be held for sharing of experiences and more efficient maintenance of their services. Churches using this plan report gratifying results.

The Organized Congregation as a Demonstration of the Good Society

Conflicting ideologies as to what constitutes "the good society" are the storm center of today's world conflict. At one extreme is the theory of unrestricted competition, the laissez-faire doctrine which would say "Hands off!" both to state and church in matters of business, industry, social organization. At the other extreme is the totalitarian concept, according to which the state, as representing society, supersedes all private ownership or control and which considers collectivism as the ideal form of government and social organization.

A Christian congregation, well organized and efficiently functioning, may demonstrate that neither extreme is necessary. Individualism is preserved, and at the same time co-operation is practiced. Intelligent self-respect is maintained along with equal concern for others. Material values are regarded but are made subservient to spiritual values. Initiative is encouraged but is enhanced by teamwork. Emphasis is placed on making this world a fit place in which to live, but always with the perspective of eternal life. The church is loved and honored, not as an end in itself, but as a means to the achievement of the purposes of its founder, Jesus Christ.

An organized and functioning Christian congregation is, therefore, more than a body of people maintaining a church. Such a congregation is like "leaven which a woman took and hid in three measures of meal, till it was all leavened" (Matt. 13:33). In a troubled and divided and warring world, such a congregation, joined with other congregations, may make real Paul's vision of a Christian world community, in which Christ "is our peace, who has made us both one, and has broken down the dividing wall of hostility, by abolishing in his flesh the law of commandments and ordinances, that he might create in himself one new man in place of the two, so making peace, and might reconcile us both to God in one body through the cross, thereby bringing the hostility to an end" (Eph. 2:14-16).

Chapter VI

Complexity Calls for Specialization

THE TYPICAL evangelical minister does not want to be an "organization man." He views with distaste the picture drawn by William H. Whyte, Jr., of the modern man so completely identified with the organization for which he works that he has lost individuality. The organization man is a cog in a huge machine; he is part of an impersonal system; he is identified by his social security number; and, like a man on an escalator, he gets to the top just by standing still. "The fault," Mr. Whyte says, "is not in organization . . . ; it is in our worship of it. It is in our vain quest for a utopian equilibrium . . . ; it is in the soft-minded denial that there is a conflict between the individual and society." [1]

Neither does the minister like to think of himself as a professional specialist. He does not want to narrow his interests to one aspect of the work of the church or one aspect of the kingdom of God. Yet in a day of specialism he is bound to admit that he cannot carry on all phases of a modern church's manifold activities equally well. Like other men, he must find his vein, develop his aptitudes, and give his major attention to that which he can do best. As a church grows in size, it grows in complexity of organization, and this complexity inevitably calls for specialization. According to New Testament practice, the teacher was no less a minister than the prophet and was commissioned equally by the laying on of hands (Acts 13:1–3). The specialized services of ministers of education and of music are necessary to the ongoing of many churches.

Professional Standards for Christian Service

The word "professional" came early to have a distasteful connotation in American Protestant circles. The minister was "called of God," and this was looked upon as his chief qualification for ordination. Ordination set him apart, and thereafter he was a dedicated man, under divine guidance, with only incidental dependence on the human element of special training. In the earlier years of American history the evangelical minister was primarily a preacher, and the test of his preaching was not his scholarship but his effectiveness in moving a congregation to demonstration and action.

Following the period of revivalism, churches of the nineteenth century began to make heavier requirements of their ministers. Ordination often was withheld until educational requirements were met. With the gradual raising of the standards of the churches, young men intending to be ministers realized the importance of college and seminary education. All of this was in line with the trend of public demand for professional competency. Doctors, lawyers, teachers, and others similarly serving the public came to be known as "professionals" and were required to meet certain tests before being admitted to practice.

Notwithstanding the deep-rooted tradition of distinctiveness of the minister's calling, it was inevitable that he should be required by common consent to measure up to certain professional standards. Ordination, in the evangelical concept, does not confer on the minister divine rights or put any imprint on his soul that makes him different from other men; ordination is, rather, the recognition of his sense of mission and his competence in fulfilling it. When he is set aside, it is not to a life apart from his fellow men nor to another realm of existence but to the highest office, in which as a man of God he deals with the highest values, serves the highest needs, relates men to God and God to men and men to one another through Jesus Christ.

He is the friend-at-large of all who need him, without money and without price. He has access to the lives of persons in their deepest crises, and they have the right to turn to him as one who has divine resources for their human needs. He is an apostle, one sent, a missionary representative of Jesus Christ. He is a prophet, a preacher and interpreter of truth as it is found in Christ and in the

Bible. He is an evangelist, an announcer of glad tidings to individuals and companies, his good news being that of salvation for all who will repent and believe. He is pastor and teacher, shepherd of a flock and principal of a school. We could easily say that his are the most varied and exacting demands made on any man in our culture.

The Evolution of the Church Staff

Complexity of organization resulted from pressure of needs that were inescapable. In the main, the evangelical church bodies of America followed a rural pattern at the beginning. Scattered families came together on Sunday for preaching. A one-room building sufficed. Little organization was needed; hence, little was developed. As communities grew, demands on the churches increased. To the preaching service was added a teaching service, and the Sunday school brought a variety of organizational demands. Stirred by the challenge of missions, the women organized societies which branched out in many directions. The youth movement met a felt need and from the beginning was characterized by organizational complexity. Evangelism developed along lines that called for intensive promotion and skilful management.

Rapidly growing population brought social and civic problems which churches and their pastors were called on to help solve. Crude buildings had to be replaced with more adequate houses of worship and work. A continuously rising level of education made heavy demands on the minister for scholarly as well as inspiring preaching. The difficult years of war and depression and more war brought a stream of distressed persons to the minister for pastoral care and counseling. Community and denominational duties added to his heavy load. Increased church membership multiplied responsibilities and burdens until ministers reached the breaking point.

The answer could no longer be found in one-man leadership, even with many volunteer helpers giving of spare time. Some relief came through the employment of an office secretary. Occasionally a "church visitor" was secured who took some of the burden of visitation off the pastor. Here and there a church employed a paid superintendent of the Sunday school, usually a layman who gave full time to the affairs of the church school. Now and then a church employed an assistant to the pastor, often a young minister just out of school who needed experience.

Gradually it dawned on pastors and deacons that a church beyond a certain size can no more be operated by one man than can a similar business. It was seen that the New Testament principle of a multiple ministry was sound and needed to be implemented continuously in the light of modern conditions. Men and women of ability in business and industry began to bring to the church the concept of management through division of labor and responsibility that has given stability and efficiency to other successful enterprises. Since no man can be a many-sided specialist, equally adept in meeting the varied demands of a modern church, planning began to take the place of haphazardness in securing for the pastor adequate assistance.

A church operating on a full-time basis is quite a different institution from the Sunday church of another generation. Today's church opens its offices each morning and maintains a schedule of activity throughout the day. According to the size of the church and the needs to be met, staff members will carry on specialized operations just as in any other well-ordered institution. The same principles of efficient office practice will be followed in the operation of the church office. The same requirements of courtesy, promptness, system, initiative, and teamwork will be met. The same tests of organizational efficiency will be applied, the distinction being made that, ideally, effort will be motivated by devotion to Christ and love of people more than by monetary reward. The business of such a staff, working as a team, will not be to relieve church members of their duties but so to organize, systematize, delegate, and supervise as to engage the largest possible number of members in the most fruitful possible service. This staff ideal follows very closely the pattern of the first churches as pictured in the New Testament. It represents not a departure from, but a recovery of, the New Testament ideal.

Types of Staff Organization

On the simplest level the church staff may consist of pastor, secretary, and caretaker. A competent church secretary is more than an office girl and typist. Her first responsibility is to assist the pastor and to relieve him of unnecessary details. She will handle the church correspondence, record the minutes of important meetings, supervise the keeping and use of accurate records, maintain an orderly filing system, communicate notices of meetings, receive and transmit messages for the pastor, record and remind the pastor of engagements, arrange conferences for those who need to see the pastor, conserve his energy by attending to matters which need not reach him, safeguard his study hours with full appreciation of the demands made upon him as preacher. The secretary herself needs to be protected against undue demands made on her time by officers and members of the church. She is not at the beck and call of those who need errands run, telephone calls made, notices sent out, programs mimeographed, socials arranged, and the like. She is not on duty at all hours of the day or night. She must have regular hours with time off for recreation and study lest she become stale. Since her responsibility also has a spiritual quality, she must not be thought of as the church's "hired girl." Her pay should be commensurate with her responsibilities, not lower than that of women in other like jobs because she is doing the Lord's work. She should be a woman of intelligence, discretion, tact, initiative, competence. Blessed are church and pastor who have such a treasure!

The caretaker of the church's property is more than just a janitor who sweeps the building and tends the furnace. He should be thought of as a member of the team. He should take pride in keeping the building and grounds attractive, clean, usable, comfortable. The outward appearance of the house of God reflects to the public the congregation's sense of the worthiness of religion. The Bible does not say that "cleanliness is next to godliness," but it might well have said it. Worship is hindered by an untidy, uncomfortable sanctuary. Teaching is handicapped if the rooms are disorderly, poorly ventilated, improperly lighted. Visitors are repelled and the sensitive are made unhappy if windows are dirty, if the carpet is frayed and worn, if the communion table has a miscellany of books and bulletins and misplaced articles on it, if the air is musty, and if the temperature is too high in summer and too low in winter. The caretaker needs to know well in advance about special occasions when the building should be prepared and open and about committee meetings which call for comfortable rooms opened at the right time. Otherwise, conflicts may arise that leave deep wounds if misunderstandings develop over the use of the building. Property damage may be avoided by the exercise of foresight. Many a care may be removed from the pastor and secretary by the right kind of caretaker.

A second level of organization is reached when to pastor, secretary, and caretaker are added ministers of education and of music, frequently with additional secretarial service made necessary by this staff enlargement. Sometimes the duties of minister of education and minister of music are combined in one person. Experience indicates that as soon as the church can afford it the offices should be separated in the interest of efficient service in each field.

A church whose membership has reached five hundred to a thousand needs a minister of education. The basic qualification is a sense of divine call to this ministry as a lifework. According to New Testament practice, as teacher he has as much right to ordination as the preacher. On New Testament grounds there is clearly no issue. The reason for withholding ordination if the office is held by a woman is cared for on the Pauline principle of subordination in office, according to which women are not to be put in authority over men. The minister responsible for teaching is no less a gospel minister than he who is responsible for preaching. In the light of tradition, however, the teaching minister may wisely forego the right of ordination if it creates a difficulty. The duties of his office call for just as thorough educational preparation as that of the pastor; yet the pastor's greater responsibility for the whole church gives to him a priority which the minister of education should gladly recognize.

The minister of education, alongside the pastor, has responsibility for the guidance of the total educational program of the church. Among his major duties are the following: (1) the organization, administration, and integration of the church's educational agencies; (2) the discovery and preparation of officers, teachers, leaders of the educational agencies; (3) the guidance and supervision of the in-service leadership; (4) the supervision of records and accounting of these agencies; (5) the promotion of attendance and enlargement; (6) the counseling of those who need special help in meeting difficulties; (7) the development of a well-rounded and adequate curriculum; (8) the utilization of the educational agencies of the church for the major purposes of the church; (9) the lifting of church school teaching and training to the level of sound and fruitful education; (10) co-operation with pastor and other staff members in maintaining effective teamwork.

The minister of music is, likewise, a person of high importance in the life and work of the larger church. This place, too, may be filled by either a qualified man or woman. No longer is the minister of music thought of as merely a choir director. Music is looked upon as an integral part of the church's program of worship, education, evangelism, outreach. Of course, musicianship must be unquestioned, but equally important is churchmanship. Back of both must be thorough scholarship. College training should be supplemented by specialization in an accredited school of music, preferably a school so related to seminary as to give opportunity for courses in biblical studies and in religious education.

More specifically, the duties and responsibilities of the minister of music may be thus detailed: (1) general oversight of the total music program of the church; (2) arrangement of the musical aspects of the stated worship services; (3) co-operation with the pastor in suiting the music to the purpose of the sermon; (4) stimulation and guidance of congregational participation in the song services; (5) discovery and development of musical talent in the congregation; (6) organization and direction of graded choirs, made up of little children, older children, intermediates, young people, adults; (7) the selection and use of music that will serve the high purposes of the church in reaching, winning, and nurturing for Christ persons of all ages and conditions; (8) extending the reach of the church through mass media such as radio and television; (9) vitally relating the ministry of music to all other interests and activities of the church; (10) becoming a happy and useful member of the church staff team.

A third level of staff organization is reached with the addition of a variety of specialists. When a church's membership reaches one thousand and more, with a Sunday school of similar proportions and a multiplicity of other organizations, the demand for further division of labor calls immediately for age-group specialists. A full complement of these specialists will include (1) a director of the children's division, (2) a director of the youth division, (3) a director of the adult division, (4) a director of the junior choirs, (5) a director of the senior choirs. Leaders of these limited age groups should have fully as thorough an education in the liberal arts and in biblical and theological studies as the minister of education; in addition, there should be specialization in the psychology of the particular group and in methods of teaching and leadership appropriate to them.

In the main such workers have duties and responsibilities which may be summarized: (1) to co-ordinate all the interests and activities of the group within the total church program; (2) to lead in securing needed personnel for all units within the group; (3) to conduct conferences for the in-service teachers and leaders, looking to their ever-increasing competency and fruitfulness; (4) to maintain vital co-operation of parents with teachers and leaders; (5) to maintain a plan of continual visitation so as to base teaching and activities on known needs; (6) to plan and conduct attractive social and recreational activities suited to the group; (7) to provide music and music education for all within the group; (8) to promote worship, evangelism, stewardship, and service appropriate to the group; (9) to plan special occasions which will stimulate interest in the group on the part of the whole church; (10) to maintain attendance and the recruitment of new members at a high level; (11) to represent the division in council meetings and in congregational business meetings; (12) to keep full and accurate records, including significant events in the life of each member of the group; (13) to plan weekday religious education rightly related to the public school; (14) to seek to make the total experience of each person in the group an educative means toward creative Christian ends; (15) to do all these things and others, not in isolation, but as members of the church staff team.

The fourth and perhaps highest level of staff organization is reached in the very large church of fifteen hundred members and more when still other specialized workers are added. Among these may be: (1) the church hostess, who gives full time to the preparation and serving of meals, looks after the comfort of guests of the church, and in many ways seeks to make the church a pleasant and attractive home; (2) the church administrator, who serves as treasurer and accountant, is usually the official buyer, and often leads in devising the church budget and securing its subscription; (3) the director of recreation, who guides in the planning of the social and recreational calendar, promotes this phase of the church's life, and is skilful in the leadership of social affairs; (4) the librarian, in charge of the church library, including books and audio-visual aids, and responsible for promotion of the widest possible use of the library's resources, both by individual readers and by teachers and leaders; (5) the church visitor, whose special ministry is usually to the sick, the shut-ins, the bereaved and distressed, the inactive and backslidden, newcomers and prospective members; (6) the assistant or associate pastor, serving alongside the pastor in all his ministries, often with special responsibility for pastoral counseling. Obviously, not many churches will have all of these special workers, although an occasional church may have even more. The pressure of need and the growth in numbers broaden the demands made on the church. These demands must be met, as in other fields, by an enlarged staff with specialized functions.

The Pastor as Chief of Staff

How does the pastor fit into this scheme of staff organization? In the democratic ideal, he is *primus inter pares*—first among equals. No matter how democratic the organization, someone must be first in headship and authority. Confusion and inefficiency would result if each member of the staff were to assume his or her autonomy. Equally unfortunate would be the consequences if the pastor were to assume the role of dictator. No matter what the position of the staff member, he or she needs someone to whom to turn for counsel, constructive criticism, encouragement, authorization. Likewise, the pastor needs trusted helpers whom he can consult, with whom he can share his dreams and plans, and among whom he can divide the burdens of the work. There are few enterprises in which mutuality is so necessary as in the management of the church enterprise.

The pastor sets the spiritual standards of the staff. The church team is different from other teams. In athletics the objective is to win the game. In politics it is to win the election. In the professions it is often to gain distinction. In business and industry it is to make profits that will establish financial security. In social service it is to benefit needy persons. In the church it is to do the will of God and to win others to Christ and his service. Certainly those in other enterprises will have this high aim as Christians, but their work contributes to this end rather than being done in an enterprise that has this end as its sole objective. The pastor will render his highest service to the staff by keeping their eyes fixed steadfastly on this goal.

The pastor unifies the work of the staff. Each member of the staff has a different field of operations. Each naturally feels that his or her part is of paramount importance. Absorption in this special interest may lead the staff member to overlook the importance and value of the contribution of other staff members. Notwithstanding their high ideals, these staff members are human and may be guilty of unconscious jealousy. They cannot work so closely together without overlapping of responsibility and duplication of service. Tensions may arise through overstepping of bounds, through lack of considerateness of one another, through misunderstanding of limitations, through hurt pride and a sense of injustice. Perhaps even more hurtful to the best interests of the church is the development of a spirit of isolation, each member of the staff building a wall between himself and other members across which there is little or no communication. All of these unfortunate possibilities can largely be prevented by the pastor who unifies the staff around the person and purposes of Jesus Christ and who develops greatness of spirit among his colleagues because he himself is a greatheart.

The pastor looks ahead and plans for the future. The staff member, in his or her localized position, may have difficulty in maintaining perspective. Immediate results may be disappointing; inevitably there will be criticism; cherished plans may fall through. Taking the short look, the staff member may feel that he or she is a failure. The pastor's part is to look ahead, to think ahead, to plan ahead, and so to project the work as to lift the eyes of the staff from the immediate to the ultimate. This setting up of five- to ten-year objectives, and even beyond, gives to the staff a sense of security that they cannot have if their efforts are measured by the week or the month or even the year. Prophetic preaching as well as prophetic leadership is not to be confused with the vain effort to predict the future in terms of a secret code derived from the apocalyptic literature of the Bible. Rather, it consists in projecting the cause of Christ into the future on the basis of past experiences and in the light of the Christian hope. An impatient, shortsighted pastor, demanding quick results, will demoralize any staff. The patient pastor, with a Christian view of history and of progress, will stabilize and energize the staff and through them keep his church faced toward the future with courage and optimism.

The pastor provides the security of authoritative leadership. Long ago Paul asked, "If the bugle gives an indistinct sound, who will get ready for battle?" (1 Cor. 14:8). Church work, like life itself, is full of uncertainties. He who takes counsel of his fears will accomplish little. In almost every congregation there are reactionaries who revere the past and want to let well enough alone. In contrast, there are almost certain to be liberals who are dissatisfied with whatever is traditional. In between may be objectors who are habitually opposed both to the old and to the new. To please all parties is obviously impossible. To do nothing is to displease everybody. The steady hand and the positive voice of the pastor are needed to give encouragement and direction to the staff member who would otherwise be frustrated.

There is a difference between authority and authoritarianism. True authority is internal, stemming from character, conviction, and courage. It is said of Jesus that he spoke with authority and not as the scribes. His was not the authority of official position or of reiteration of inherited rabbinical teachings. His authority was that of truth incarnated in flawless personality. Within the limits of human imperfection this is the sort of authority that the pastor should strive to possess. When he becomes dictatorial, presuming on his ordination and office, he has come wide of the mark of true authority. Exercising Christlike authority, the pastor becomes to the staff, as to the church, "like a hiding-place from the wind, a covert from the tempest, like streams of water in a dry place, like the shade of a great rock in a weary land" (Isa. 32:2).

Problems of Interpersonal Relationships

Happy staff relations, like happy family relations, do not just happen. Charles Ellwood, a Christian sociologist, sums up "the social problem" as essentially that of diverse persons getting along together.[2] In the close fellowship of Christian service it would seem that this problem should rarely appear and that it would be easy of solution should it occur. Experience does not vindicate this assumption. The problem of relationship of pastor with staff and of each staff member with his fellows should be given careful consideration.

How the relation is formed is important. The tradition is deep rooted that pastors are "called." This recognition of divine commission saves the pastor in some measure from being subject to the whims of church officers or the congregation. The impression is not nearly so general that staff members likewise are divinely called. When a staff member seeks employment by the church, it is often assumed that he is saying in effect, "Treat me as one of your hired servants." The employment of the staff member may not even be thought of as the congregation's concern. He may be hired by the pastor or a committee or a board and is thereafter looked upon as subject to their orders and dismissal.

There are, of course, human elements even in the locating of the pastor on a church field, and certainly there are human elements in the employment of the staff member. Yet should not there be a divine element in the latter case just as really as in the former? "Nobody can be as wise as everybody" may well apply to the selection of staff members through prayerful consideration and approval by the congregation rather than by an individual or a small group. The relation, therefore, should be formed after careful investigation, prayerful consideration, the mutual seeking and finding of the will of God.

The terms of the relationship are important. At the outset certain matters should be clearly understood. While rigid distinctions cannot be made between the duties of the pastor and of the staff member, and between the duties of one staff member and another, care should be taken to set up general boundaries. There is wisdom in agreeing that staff members, other than assistant or associate pastor, shall not perform the functions that are peculiar to the pastoral office, such as preaching, performing wedding ceremonies, conducting funerals, administering the ordinances. At the same time, the pastor should not perform the specific duties of staff members. The same understanding should hold with regard to the distinctive field of each member of the staff in relation to each other member. Equally clear should be the understanding that there are certain duties and privileges which pastor and staff have in common, such as sitting together in planning conferences, selecting and training personnel, visiting and personal witnessing, sharing in the solution of problems, praying together and bearing one another's burdens.

No room should be left for misunderstanding as to the person or persons to whom staff members shall be responsible. Always there is responsibility to the pastor as chief of staff, but he will be wise if he has a strong personnel committee with whom to share this responsibility. Staff members should not be under direct authority of any individual or church organization. The most satisfying concept of interpersonal staff relationships is that of teammates in an enterprise in which every member of the team is equally important.

Mundane matters need clarification at the beginning. These practicalities include salary and promotion, tenure and security, vacation and attendance on conferences, expense budget and sick leave, hours of work and of leisure, and the like. No contract need be drawn, but frank understanding in advance may save confusion and difficulty later on.

Maintaining the relationship is important. It is significant that Jesus gave specific directions concerning life within the church at only one point. When fellowship has been broken, reconciliation is to be sought by the offended person; if this fails, a small group of friends should intercede; if this fails, the concern of the church is to be invoked; if all this fails, broken fellowship must be declared and the unyielding offender treated as any other unsaved sinner. Jesus anticipated that breaches will occur, but he solemnly warned against their continuance.

A questionnaire sent by the author to a selected number of veteran pastors raised the question as to the causes of interpersonal tensions among staff members and church leaders. In the experience of these pastors, the frequency of causes of strained relationships was listed in this order: (1) wounded pride—the deep sense of hurt that comes when one's personal dignity is violated; (2) egotism—the assumption of superiority on the part of one person which threatens the ego of another; (3) unfairness—selfish advantage sought at the cost of another's rights; (4) criticism—depreciation of another in the interest of one's own elevation; (5) exploitation—using another as means to one's ends; (6) high-pressure methods—promotion that is more concerned with outward show than qualitative results; (7) hypersensitivity—the "chip on the shoulder" attitude that misinterprets the motives of fellow workers. Avoidance of these causes of disturbance in the Christian community should be sought prayerfully and diligently.

How may good interpersonal relationships be maintained? A few simple rules emerge from wide experience: (1) Be a good listener; this is the heart of the art of counseling and goes far toward winning the confidence of others. (2) Be a student of people. A church is a laboratory of life where the most fascinating of all studies may be carried on for the acquisition of insights into human nature and conduct. (3) Take an objective attitude. Refuse to become involved in personality clashes; stand on the side lines and analyze causes and effects with a view to the promotion of unity and harmony. (4) Respect personality, no matter whose. See the best in others; look with optimism on the possibilities in Christ of the least promising; put into practice Christ's commandment to love one another. (5) Be appreciative. Practice the art of expressing gratitude for even the smallest of favors and efforts. (6) Seek to understand and utilize group dynamics. Harness to the cause of Christ and the church such powerful drives as faith, hope, love, aspiration, the longing for recognition and significance. We may fail to love, but Paul is right: "Love never fails."

Severing the relationship is important. It is well known that ministers change pastorates frequently. John Wesley and his successors thought that maximum usefulness was exhausted in a four-year term of service on a given field. Lately, the advantages of a long pastorate have been increasingly recognized. There are even stronger arguments for continuity of service on the part of staff members. In some churches the tradition has developed that when the pastor resigns or is transferred, the staff members should be let out in order that the incoming pastor may have "a clean slate." That this policy is unfair and wasteful can scarcely be debated. At the beginning of their service staff members should have it clearly understood that their tenure is not dependent on the term of service of the pastor any more than his is dependent on theirs. Each person should serve to the point of his maximum capacity and usefulness.

There comes a time when a change of field is indicated. Often the reasons for such a change are inadequate, if not groundless. Rarely should one resign because of the following reasons: (1) There are too many problems and difficulties; ordinarily these should constitute a challenge to patience and perseverance. (2) There is opposition to proposals and plans; this may prove to be the needed testing for refinement and clarification of ideas. (3) Criticism is made by a disgruntled few; brakes are needed as well as an accelerator, and critics may perform a useful if not indispensable service. (4) There is lack of immediate visible results; a squash may mature in a few weeks, but it takes years to grow an oak. (5) Pressure to go elsewhere is great; distant pastures are greener, and inducements held out should be viewed in the light of searching inquiry as to whether one's work is done where one is.

There are, of course, adequate reasons for changing one's work. Among these may be listed: (1) Unresolvable conflict with pastor or other staff members or church leaders; it is far better to leave than to be the occasion of strife, no matter how righteous one's dissent. (2) Conviction of unfitness for the demands of the situation; there is no disgrace in admitting the futility of trying to fit the square peg into the round hole. (3) Full realization that progress is impossible; life is too short to mark time indefinitely. (4) A clear sense of call of God to another field; the Commander has a right to move his men where he needs them most. (5) Failing health or advancing age; "quitting sense" is a mark of that high devotion to the cause of Christ which makes retirement a blessing and not a tragedy.

A Parable for Staff Members

Once upon a time a church called successively three members to serve on its staff. The first said: "Here I am; now your troubles are over. I will do everything that needs to be done." So he took over, coming to the church early and staying late, attending to an infinite multitude of details, relieving everyone else of all possible responsibility. But it came to pass that other staff members and the congregation grew weary of his superindustriousness, and his job was given to another. The second said: "Here I am. You do the work while I do the planning and give the orders." And so he installed push buttons on his desk, announced changes, and publicized elaborate proposals, until the church was continuously astir with activity like unto a beehive. But again it came to pass that colleagues and congregation grew weary from overwork and exasperated from taking orders; so his place was declared vacant and given to another. The third said: "Here I am. Let us pray and plan and work together, that we may serve him who has chosen us and appointed us that we should go and bear fruit and that our fruit should abide." And the seeds which they sowed fell in good soil and brought forth abundantly.

Chapter VII

The Teaching Church Has a Winning Strategy

TODAY'S CHURCH IS A school, and its pastor is an administrator of religious education. The church school, or "Sunday school," as it early came to be known, expresses the genius of American Protestant Christianity more than any other institution. "Sunday school," generally indicating an hour on Sunday for Bible study, has become entirely inadequate as a description of the modern church at work teaching. The conception of the Sunday school as the "school of the church" has in large measure given way to the conception of "the church as a school." The organization and administration of the educational program of the church call for insights and skills which are an essential part of the minister's equipment.

The Need of an Adequate Strategy

War has made us conscious of the importance and value of strategy. Generals know that it is not enough to take single or isolated objectives. There must be an over-all plan of campaign, the mapping of a series of objectives, and, usually, concentration on an area which if taken will mean success up and down the line. Pastor and church leaders should be strategists.

There are several possible strategies. A church may measure success in terms of the number of persons who attend its worship services. In this case, the most important features are the music and the preaching. In contrast, a church may measure its success in terms of the quality of its membership. With this view, the strategy is to attract and hold individuals and families of outstanding ability and influence.

A church may measure its success in terms of evangelistic results, the number of persons led to a profession of faith in Christ and to church membership. The strategy, accordingly, will be that of the revival or the evangelistic crusade or the perennial effort to win souls. At the other extreme, a church may measure its success in terms of Christian nurture, seeking to bring the children of the church into the fold early and developing them in knowledge and grace. This strategy puts the family at the center and makes the church a household of faith, often with no great concern to reach those who are on the outside.

A church may measure its success in terms of personal salvation, the cultivation of the spiritual life of the individual, the realization of peace of mind and peace of soul. The strategy of such a church is to draw together like-minded persons who crave emotional satisfactions and who are bound together by their otherworldliness. In contrast is the church that measures its success in terms of social action, the improvement of human conditions, the bringing in of the kingdom of God on earth. Its strategy is to bring together persons of tender conscience and active minds who seek to put religion into practice, whose picture of Jesus is that of one who "went about doing good," and whose human model is the good Samaritan.

Contemplating these varying and conflicting standards and strategies, pastor and church leaders may find themselves confused. Each viewpoint has its advantages and disadvantages. None can be exclusive of all the others. Is there a strategy which will enable each of these to achieve its full purpose? The concept of the church as a school may well provide such a strategy.

The New Testament Pattern: The Church as a School

The Jewish synagogue provided the pattern of church school with which Jesus was familiar in his childhood and youth. We are told that he went into the synagogue on the sabbath "as his custom was." That he attended the synagogue school at Nazareth may be taken for granted. His attitude toward the synagogue was that of respect and affection. Matthew records that "Jesus went about all the cities and villages, teaching in their synagogues" (Matt. 9:35). He was given the name "Teacher" more than any other title. He spent more of his time teaching than in any other activity. Those whom he gathered about him were known as his "disciples," that is, learners. His "church" was far more like a school than the later institution of formal worship and preaching. The early Christians followed this pattern of Jesus and made their churches schools. Paul, trained as a rabbi, was basically a teacher, and the churches which he constituted were places of learning. The teaching function of the church and the ministry was primary in the first three centuries of Christian history, when Christian conquest was at its best.

The deterioration of Christianity followed closely the gradual abandonment of this teaching ideal. The time of instruction of catechumens was progressively shortened until, instead of months and even years, a brief period preceding Easter sufficed. Lack of teaching led to increasing sacramentalism, which in turn lessened the requirement for intelligent understanding of the Christian faith. Thus the church, as we have seen, became a saving institution rather than an institution of the saved.

The success of the Reformation was due in large measure to the restoration of the ideal of the teaching church. Luther and Calvin saw clearly that through preaching and teaching, which must never be dissociated, the reforms they sought would be made permanent. Wherever an effective program of preaching-teaching was carried out, the reformed churches became firmly planted. Catholic statesmanship recognized this strategy. The Counter Reformation was largely an attempt to meet Protestant education with Catholic education. Thus arose the system of Catholic parochial schools which gave to the hierarchy its new lease on life. The map of Europe will show that wherever Protestantism secured a firm foothold and established teaching churches the territory became dominantly Protestant; wherever the Catholic Church became a teaching church, establishing and maintaining a strong parochial school system, the territory remained Catholic.

The wisdom of the New Testament is vindicated by history—a church is strongest when it functions as a school. Much of the strength of Catholicism in America is due to its system of parochial schools. Rejecting the parochial system in the main, the strongest American Protestant bodies are those that have supported the public schools and made their churches effective schools. No sharp distinction is made between preaching and teaching, between worship and service, between the curriculum as subject matter and the curriculum as experience. Christian education is thus an all-embracing term, the administering of which is at the heart of the minister's purpose and is the essence of the church's strategy. Teaching is at the heart of the church program.

The Sunday School in American Church Progress

The Sunday school had its humble beginning in England in the latter part of the eighteenth century. The story of Robert Raikes and his "ragged school" in Gloucester is well known. The heart of this printer-publisher was touched by the destitution of underprivileged children in the factory district of his city. As a result, he rented a building and employed four women to teach on Sunday such children as might be induced to come. To the fundamentals was added the catechism, which entitles the enterprise to be termed "religious education." A Baptist deacon of London, a man of considerable means, saw the possibilities of the "ragged school" and sought to extend it to other communities. So striking was the transformation wrought in the ragamuffins who attended the school that the queen gave it her sanction and popularized the movement among the nobility. John Wesley and his followers were quick to see the possibilities of this kind of popular religious education and incorporated it into the Methodist Church. Leaders of the democratic movement in England saw the necessity of an educated citizenship and sought support of charity schools by taxation. Thus arose the public school system, paralleling the Sunday schools, which had been largely adopted by the churches and made more and more definitely religious.

The Sunday school came to America in the last decade of the eighteenth century. The plan of popular teaching of the Bible in and by the churches fitted naturally into the genius of American democracy. At first the Sunday school was nondenominational in character. Soon Sunday schools became a feature of many New England churches. In 1824 the American Sunday School Union was formed, primarily for the promotion of the Sunday school movement. In 1832 the first meeting of the National Sunday School Convention was held, bringing together ministers and laymen who were interested in making the Sunday school more effective as an educational and evangelistic agency. State and regional conventions were held with impressive attendance as more and more Sunday schools were established.

The War Between the States disrupted the work both of the Sunday School Union and of the Convention. Following the war, the movement was pressed with increasing vigor. A period of amazing expansion came with the adoption of the plan of uniform lessons in 1872. Extension of the movement to other lands brought change of name to International Sunday School Association. Denominational publishing houses sprang up, providing inexpensive lesson helps in vast quantities for Sunday school pupils and teachers. Sunday schools, principally for children, were established everywhere, sometimes under sponsorship of a church, often as a community enterprise which later grew into churches. The Baraca-Philathea movement brought large numbers of young people and adults into organized classes. By 1900 the Sunday school had become a major feature of many, if not most, of the evangelical churches of the United States. No other institution in American Christianity has so greatly influenced the life and work of the churches as this "school of the church." Scarcely any aspect of American church history could be written without taking into account the Sunday school movement.

Today's Church Organized for Christian Education

In America, the Sunday school at first met with considerable clerical opposition. This is understandable when we consider the low educational level of the Sunday school, its dependence on untrained officers and teachers, its lack of adequate curriculum materials, its incompetent administration, and its poverty of equipment. Yet it provided certain essentials of democratic church life—the popular reading of the Bible, the bringing of the constituency of the church together in congenial classes, the utilization of great numbers of lay people, the implementation of the congregational ideal, the provision of opportunity for effective evangelism, the assimilation of new members into the church body. The Sunday school succeeded not just in spite of its low educational standards, but even because of the lack of educational requirements. No one was too underprivileged to be sought for enrolment in this school, almost any willing Christian was acceptable as teacher or officer, promotion was automatic, the objective was not so much sound learning as conversion.

Near the turn of the twentieth century concern began increasingly to be felt to make the Sunday school a school. A great step forward was taken when closely graded lessons were introduced. These lessons recognized the fact that abilities and interests change with age. Lesson materials and helps for teachers were thus devised to meet the needs of the several age groups and within these groups to make adaptation for each successive year through high school.

Graded lessons called for graded departments and teachers, and all this in turn called for graded building and equipment. Thus, provision was made for the Nursery children, who are promoted in due time to the Beginner Department, who then successively become Primaries, Juniors, Intermediates, Young People, Adults. Since the adult life span is twice that of the preadult, recognition has come of the need of grading adults also into age-span departments and classes—young adults (25–34), middle adults (35–49), older adults (50 and above). While an age basis of grading may not always be rigidly required, it serves as a simple and practical means of maintaining teachable units. Annual promotion by classes and departments keeps the school graded and furnishes incentive for meeting certain minimum standard requirements.

The church school from the beginning was a lay institution. Its officers and teachers have been drawn from the congregation and have served on a voluntary basis. Devotion and willingness have, in the main, been the chief qualifications of service. With the growth of the Sunday school and its departmentalization and grading, an ever increasing army of volunteers has been necessary to carry on its work. Studies have shown that, on the average, one worker must be enlisted for every ten persons enrolled. The training of these lay workers, not only for the Sunday school but for other church responsibilities, becomes a matter of first importance.

Administering the Program of Training

Early in the Sunday school movement courses were devised for the training of officers and teachers. A miscellany of books appeared, intended to give help in understanding and teaching the Bible, in organizing and administering the Sunday school, in developing skills in the use of methods, and in giving insights into pupil life. Gradually these miscellaneous books and haphazard plans were unified as standardized leadership training courses, with requirements as to hours and conditions of study, competency of teachers, and examinations leading to awards.

The International Council of Religious Education (now the Division of Christian Education of the National Council) popularized interdenominational leadership schools, which have done much to lift the level of teaching and administration in the Sunday schools of America. Denominations, individually and co-operatively, have promoted leadership training with varying degrees of success. Studies have indicated that there is a close correlation between the effectiveness of a church and the quality and continuity of its leadership training program. Obviously, pastor and staff must assume principal responsibility for administering the plans for leadership training not only for Sunday school officers and teachers, but for all volunteer leaders in the life of the church.

The youth movement in American churches, which later developed into programs of fellowship and training in church membership, had its beginning in England in the formation of the Young Men's Christian Association in 1844. Brought to America in 1851, the movement spread rapidly. Thirty years later the Young People's Society of Christian Endeavor introduced the youth movement into the churches. The organization caught the imagination of Christian young people and spread with almost incredible rapidity.

The society, vigorously promoted from its Boston headquarters, was nondenominational. By the turn of the century Christian Endeavor had proliferated denominationally into such organizations as Epworth League, Westminster League, Luther League, Baptist Young People's Union. At first these leagues and unions were Christian Endeavor societies with a denominational label. Later they developed distinctives along two main lines: (1) as church agencies for the promotion of fellowship among the young people of the churches, and (2) as agencies for leadership training and training in church membership. Representing the former emphasis is the Youth Fellowship; representing the latter is the Training Union, meeting Sunday evening, with departments for all ages corresponding to the fully graded Sunday school.

In many churches the Youth Fellowship takes the place of the Sunday evening worship service. Difficulties of maintaining the Sunday evening service of song and preaching have become intensified in many sections of America. Often the people are scattered and live at distances from the church. There are multiplied bids for their Sunday time. The competition of radio, television, and Sunday amusements and sports is keen. Some feel that Sunday evening should be kept for the family at home. The group to whom a service at the church will appeal strongest are the young people, and the strongest appeal for their attendance is that of fellowship. Thus, programs are prepared and presented that are designed to capitalize on this desire of young people to be together and at the same time to deepen their spiritual lives and strengthen their Christian and church loyalties. Obviously, these programs and meetings require continual promotion and supervision by pastor and staff in order to be effective.

The Training Union, brought to its highest development of effectiveness among Southern Baptist churches, assumes that Sunday evenings can be spent with profit and enjoyment at the church. Pastor and people refuse to yield to the pull of other attractions and dare to believe that the Sunday evening worship service can be maintained. They are convinced that every church needs trained members and that every member needs training. They realize that an hour of Bible study in the morning followed by a worship service is not enough to sustain the spiritual lives of Christians and that the Sunday school as a teaching agency should be supplemented by an organization for training in church membership. They are quite aware of the difficulties in the way, but they are determined to overcome these difficulties. As a consequence, large numbers of churches —practically all within the Southern Baptist body not extremely weak and small—maintain well-attended services of worship with strong evangelistic flavor. This training program associated with an evangelistic evening service is said to be a major factor in the remarkable growth of Southern Baptists during the past half century.

A membership training program for all ages meets a deeply felt need of today's churches. The preacher and the Sunday school teacher provide impression that needs to be given expression. All too often church members "keep silent" in the "holy temple" until their powers of expression are atrophied. Freedom of discussion requires occasion for exercise, or it is in danger of being lost. Thinking is more than listening to the thoughts of another—it is problem-solving in which one takes part vocally. There is keen enjoyment in such participation in discussion with a congenial group. Qualities of Christian personality are developed that otherwise would lie dormant.

Skills are acquired in such a continual program of training that are essential to effective churchmanship. In the Commission of Jesus the supreme command is that the disciple be a witness. Effective witnessing for Christ is an art that must be learned by practice. The lips of many Christians are silent when opportunity arises for witnessing because they have had no experience in putting into their own language what they believe. To take part on programs that call for individual expression of Christian faith is to acquire skill in communicating one's faith to another when the opportunity arises. Activities connected with the training program develop skills in church work that make relatively easy the recruitment of teachers and officers for the Sunday school and leaders for the other church organizations.

Convictions are deepened and released in action by examining and clarifying them in the discussions and studies carried on in an organization for membership training. An embarrassingly large number of church members do not know what they believe or why. They have had explanations from the pulpit and the lectern, but there are areas of confusion that have not been cleared up and questions that remain unanswered. In unhurried discussions among his peers, the child or young person or adult is given opportunity to learn for himself what he cannot be taught by another. Indoctrination thus conceived is not brainwashing but truth-discovery that, as Jesus promised, sets the learner free.

Training by groups that include all ages utilizes a method, borrowed from the early Christian churches, that accounts in large measure for the success of communism. The Communist "cell" binds together a group wholly committed to the interests of the Party, no matter what the cost in personal sacrifice. The group plan of organization for training does not go to any such extreme, but provides the cohesiveness that makes for far greater effectiveness of Christian service than the large and inchoate congregation. The sense of belonging is a powerful factor in maintaining loyalty and devotion. To feel that one is missed if not present is a strong incentive to be regular in attendance. The satisfaction that comes from the sense of recognized and appreciated achievement stamps in the learning that occurs from participation in study. It is not surprising that members of training groups become effective agents for the church to which they belong.

Provision for children, even for infants, is made on the grounds that a church is a family affair and that Sunday evening can be profitably and happily spent "at home at church." The babies are cared for by trained attendants in an attractive and comfortable nursery. Children of Beginner age (4 and 5) have a happy time in attractive quarters under direction of skilled leaders. Children of Primary age (6–8) are led in activities and studies suitable to their interests and needs. Supplementing what they are receiving in Sunday school, and closely correlated with it, Training Union thus affords educative experiences that lead toward Christ and church membership and are obviously of much greater value than Sunday evenings spent at home viewing television or listening to radio. For boys and girls of Junior age (9–12) and of Intermediate age (13–16), discussion groups, projects, Bible drills, and a variety of studies of Bible truths applied to life are conducted; studies of history, biography, missions, stewardship, service, worship, and like subjects adapted to their interests and needs provide situations in which those not already Christian can be led to intelligent decision and commitment and those already church members can be trained for effective Christian living and churchmanship.

The need of a special young people's organization is obviated when they are included in the Training Union and integrated into the church family circle. They lose nothing of their identity as a youth group and at the same time are identified with the larger body of believers. The danger that they may become detached or even develop undesirable attitudes and practices is almost completely avoided. Adults of various ages form congenial groups that meet the growing need of continuing adult education. Furnished basic guidance materials, they may adapt them to suit their purposes and capacities. Many adults bear witness to the enrichment brought to their personal lives, the enlargement of their contacts and horizons, the stimulation of their intellectual lives, and the deepening of their loyalty to Christ and the church. From these adults, with this background of study and activity, will come the church's leaders in almost all its activities and services.

The training program thus conceived goes beyond Sunday. A notable feature is the daily Bible readers' course, a plan for systematic devotional reading of the Bible which covers the whole of the Scriptures every five years, with appropriate comments. To weekly programs are added book studies, the well-written and inexpensive texts dealing with a wide range of subjects, appropriate to the interests and needs of the several age groups, and taken individually or in weekday classes. A "calendar of activities" suggests suitable seasonal things to do that put into practice what has been learned. On occasion, the Training Union forces may be mobilized in the service of a building enterprise, a stewardship campaign, an enlargement effort, an evangelistic mission, a missionary drive, or similar project. Social events at home and attendance on colorful assemblies add zest to the work of the training organization.

No claim is made that it is easy to maintain such a training program. Pastor and staff and church must be convinced of its worthwhileness and must be willing to pay the price of unceasing concern and effort; but the claim is not only made but demonstrated that such a plan of training is worth what it costs.

Essentials of Educational Administration

A number of factors complicate the problem of educational administration in a church. Too few people consider church school education as important as public education. Being unpaid and under no contract, officers and teachers are often prone to take their responsibilities lightly. Traditionally, standards of teaching and learning are lacking and, if established, are unenforceable. Attendance is, of course, voluntary and, for the majority, irregular. Little has been done in the way of tests and measurements to determine values and achievements. Methods are rarely carried out under supervisory criticism. Willingness more than competency is often the accepted qualification. The teamwork necessary to joint enterprise may be hard to secure and maintain. Standards are set up that furnish guidance but are often ignored. The time element makes difficult fruitfulness in teaching and learning. Pastor and staff may have a sense of futility in seeking to bring the church as a school up to the level of educational respectability.

In the midst of these difficulties, ways of working have been developed which secure satisfying results:

Standards of excellence have been devised with which to measure strength and weakness. These standards, in the main, indicate requirements for success, growing out of experience, by which the educational work of the church may be tested in such areas as these: (1) Right relationship to the church, according to which the church elects officers and teachers, provides necessary building and equipment, finances the enterprise through the church budget, receives and approves regular reports. (2) Challenging measure of enrolment, according to which the Sunday school, for instance, shall maintain an enrolment equal to the total resident church membership. (3) Carefully determined basis of grading, according to which classes and departments are set up in teachable, congenial, dependable, and manageable groups. (4) Well-chosen curriculum materials, selected with a view to meeting the needs of pupils at each succeeding stage of the life cycle. (5) Insistence on the use of Bibles by teachers and in classes, so that this chief textbook of the school will become familiar as a guide toward, to, and into the Christian life. (6) Promotion of loyalty to the worship services and the total program of the church, including emphasis on systematic and proportionate giving. (7) Continual emphasis on responsibility of officers and teachers for the evangelization of their pupils and the nurture of the Christian life. (8) The bringing together regularly of pastor, staff, and all officers and teachers for conference and planning. (9) Promotion of continual enlistment, training, and supervision of all who are responsible for the teaching work of the church. (10) Concern for worldwide missions, expressed through study, prayer, giving, witnessing, and service.

With a standard such as this, pastor and staff and administrative lay officers may check with reasonable objectivity the points at which the church school is strong or weak. In the light of results steps may be taken to capitalize on the strong points and to strengthen the weak points.

Meetings for planning and study will give concentration to the varied duties and activities of the large group of lay people necessary to the operation of the church school. Two types of meetings are needed.

First, the workers' council will meet at least monthly for conferences concerning administrative matters. Pastor, staff, and general officers will receive and review reports for the month, spotlight points of success and failure, discuss problems and share ideas, plan to reach prospects and visit absentees, revise class rolls, supply vacancies in the teaching staff, and pray together for divine blessing on their efforts.

Second, the officers and teachers will meet weekly; plans of the meeting will include a fellowship meal, a brief period of announcements and promotion, the correlation of efforts toward common objectives, and then separation by departments for intensive preparation for the Sunday services just ahead. In these departmental meetings attention will be given to matters brought from the workers' council; department superintendents and teachers will check on their responsibilities for prospects and absentees; plans will be made for assembly programs, with chief emphasis on co-operative study of next Sunday's lesson or lessons with a view to effective and fruitful teaching. Churches that consistently follow this plan have found most of their administrative problems solved.

Clinical training of officers and teachers has been found gratifyingly effective in maintaining an educational standard for the church school. Improvement of administration and teaching through books and lectures has obvious limitations. Principles may be clearly presented and understood, but there is no guarantee of carry-over into practice. As a rule, in these study courses or lectures little opportunity is given for interpretation of generalizations in terms of specific situations of need and difficulty.

Clinical training takes up where book study leaves off. The "workshop" plan is followed, according to which officers and teachers bring their problems to the table. Felt difficulties are broken down into particulars, alternatives are suggested, sources of help are sought, group discussion is conducted with a view to sharing of ideas and experiences. Conclusions then are reached that can be tried out tentatively. Reports of disappointment or progress may be made at successive meetings, until improvement is actually achieved and maintained. Clinical training in the church school is analogous to on-the-job training in industry. Successful operation of the plan calls for careful planning on the part of pastor and staff, the utilization of resource persons, the availability of source materials, some understanding of the dynamics of group leadership, with clearly defined objectives that are measurably obtained.

Classroom and department supervision will almost certainly insure improvement in the church school. "Superintendents," whether of the whole school or of departments, often hold this title in name only. Traditionally, the superintendent is just a presiding officer or the conductor of opening exercises that often open nothing and exercise nobody. Sometimes the superintendent has executive and promotional ability. Rarely is the primary function of this officer conceived as the supervision of instruction, with skill in failure prevention and teaching-learning improvement.

If supervision is to become effective, pastor and staff must take the lead. By prearrangement pastor, minister of education, or other staff members sit in on department assemblies, visit classes, and make mental notes in answer to such questions as these: (1) Was the physical situation maximally favorable? (2) Were aims definite and clearly understood? (3) Was interest secured and maintained? (4) Were learning activities of pupils in evidence? (5) Were sound teaching methods used? (6) Was there a happy pupil-teacher-superintendent relationship? (7) Did superintendent or teacher dominate the situation too much? (8) Was there vital participation through use of hymnbooks, Bibles, notebooks, questions and answers, discussion? (9) Were activities and teaching life centered, designed to meet pupil needs and to carry over into conduct and character? (10) Were there measurable evidences of satisfactory outcomes?

Following prearranged visits, pastor and staff members should sit down with individuals and department groups to discuss in friendly and constructive fashion the questions raised above. Superintendents should be encouraged and aided to take over much of this responsibility, conferences being held with individual teachers and with members of the department, looking to practical helpfulness in the improvement of instruction and its outcomes. Always such supervision must be carried on with the consent of teachers, tactfully and by prearrangement. When teaching and learning thus are taken seriously and improvement on the part of every teacher and officer sought through skilled supervision, a new era in religious education will emerge.[1]

Reaching the People for Religious Education

The plain fact is that the people are not being adequately reached for Bible study and the teaching of religion. Enrolment in church schools has not kept pace with increase in church membership and in the population. Survey after survey has indicated the vast and growing religious illiteracy of the American public. The typical

American adult, even though a church member, has little apparent concern for his biblical and spiritual ignorance and not much more concern for the tragic lack of education of his children in this supremely important area of their lives. The American school system has gradually eliminated the teaching of the Bible and of moral and spiritual values until secular education in many quarters has become all but pagan.

Facing the consequences of an era of neglect, Protestant churches generally have been aroused to the urgent necessity of paralleling the reach of the public schools and of mass media of communication with a far-reaching effort to provide religious education for all the people. That people in great numbers can be reached and taught is being successfully demonstrated. Plans of enlargement have been tested to the point that they deserve to be thought of as scientific. It is all but axiomatic that, given people to be reached, a church may enrol for religious education as many persons as it will adequately provide for. Tested procedures are as follows:

Discover those to be reached. Enrolment in the church school is a person-to-person matter. Announcements, letters, advertising, and other forms of publicity may create interest and favorable attitudes, but enrolment in a school, with its implied responsibilities, is a face-to-face selling job.

The annual religious census has become standard practice with churches that propose seriously to reach individuals not already enrolled in a church school. The census may be taken co-operatively or by a single denomination or by a local church, following these tested procedures: (1) A map of the area is drawn, with delimitation of territory in which a given church group will take the census. (2) The area is subdivided so that a team, under a leader, will know exactly its responsibility. (3) Two persons will be allocated a certain number of residences which they will visit together, seeking exact information concerning every member of the household. (4) Census cards will be prepared on which will be secured such essential information as name, sex, street, telephone, age, church member, Sunday school attendance, denominational preference, local church preference. (5) Census teams having been formed, they will be brought together for careful instructions. (6) On a given Sunday, following the morning worship service, the census takers will come together for light lunch, receive their final assignments and supply of census cards, and go forth as representatives of Christ to secure the desired information. (7) The cards, accurately filled out, will be returned to the church immediately and sorted so as to eliminate those who are not legitimate prospects, after which the prospects will be sorted by age groups. (8) Triplicate copies will be made from the cards, giving by classes and departments the names and other information; one of these lists will be kept as a permanent file, one will be turned over to the appropriate department, the other will be given to the teacher. (9) Follow-up will be made to complete the information for those who were not at home when the concerted census was taken. (10) Person-to-person visitation will then be conducted, attractively and persuasively, with a view to enrolling each of the prospective members in the class and department in which he or she belongs.

Provide for those who are discovered. A familiar slogan reads, "Business goes where it is invited and stays where it is well treated." All this seeking of prospects will be in vain if the church has insufficient building and organization to take care of those who are invited. On the basis of census returns, the building should, if necessary, be remodeled or enlarged to take care of all who have been discovered. When a building reaches the saturation point, the enrolment of the church school ceases to grow. It is therefore imperative that sufficient space be provided for an adequate number of departments and classes to meet the need of possibilities. From existing departments and classes new units should be formed, even though their constituency be mainly the names of those who have been discovered in the census. Innumerable instances can be cited of departments and classes, thus formed, soon becoming as large as the older units from which they came.

In many, if not most, cases this program of enlargement will call for a change in pattern from single departments to multiple departments, from few classes to many classes. It will also call for the multiplying of officers and teachers, who must be discovered, enlisted, pretrained. It is all but hopeless, in this day of severe competition for people's time, to expect to hold for regular attendance those who have been enrolled unless when they come they receive something worthwhile. The popular mass meeting type of Sunday school, with increase in enrolment brought about by campaigns and contests, signally fails to meet the demands of the modern public. The school of the church is the church at work fulfilling its central mission—reaching, teaching, winning, enlisting individuals for Christ and his kingdom.

Some Requisites to Efficient Church School Administration

Many people think of a church as an institution that operates only on Sunday. Such a church would not be expected to pay the same kind of attention to enrolment, attendance, grades, promotion, curriculum materials, tests and measurements, student counseling, teacher efficiency, administrative skills, and the like, as of course would be the case in any other school. Yet the tremendous pressure of need to make the church school a real school, comparable in importance with the public school, calls for facilities and processes of comparable effectiveness.

Adequate records, accurately kept and effectively used, are essential to administrative efficiency. Such records and their use will meet these minimum requirements: (1) A master card file, with complete enrolment of church school members, alphabetically indexed and with basic information concerning each person—name, sex, age, birthday, address, telephone, occupation, family connections, relationship to the church, educational status, when enrolled, and space for remarks. (2) Specialized card index files for each department by classes, with spaces to indicate promotion to and from the department and within the department, regularity or irregularity of attendance, co-operativeness and responsiveness, evidences of religious growth, special needs and problems, personal visits by teacher, conversation with the pastor, loyalty to the church and its services. (3) Classification forms in duplicate, to be filled out when any new member enrols, giving basic information to be typed onto permanent cards for the files. (4) Classification officer, who will see that each new member is properly enrolled and that department superintendent and teacher receive duplicate copy of information. (5) A record system, according to which each member will be marked each Sunday on such essentials as attendance, punctuality, giving, the bringing of a Bible, previous lesson study, attendance on the worship service; allowing thirty points for prepared lesson, twenty points each for Sunday school and worship attendance, and ten points for the other items, the student may thus be rated, averages for class and department computed, and results objectively measured.

(6) Secretaries of departments, carefully trained to see that records are accurately kept in each class and department, averages computed, returns made to department heads and teachers, and results made available to the church and school each week, with modification of these items for the younger children. (7) Report cards, prepared and sent quarterly to parents, indicating grades as noted above, with comments which will be helpful to maintain a vital relationship between parents and teachers.

Regular reports should be made, to the end that the church and all concerned may be kept informed about the school. At monthly church council meetings there should be comprehensive summaries, with full details given at each weekly meeting of officers and teachers. At least quarterly, summaries should be given to the church in its congregational business meeting, with a complete report presented annually. These reports ordinarily should be mimeographed so as to avoid the tedium of reading them to uninspired listeners.

Personnel survey and nominating committees should be regularly appointed and carefully instructed, with a view to discovering and enlisting the best available persons as officers and teachers of the school. The personnel survey committee will regularly study the entire church membership roll, looking for men and women who have leadership possibilities. Such persons will be approached with the purpose of enrolling them in pretraining classes, interesting them in opportunities for service, acquainting them with the needs and opportunities of the school. A well-chosen nominating committee, under leadership of pastor and educational director, will undertake annually to provide replacements, find and enlist new officers and teachers, and after prayerful consultation will nominate to the church all who are to serve in this high capacity of faculty and staff members of the church school. No matter what is the polity of the church, there is great advantage in having the roster of officers and teachers presented to the congregation for their information and approval.

Scheduling and routinizing the meetings and activities of the school should be given careful attention. The Sunday session should be at least an hour and a quarter in duration, often with extended session for the younger children. For the older groups, the assembly period should be brief, spirited, and confined almost wholly to two purposes: to give opportunity before all the classes of the department for announcements and promotional matters and to prepare minds and hearts for the lesson which follows. Nothing should be allowed to encroach on the time of the teachers, most of whom need thirty to forty-five minutes for the discussion of the lesson. In the younger departments there would be, of course, a variety of activities, the briefer span of attention of children being kept in mind.

Weekday activities should be carefully scheduled, attention being given to proper spacing on the calendar, the seasons of the year, requirements of time on the part of other church activities, conservation of time and energy being sought through correlation of events that avoid duplication and overlapping. The term "Sunday school" is a misnomer in the light of the many activities and events which make the church school a weekday affair just as really as it is a Sunday affair. Scheduling of the school's weekday activities should be done in order to prevent conflicts with the calendar of the public school and demands made by community interests.

An extension program is a responsibility of today's church almost equal to its services within the walls of the church building. This extended service may take several forms: (1) Ministry to infants through the Cradle Roll or its equivalent, by means of which every baby in the community is brought under the loving care of a church through visits in the home, recognition of birthdays, concern at times of illness, enrolment in the church nursery wherever possible. (2) Promotion of Christian home life, through personal conversation with parents, the distribution of literature on Christian homemaking, the sponsoring of family welfare clinics, the winning of parents to Christ and the church. (3) Sponsorship of a program of Christian fellowship and recreation in the social rooms and on the grounds of the church, in parks and other recreation centers, and in the homes of members. (5) Concern for social welfare and action, expressed through the molding of public opinion on issues of civic and social righteousness, and in active participation in movements for the public good. (6) Establishment of branch Sunday schools and missions in neglected areas, seeking to bring the values of the mother church to groups who otherwise would be deprived of religious education. (7) Devotion to missions at home and abroad, through prayer, mission study, generous giving, recruitment of missionaries, in the conviction that the mission of every Christian and every church is missions. (8) Ministry to the shut-ins of the community, carried on through an alert extension department, thus extending basic values of the church school to the sick, the aged, those who must work on Sunday, or any others whom circumstances prevent from attending the regular sessions of the school. (8) Sessions of the school held at other times than on Sunday, particularly in localities where people do shift work, who on successive evenings of the week could attend the church for Bible study even though shut out from attendance on the Lord's Day. (10) Not to be forgotten are students away from home in college or otherwise engaged and the men and women in the services of their country; their continuation of Bible study should be encouraged, with literature sent them regularly and reports secured concerning their reading and study.

Progress Proceeds Through Testing and Measuring

Compare present instruments of manufacture, transportation, merchandising, and communication with those in use fifty years ago. Vast improvements in these and other fields have been in large measure due to scientific processes of testing and measuring. Advances in general education owe much to the theory and practice of tests and measurements. Educational administrators are keenly aware that progress will be hit or miss unless there is continual attention given to experimentation and evaluation of outcomes.

Much more attention than ever before needs to be given to testing and measuring in religious education. Instruments have been devised for testing biblical knowledge, for measuring attitudes and choices, and for evaluating outcomes in terms of conduct and character. These instruments need to be perfected and standardized. Immense areas of progress are opened up in the contemplation of the application of scientific principles of testing and measuring to religious teaching and learning. While there is much in the realm of religion that is not subject to exact measurement, there is much that can be done to determine the effectiveness of teaching, worship, preaching, religious activities, conduct guidance and character education. Administration will not have fulfilled its duty until it explores this sphere and makes practical use of results.

Administration in religious education is means to ends. The *how* must never replace the *what* and *why*. Content, motive, and method are interdependent. The ministry of teaching and preaching will always go limping without the aid of competent administration.

Chapter VIII

The Worshiping Church Possesses Spiritual Power

I T IS REPORTED that a church bulletin carried the disturbing announcement: "Due to lack of power, there will be no worship service tonight." With electricity cut off, the lights would be out and the organ silenced; so the evening service had to be canceled. The announcement for any church might read: "Due to lack of worship, there will be no power in the church services." The failure of worship represents a disastrous break in the spiritual power line.

The Problem of Power

Power has become civilization's greatest problem. Always there have been unlimited resources of power, but not until now have men realized its vastness and possessed so much control over it.

A new era in human affairs came with the discovery of the expansive power of steam and the invention of engines driven by this power. The harnessing of electricity broadened the scope of man's development and use of power that has replaced human effort in a thousand ways. The new physics has discovered the power hidden in the atom—the same kind of power that holds the planets together and tears them apart. Atomic fission has put into men's hands the power to annihilate all life on the earth. The question of questions is whether this vast power will be used for constructive or destructive purposes. From washing the dishes to the survival of the human race we confront the problem of power.

What is power? We once thought that it was an external force applied to an object to overcome its inertia. We now know that power is the release of energy from within, as indicated by the splitting of the atom. The power of the sun, which we receive as light and heat, comes from a continuous atomic explosion when carbon and hydrogen unite at tremendously high temperature, producing helium that radiates immeasurable energy. When there is momentary cooling following the explosion, the carbon returns to its original state with almost imperceptible loss, whereupon another explosion occurs, thus perpetually supplying the light and heat without which there would be no life on this planet.

The marvels of the cosmic order, the uniformity of the laws of nature, the amazing relation of the unseen to the seen, the infinite variety of the forms and expressions of energy demand some explanation of origins. Could there be such design without a designer? Could all that our intelligence is discovering have occurred apart from creative intelligence? Could that which science, with all its knowledge and instruments, seeks to reproduce have originated by accident? Could a universe, whose vastness in the macrocosm and the microcosm staggers imagination, have created itself? Could power have sprung from that which was in the beginning "without form and void"? Inquiring minds cannot be satisfied with the reply of the agnostic, "We do not know, and we cannot know."

The Source of Power

Thoughtful scientists, as they probe for the answer to origins, are thrown back on the ancient revelation: "In the beginning God created the heavens and the earth" (Gen. 1:1). To them the word "created" is no longer the vocabulary of prescientific man but is the key that unlocks the mystery of the universe. To create is literally to bring into being from nothing, to cause to exist. Since it is incredible that matter created itself, or that it has existed eternally, the only possible explanation is that it came from a Creator. There are those, having made this necessary admission, who would speak of the creative energy as power or process, denying the quality of personality.

Is the source of power personal or impersonal? The personal can readily be distinguished from the nonpersonal. To be personal is to possess life of a kind forever removed from the subpersonal. The highest animal is not a person and cannot be. If it is said that man is personal because he thinks, feels, and wills, it may be replied that animals have an elementary ability to think, that they certainly feel, and that they are capable of exercising a degree of will. The infinite difference appears in the possession by man of mind, or, in biblical language, soul. The human mind is a vast energy system, not to be identified with brain, but having the power to communicate and to create.

It is of the essence of personality to communicate through symbols. Thoughtful students of personality find a clear relation between language and the quality of being a person. Without speech or its equivalent in signs, personality as we know it would be impossible. Personality is developed through communication. Next to the urge of life itself is the urge to communicate. An infant deprived of all opportunity of communication with others would not develop true selfhood. Personality inheres in communicativeness.

The mark of personality is creativeness. On the human level, creativity is always relative. Humanly, to create is to make or produce by means of new combinations of that which already exists and by investing these combinations with new forms and qualities. The inventiveness of persons seems to be without limit. Persons express their creativeness as they reproduce after their kind, as they construct all manner of plants, as they invent endless types of machines, as they communicate ideas through art and literature, as they express their aspirations in social and political ideologies, on and on. Creativity is of the essence of personality.

Power, on the human level, flows from personality. The powerful locomotive, airplane, automobile, factory machinery, or atom bomb is actually powerless of itself. The potential physical power awaits release and direction through the intelligence and skill of persons. All the power now available for them was present from the beginning but has become actual only as persons have discovered how to employ it. Remove the element of personality from physical power and it becomes blind force. Put power into the hands of evil men and it becomes destructive force. Let wise and good men control power and it becomes constructive and beneficent force. Power becomes meaningful only in terms of personality.

God communicates himself to those whom he has created in his image. God's supreme creativity is not expressed in his inanimate and brute creation but in his creation of persons. In persons, not things, God finds his self-fulfilment. Within the limits of finiteness, man has been endowed with creative power like that of God's. God not only communicates with and through man but he makes man the agent of his communication and creation. Thus man finds his highest soul fulfilment in God.

Paul's words about God and man are as true scientifically as theologically: "In him we live and move and have our being" (Acts 17:28). Augustine was as sound in his psychology as in his theology when he said, "Thou, O God, hast made us for thyself, and we are restless until we find our rest in thee." Man's quest for power, both physical and personal, leads to disaster and despair unless he finds its source in God.

The Meaning and Value of Worship

A group of thoughtful students, having examined the many attempted definitions of worship found in the literature of the subject, came up with these composite definitions:

Worship is an individual or corporate awareness of God, involving a direct relationship with him as he is revealed to us in and through the person of Jesus Christ. It is a recognition of God's worth, involving a direct inner contact, a mutual intercourse, a conversation—which should result in action in accordance with his will.

Worship is the response of man to God's revelation of himself—which includes a revelation of his holiness and worth—as man humbles himself and confesses his sin and asks for cleansing. God then responds with a further revelation of himself by cleansing man and calling him for service, to which man responds.

Worship is that real and vital experience in which we commune with God, the creature with the Creator, the trusting child with the loving and all-wise Heavenly Father. We feel a yearning within us to have fellowship with our Maker who made us for this very purpose, and recognizing our need, we approach him in adoration and reverence and thanksgiving.

Worship is an experience involving both the acts and attitudes of men in their responses to the recognition of a Holy God, and in fellowship with him, resulting in a commitment of the self to him.

Worship is the soul's sincere outreach toward God in an act of reverence toward the "worthship" of the divine Lord. It is based on the biblical insights as revealed in the person of Jesus Christ and has as its goals the glory of God and the edification of the saints through a self-dedication and renewal of life.

W. R. McNutt, in *Worship in the Churches,* after having reviewed a number of definitions, arrives at this comprehensive statement:

Christian worship (in the churches) is that varying and ascending series of experiences—emotionally charged, and sustained throughout by the appropriate attitudes—which arises in some awareness of God the Father of all men, moves forward through vision, sense of impotence and reassurance, toward climax in dedication of life, thence descending through a feeling of peace, power and conviction of social responsibility.[1]

Obviously, no one of these definitions is fully adequate, for worship is an experience that surpasses explanation. Fortunately, the value of worship does not depend on rationalization. Worship brings recognition to man that he is more and other than animal. Worship lifts man's gaze to a world higher than that of things. Worship reminds man that there is One greater than himself to whom he owes homage that breaks the bonds of selfishness. Worship of the All-Holy induces humility as man by contrast recognizes his sinfulness. Worship throws the white light of God's character as revealed in Christ on the defects of man's character, thus bringing him to repentance. Worship discloses an ethical standard far above man's and stirs in him aspiration to seek its attainment. Worship provides fellowship with other worshipers, thus reinforcing the individual with the dynamics of the group.

Worship leads to selfless service, demonstrating the truth that it is more blessed to give than to receive. Worship not only motivates service but sustains it as a way of life. Worship conquers fear, making it possible to live victoriously and to die fearlessly. There are no values for human living that are not enhanced by worship and none that are not degraded by false worship or failure to worship. A church may do many things, but its supreme contribution is to provide and enrich worship.

The Administration of Worship

The experience of worship needs to be stimulated and guided. The pressures of everyday living may well tend to obscure the consciousness of God. Wordsworth truly said, "The world is too much with us; getting and spending, we lay waste our powers." Worship is not confined to a church building, nor is it induced only by a church service. Yet men universally have found the need of a place of worship and an order of worship. Among the most important functions of ministers of religion is the administration of worship.

Ministers by virtue of their calling and office are leaders of worship. Since worship is an art, the leader of worship should be an artist. He should incarnate the spirit of worship, exhibit always the attitude of worship, inspire in others a sense of reverence, and develop the skills that will enable him to lead worship acceptably and attractively.

The minister as leader of worship needs competent assistance. Where is his administrative ability more conspicuous for its absence than when he assumes a monopoly of responsibility for the planning and conduct of the worship services of the church? The perceptive minister will not concentrate all his attention on the preparation and delivery of the sermon; he will give equally careful attention to the planning of the service of worship. Such planning requires a fine measure of teamwork as the minister seeks to relate himself and his part to those who are his associates.

The worship service in a typical evangelical church falls into two main parts, inspiration and illumination—the service of song, prayer, testimony, and giving, and the interpretation and application of the Scriptures in the sermon. These are not two separate parts of the worship service but common halves of a whole. The purpose of worship preceding the sermon should be the same as that proposed by the sermon. If this integration is to be achieved, the preacher and those responsible for other aspects of the service must get together. Effective teamwork requires continual co-operation, mutual understanding, agreed objectives. The minister of the Word and the minister of music are teammates, each reinforcing the other. The musician or musicians belong to the team and should always be in the consultation when the worship program is being devised.

From time immemorial the choir has been an indispensable adjunct to worship. There were choirs in David's day, and some of the most beautiful of the Psalms were written for choral use. The preacher and the minister of music have joint responsibility for selecting and training the choir or choirs.

According to the policy established by the church, members of the choir should meet certain basic requirements. They should be members of the church in which they serve, vital Christians and faithful attendants, worthy witnesses of the gospel which they sing. The choir should be recruited as carefully as Sunday school teachers and officers or leaders in any other of the church's organizations. Some churches wisely nominate choir members to the church for election just as others who are chosen for responsible office. Usually, they should be selected after conference and audition, to the end that the best musical talent of the church may be obtained. They should commit themselves to regular attendance on rehearsals and to be present and in their places for the stated services of worship. Their behavior should be above reproach, both within and without the church house.

Robes for the choir are becoming increasingly acceptable to churches that once rejected them as too formal and ceremonial. Robes cover a multitude of distractions of millinery and dress. Uniformity distinguishes the choir from the congregation and gives added recognition of their service as ministers of music. Their functions as leaders of the congregation in singing should be kept primary; yet their specialized talents and training can add much to the beauty and attractiveness of the service. Good administration calls for the continual training of the choir in the meaning and significance of their leadership of worship.

Fruitful Ways of Worship

The obvious purpose of corporate worship is that those present may together have an experience with God which will in some measure change their lives. Not all worship services will bring about this result. There are occasions when the presence of God is scarcely felt at all. On other occasions his presence is very real.

The planning of a worship service is not with a view to compelling the divine presence or coercing a response from the congregation. Like the wind which blows where it wills, the Holy Spirit is not subject to man's orders, even at church! The planned program of worship should, however, seek to provide maximally favorable conditions for a fruitful meeting of God with his people.

Favorable conditions for this meeting of God with his people should be carefully studied and provided. Man's part in the experience is important. There are ways of worshiping that hinder and ways that help. Perhaps there is no one best order of service that meets all the conditions for everybody at all times. Like almost everything else that we do, our planned services may be rated as good, better, best; or bad, worse, worst.

The service of worship may be planned rigidly and prescribed by church authority. Fairly early in church history services began to be standardized. Rituals of confession were provided for those who had sinned and sought restoration. Ceremonials of consolation were prepared for those bereaved by death, especially in the case of martyrs. The baptismal rite came to be according to a fixed formula, and the Lord's Supper was observed with "words of institution." Gradually, elaborate liturgical forms were developed, often beautiful and meaningful. There was the "liturgy of the Word," the ceremony accompanying the sermon or homily; then followed the "liturgy of the upper room," when the Lord's Supper was observed.

In the course of time the sermon all but disappeared, and in its place were the Catholic ceremonials climaxed by the Mass, representing the repeated unbloody sacrifice of Christ wherein the bread became his actual flesh and the wine his blood. On the calendar of the church year were fixed the growing number of holy weeks and holy days, for each of which there were prescribed orders of service. Reduced at length to exact uniformity, these services are the same, with slight variations, in Roman Catholic churches throughout the world. Much use is made of regalia, candles, images, recited prayers, responses by the congregation from memory or from the prayer book, choral music, with accompanying ancient symbols. To the faithful Roman Catholic, this prescribed observance may have a measure of spiritual value, but it tends to become formal and meaningless.

At the other extreme, the service of worship may be loosely planned or altogether unplanned. Rejecting all formularies, the congregation may worship "as the Spirit moves them." Such formless worship occasioned Paul's rebuke of the Corinthian Christians. With confusion of voices and speaking in tongues, they had made their worship services disorderly and unintelligible. Paul thus argues for orderly worship: "If, therefore, the whole church assembles and all speak in tongues, and outsiders or unbelievers enter, will they not say that you are mad?" On the other hand, if there is orderly and intelligent worship and an unbeliever is present, "the secrets of his heart are disclosed; and so, falling on his face, he will worship God and declare that God is really among you" (1 Cor. 14:25).

The argument made in favor of unplanned, extemporaneous worship is that it is more directly under the guidance of the Holy Spirit. The fallacy involved is that the Holy Spirit cannot or will not give guidance to the planning of the service. Is there not even more opportunity for the Holy Spirit to lead a praying minister and his colleagues to plan a service wisely and well than to give such leadership when the congregation has assembled without previous preparation on anybody's part? Laziness and presumptuousness may manifest themselves in either way—the following of a set service which has cost no thought or effort, or the escape from thought and effort by depending on the mood of the moment.

Good worship administration will avoid the error of either extreme. The minister and those responsible with him will review the order of service frequently, observing the extent to which it may be growing threadbare and in need of change, yet being careful not to make changes so often as to confuse the congregation. The ideal is freedom within the limits of an orderly pattern. Since it is agreed that the sermon is at its best when carefully and prayerfully planned, may we not agree that the accompanying worship activities are also most fruitful when thus prepared?

The Improvement of Worship

The human aspect of worship, like any other finite endeavor, needs continual improvement. The temptation is to develop a reasonably satisfactory order of service and repeat it ad infinitum. It may be that the only change made in years has been the hymn numbers and the sermon subjects. Any activity repeated thus invariably tends to become monotonous and to lose effectiveness. Improvement may be effected in a number of ways.

The preacher, the minister of music, the musician, and selected choir members may sit together at regular intervals to ask: What have been the most satisfying aspects of our worship recently? What have been the weakest points? What needs changing? Sympathetic appreciation of one another and prayer for guidance undoubtedly will bring suggestions for improvement.

The ushers have a significant part in making the worship service satisfying. They, too, should be called together for conference and similar questions discussed. Do ushers realize that they are the church's hosts? Are they always present ahead of time, each in his appointed place, prepared in mind and heart to serve? Do they observe utmost courtesy in greeting and seating the worshipers? Are they careful to fill the front seats first, so as to reserve the back seats for latecomers? Are they quick to detect discomfort from lighting, ventilation, heating, cooling? Do they watch for visitors and make them feel comfortable and welcome? Do they observe the effect of the service on the congregation with a view to suggesting improvements? Skilful and spiritual-minded ushers can do much to make the worship services more satisfying.

The congregation may be taken into the confidence of those who lead the worship services. Their opinions may be sought through a quietly conducted poll as to the aspects of the services which are more or less enriching. Their preferences as to the music may be taken into account. Their views may be very helpful in the selection of the hymns. After all, the worship services are primarily for the benefit of the congregation, not for the gratification of the worship leaders.

Improvement of worship goes back to the need of training in worship. It is too late and untimely to instruct as to ways of worship during the worship service itself. Such effort at instruction is usually an interference with the experience of worship. Training in worship has its beginning in the home. Worshipful church members come from worshipful homes. Strong emphasis should be given and help provided for the conduct of family worship. Assembly periods of Sunday school, Training Union, and other church organizations furnish excellent opportunity for training in worship. The chief value of these assembly programs preceding meetings for study and discussion is that they provide an atmosphere of worship and an occasion for learning how to worship. Leaders of the church organizations hold in their hands the key to improvement.

Rather than the traditional "music committee," there may be greater value in a "worship committee," a small but representative group of persons whose responsibility is to observe every phase of the life of the church with a view to making every activity and every service more worshipful. They will serve as consultants to the pastor, the minister of music, the musician, the choir, the ushers, the leaders of the church organization and their departments. To them the improvement of worship will be a matter of major importance, and from them will come suggestions of much practical value.

Guiding Principles of Worship

Worship, the response of the creature to the Eternal, cannot be confined to a ritual or reduced to an order of service. Worship is a vital experience with a living God and takes as many forms as there are worshiping persons. These experiences may be classified according to general types: prescribed or free, ceremonial or spontaneous, orderly or disorderly, rational or irrational, Christian or pagan. The Bible describes many experiences of worship, which may be classified as characterized by importunity, thanksgiving, praise, petition, intercession, penitence, submission, dedication, sacrifice. Services of worship may be planned to emphasize one or more of these elements, but the experience itself cannot be forced into a mold. The response sought may be foreseen and appropriate means used to secure it. Worship may have an orderly movement toward a desired end and can therefore be conducted according to certain guiding principles.

Worship should be reverent. The leader of worship should never forget that it is directed first of all to God. He is the object of worship, and its conduct should be pleasing to him. Worship seeks response from the people, but it is a response to God, not just to the music and the sermon. In the presence of the Almighty we should be filled with awe, respect, humility, affection. Anything bordering on irreverence is out of place in a service of worship.

Worship should be dignified. True dignity in worship springs from a recognition of God's majesty, Christ's lordship, the Holy Spirit's power. There is a stiffness that sometimes is mistaken for dignity; but, rightly understood, dignity in worship calls for warmth of feeling as well as loftiness of thought. Frivolity and clownishness have no place in worship.

Worship should be genuine. Jesus said that "the true worshipers will worship the Father in spirit and truth, for such the Father seeks to worship him" (John 4:23). The touchstone of worship is reality. Jesus condemned hypocrisy more than any other single sin. Whatever is insincere must be rejected, for of necessity it cancels worship.

Worship should be relevant. We worship a living God through the mediation of a present Christ. Dead forms, however sanctified by the past, are of no value to living persons who come into the presence of a God who is immanent as well as transcendent. Worship does not call us away from the affairs and concerns of life but brings us with all our sins and cares into God's presence for his guidance and help in dealing with them. Worship is a sharing with God of our interest in the human situation, not a withdrawal from it. Worship as an abstract performance is not true worship and will not be pleasing to God.

Worship should be beautiful. Goodness, truth, and beauty are inseparable. David sang: "Give unto the Lord the glory due unto his name: bring an offering, and come before him: worship the Lord in the beauty of holiness" (1 Chron. 16:29, AV). There is beauty in holiness and holiness in beauty. Surely the God of goodness, beauty, and holiness does not want his house to be ugly and unattractive. There may not be rich adornment, either of the place or of the service, but there can be the loveliness of simplicity, cleanliness, harmony, and radiance. Drabness and bad taste are incongruous in worship.

Worship should be well timed. We live in an age when much of life is regulated by the clock. A worship service that begins late, drags through with interruptions and distractions, and runs overtime violates the principle of timing and is cheapened accordingly. Time is life, and worship, without being hurried, should conserve life by keeping on time. Leaders of worship must keep faith with the people by conducting the service according to schedule.

Worship should be varied. The God whom we worship is a God of infinite variety. All nature reflects God's avoidance of sameness and monotony. Variety in worship does not mean straining for effect, but it does demand differences that bring out the best in the leadership and in congregational response. In an experience as thrilling as worship may be, does not dulness somehow partake of the nature of sin?

Worship should be supremely God conscious, Christ mastered, Spirit led. This is the controlling principle—the centrality of God in all that is said and done. Let this principle be violated, and nothing else greatly matters; let it be honored, and all else will fall eventually into proper place. The high purpose of worship is fulfilled when the Commandment is kept: "You shall worship the Lord your God and him only shall you serve" (Matt. 4:10).

Growing a Worshipful Congregation

When in Colonial days a group of Christians had no house of worship, no ordained minister, no material resources, and little learning, they came together to read the Scriptures, to sing and to pray, and to bear their testimony. By deep Christian intuition they put worship first, in the confidence that other needful things would be added. In the course of time these "things added" have multiplied until they sometimes have crowded out the prime essential, worship. To restore worship is to restore a church's power.

Pastor and people may not be very far wrong when they feel that attendance on the stated worship services of the church constitutes a real measure of its success. The significance of the crowded church is not just that it compliments the preacher and the choir, or that it guarantees a good collection, or that it insures increased membership. These may be important by-products, but the real value of crowds of souls lies in what worship does for them and for the church. Paul declares that he is not ashamed of the gospel, for "it is the power of God for salvation to every one who has faith" (Rom. 1:16). But the gospel is powerless for those who do not hear it. "And how are they to believe in him of whom they have never heard? And how are they to hear without a preacher?" (Rom. 10:14). The most eloquent preacher is ineffective without hearers, and the gospel of God is without saving power to those who do not listen.

The preacher fills the pulpit, but the congregation must fill the pews. People attract people, and even more important than the pulling power of the preacher is the influence of church members on their friends and acquaintances. Pastor and staff, deacons and church officers, superintendents and leaders of the church organizations constitute an administrative team whose business it is to "pack the pews."

The potential of a place of worship filled to capacity Sunday after Sunday with participating worshipers is like to that which was realized at Pentecost when the whole body of disciples "were all together in one place" (Acts 2:1). They were all filled with the Holy Spirit, they all bore witness to the mighty works of God, so that all who heard were amazed and a little later responded to the preaching of Peter; and "those who received his word were baptized, and there were added that day about three thousand souls" (Acts 2:41). A worshiping church became a witnessing church, preaching was with power, and many souls were saved. The revival for which many wait and pray must come, as it always has, when the conditions of Pentecost are again fulfilled and the worshiping church flames with the fire of evangelism.

Chapter IX

Music Is an Essential Ministry

MUSIC IS NOT incidental and optional in the life of a worshiping and witnessing church. The administration of the program of music in a church rates high in the responsibilities of pastor, staff, and lay leadership. It is not just the business of minister of music or choir director or music committee, but should be the concern of the whole church. Music is more than an adjunct of the preaching services and a traditional part of the opening exercises of the several church organizations. Music is an integral part of the total life of the church. Its character and quality will go far toward determining the spiritual vitality and effectiveness of every phase of the church's activity.

Clarifying Conceptions Concerning the Place of Music

Misconceptions of the place of music in the church have long prevailed. From the Roman Catholic tradition comes the conception of music as inseparable from the ritual, to be performed by choir and officiating priests as unto God in the presence of the congregation. At the other extreme is the free church tradition in which music is considered routine, something with which to "fill in" while the congregation is settling itself for the sermon.

Seeking to take music seriously, a church may employ competent musicians—director, organist, accomplished vocalists—and expect from them a high quality of concert music which may or may not be worshipful or have relationship with the sermon. Realizing that this type of music tends toward the professional, that it does not have popular appeal for those who lack musical education, and that it may make little or no contribution to the effectiveness of preach-

125

ing, another church may secure the services of a director, whose function will be to recruit a chorus choir and lead the congregation in a period of lusty singing of tuneful songs that get the people ready for a stirring sermon. If the demand of the church is for something on the quieter side, the selection may be of the more familiar hymns, intended for enjoyment and uplift, often with little religious relevance, the choir's selection of special music in the way of anthem or quartet or solo frequently making little contribution to the total purpose of the service.

The statement of these conceptions of the place of music in the church reveals their inadequacy. "The ideal of church music is found in its function," declares Joseph N. Ashton.

This function is religious: to bring to stronger and clearer consciousness and to greater vitality our inherent religious nature. At the heart of church music must be the consciousness of this religious nature: the sense of the divine, of goodness and righteousness, of the Almighty, the Eternal; the sense of exaltation of human life to the divine, and accompanying this the feeling of humility into which such a sense must lead us.[1]

Such an ideal may be only approximated in some situations and, as Ashton points out, will be variously realized because of differences in cultural background, resources of musicianship, musical facilities, music traditions. Yet if music is to have a place of high importance in the life and work of the church, it should be genuinely and worthily religious in character and in purpose. Nothing in music should be admitted that would not be acceptable as qualitatively on the same high level of teaching and preaching. Any lack of sincerity, of dignity, of seriousness of purpose, of fidelity to the Christian faith, should no more be tolerated in music than in teaching and preaching. The three means of communication of truth are inseparable and deserve equal care and concern on the part of pastor and staff and people.

Music in the Service of Religion

Music through the ages has rendered service to religion. Indeed, music antedates recorded history. Archaeologists have unearthed crude musical instruments and fragments of musical notation belonging to the early Egyptian period. The rhythmic beat of drums accompanied by the chanting of priests and worshipers is a form of primitive music known from ancient time to the present. From the beginning, music seems to have been used as a part of religious ritual.

Music was of high importance in Hebrew worship. The Old Testament lists a great number of musical instruments—the harp, the dulcimer, the lyre, the pipe, the trumpet, the drum, the cymbal, the bell. A careful count discloses that the Hebrews in the time of David and Solomon possessed thirty-six different instruments.

Christianity began as a singing religion. The angels sang at the birth of Christ; Mary sang with poetic exaltation when she knew that she was to be the mother of the Messiah; Zacharias sang at the birth of John the Baptist; Simeon sang when he took the holy Child in his arms at the time of the presentation of Jesus in the Temple. The New Testament writings contain many poems that evidently were set to music. Karl Harrington writes:

While ancient Hebrew singing and its antiphonal features must have exerted more or less influence on early Christian song, it is clear that the music of the early church was based chiefly on the music of the Greeks, and that modifications of the Greek scales were long the foundation on which grew the structure of the Christian music of the European church. The origin of some of the most famous of the standard hymns of Christianity, like the *Gloria in Excelsis* and the *Te Deum* lies back in the very early Greek hymns of the Eastern church.[2]

The sixteenth century saw Roman Catholic music lifted to its highest level under the influence of Palestrina, who achieved superlative success both in composition and in the inspiration of church musicians to elevate music to a high worshipful level. Luther and his fellow reformers realized that in music they had a powerful weapon for the advancement of their cause as well as a profound help to the religious life. The Reformation brought significant change. Whereas Catholic music was for the choir, Protestant music was for the congregation. The melodies, known as "chorales," were generally based on popular folk songs, simple and full of feeling. Gradually there developed a great body of Protestant music, cantatas and oratorios being added to the popular hymns and the gospel songs.

Church music in Colonial America was restrained and severely simple. The Pilgrims and Puritans sang only Psalms to fewer than a dozen tunes and without musical instruments. There were heated discussions over methods of singing:

(1) Should one person sing for all the congregation, the others joining only in singing "amen," or should the whole congregation sing? (2) Should women as well as men sing, or only the men? (3) Should "carnal men" and pagans be permitted to sing, or only the Christian and church members? (4) Should it be lawful to sing psalms in tunes invented by men, or should the congregation sing as inspired? [3]

Within a hundred years these questions largely disappeared. The colonists had become a singing people and the new nation a singing nation. Indigenous folk music appeared and then a vast variety of popular music. Perhaps the most thoroughly creative and original American music was the Negro spiritual. A great deal of this popular music was religious.

The popularization of church music led to the necessity for organization. The church choir came into vogue toward the latter part of the eighteenth century. Singers with better voices and some training drew apart from the congregation, at first gathering about the organ or sitting on the front pew, then assembling in a space especially provided for them on the platform. Singing schools were conducted, with a view to teaching the elements of notation. Singing came to be one of the most attractive and important features of the revival. D. L. Moody and Ira D. Sankey formed the first notable preacher-singer evangelistic team. In the American tradition, music and evangelism are inseparable, just as music and worship have been from time immemorial.

The kinship of music and religion is not accidental. The ancient Greeks conceived music in terms of ethos, that is, moral quality. They recognized that music by its very nature produces an effect on attitudes, choices, character. It is commonplace knowledge that the practical doctrinal beliefs of most persons are derived from the songs they sing even more than from the teaching and preaching to which they listen.

Growing a Musical Church

A church may have a skilled director of music, a trained and talented choir, a great organ, the best of music materials, an appreciative pastor, and a music-loving congregation and yet fail to achieve the distinction of being a musical church. There are methods and means necessary to the growing of such a church.

Music appreciation can be taught. Some elements of music are intuitive; witness the little child who beats time rhythmically and the untutored primitives who chant harmoniously. From this native endowment of capacity for musical response the normal individual may progress indefinitely in music appreciation and skills.

Tastes in music vary widely. Occasionally, there are found those who confess that they do not like music of any sort. They protest that it is meaningless sound which possesses for them no significance or value. Some prefer music of the jazz or jive or bebop variety, with its noisy syncopation. Others prefer classical music, with its intricacies and complexities. Some enjoy concert music, with its many instruments played together impressively and brilliantly. Others enjoy the quieter chamber music, suited more to the home and the small company. Some would rather listen to music by skilled performers; others gain more satisfaction from participation.

Why all this variation of taste? The difference may be due in part to temperament, but in the main it is the consequence of education. This does not mean necessarily that lowbrow persons like vulgar music while highbrow persons like classical music. It does mean, however, that musical taste is cultivated and reflects total personality.

Education in music calls for standards of value. Church music may be rated on a scale of good, better, best; bad, worse, worst. Standards are not arbitrary; they have been established through long usage, through conjoint opinions of competent musicians, by means of simple criteria that are generally accepted. Worthy church music is: (1) consonant with the teachings of the Bible and the ideals of the Christian religion; (2) composed in singable, inspiring, ennobling melody; (3) identified with words that measure up to the standards of true poetry; (4) played and sung for the glory of God and the transformation and enrichment of human life. More may be desired, but less should scarcely be tolerated. The appreciation of any congregation can be moved toward this level under competent leadership with patient determination.

Schools of music may be conducted. The church school of music is a popular and effective means of promoting both music appreciation and musicianship for a single church or a group of churches.

In its simplest form, the school follows the pattern made familiar by the training school for Sunday school officers and teachers or other church leadership groups. Held at least annually, and preferably biannually, the school will concentrate within a week instruction and inspiration designed to spotlight the importance of music in the program of the church, to bring together for intensive study those already engaged in the church's music activities, and to recruit additional persons for orientation and enlistment. A faculty of high quality should be engaged, all available persons in the several age groups should be pre-enrolled, attractive publicity should be given, books and other materials should be provided, and the support of the entire church should be sought. Classes will be conducted by departments; then all will be brought together for a brief period of concerted singing. The closing session may be held on Sunday evening, the entire hour being given over to the massed choirs in impressive demonstration of what has been learned. The plan of the local church school may be expanded to include the churches of an entire area, which will come together for a joint school, climaxed by a sacred music festival, with individual and massed choirs from many churches participating.

Special occasions may be planned. Many opportunities are afforded throughout the year for emphasis on music. Christmas and Easter may be celebrated with appropriate cantatas. "Hymn sermons" are attractive and effective. Hymns gathered about a great Bible theme, such as faith or hope or love, and related to appropriate Scriptures, may make the points of the sermon after the fashion of the homiletically prepared discourse. Music may be the main feature of celebrations, such as baptism, the Lord's Supper, the church's anniversary, Thanksgiving, Home-coming, and other events in the church calendar. An organ concert, a service of meditation through music, a "singspiration," a Children's Day service, a memorial service, or a service in appreciation of pastor and staff and their fellow workers may be made fruitful and memorable through the use of music.

Music may be a creative experience. Music has been described as "a meeting between sound and human consciousness." If there were no vibrations entering the ear, there would be no music; and if there were no apparatus of hearing, connecting sound with consciousness, there would be no music to the person. The question arises, What is music for? The pragmatist may say, "Music may be beautiful, but if it hasn't any use, what good is it?" Music produces no food, no clothing, no shelter, none of the necessities of life. But music does induce an experience, and experience is one of life's most precious realities!

The values derived from such creative experience may be suggested as: (1) An emotional sense of well-being—physically, emotionally, spiritually. (2) The stimulation of memory and imagination—associative recall that relates one not only to a personal past but to a racial past, with associations that stimulate the exercise of creative imagination. (3) The expression of emotion—the provision of a satisfying channel through which feeling may flow constructively. (4) The enrichment of intelligence—the opening up of new fields of thought and reason, in an aesthetic world that gives evaluation to all other values. (5) The directing and strengthening of volition—the clarifying and energizing of judgment, decision, will. (6) The recognition and utilization of suggestion—the implanting in the unconscious of ideas and ideals; the purging of the soul of ugly and forbidden desires; the release of latent aspirations and capacities, all the more effectively because without tension and struggle; in Christian language, the willingness to "Let go and let God," as the Holy Spirit is given opportunity to do his work.[4]

Music in the Service of Christian Education

Music is no longer incidental in the curriculum of religious education. Once thought of as subject matter in books or periodicals or quarterlies, the curriculum in a sounder educational theory is conceived as consisting of all the elements in the total situation to which the learner responds. Never before in the history of education has music played so large a part as in the present era. Today's child is exposed to more music than any other child since time began. He is often awakened by the music of the radio and continues to listen until time to go to school. At school almost daily he hears recorded music, and he may belong to orchestra or band. Returning home, he is exposed to more music by way of radio and television, and if he attends a motion picture, the story on the screen will be told to the accompaniment of music. Instruction in music is a part of the student's daily routine.

The consequences of this exposure to music—good, bad, indifferent—are not easy to assess. Unquestionably, there is unprecedented broadening of the scope of music experience, with tremendous possibilities of good and of evil. The situation is somewhat analogous to that of the child's exposure to reading. The responsibility of Christian education is much the same in each case—that of teaching discrimination, selection, appreciation of the worthy and rejection of the unworthy, utilization for Christian ends. Essential aims in an effective program of Christian education through music may thus be listed:

Acquaintance with the best in music can be cultivated. Music appreciation is not enough. There is need of exposure to many types of music. Value judgments involve comparisons. How is one who has heard nothing but hillbilly music to know that Bach chorales are superior? How is one who knows little but Bach to realize that hillbilly music can be quite enjoyable? A congregation brought up on light though tuneful gospel songs and choruses may not know what it is missing through failure to become acquainted with the great classical hymns of faith. By the same token, a congregation accustomed to classical hymns and anthems only may fail to recognize the heart-warming evangelistic power of simple gospel songs.

When we speak of "the best" in music, we may well ask, Best for what? In the selection of church music, art for art's sake is avoided; art is for Christ's sake and for the sake of persons. While correct standards of composition and rendition are always to be upheld, acquaintance with a wide variety of music is to be sought and utilized for educative purposes. Thus, discrimination is taught rather than a rigid scale of values which would reduce church music to an arbitrarily limited category.

Attitudes and skills can be developed through music. Religious educators make much of attitudes. Religious living is more a matter of direction than of keeping moral rules and regulations. Music possesses potent influence as a determiner of attitudes. Teachers in the field of religion particularly know how difficult it is to secure satisfying results if students are apathetic or inattentive, prejudiced or antagonistic, skeptical or cynical. A favorable frame of mind is important for the teaching of any subject but is prerequisite to fruitful teaching and learning in the field of religion. Appropriate music plays an indispensable part in creating and maintaining such an atmosphere. At the same time, inappropriate and poorly performed music may have the opposite effect. For the ultimate purpose of religious education, the kind and quality of music played and of songs sung are almost, if not quite, as important as the biblical materials selected.

Skills are closely associated with attitudes. As a rule, we do better that which we like to do. The learning of religious songs calls for much repetition. Mere repetition soon grows monotonous and tiresome, but repetition of good music enhances enjoyment. Repetition is education only if what is repeated proves satisfying. Few skills are more satisfying than those developed through participation in music. Musical skills thus developed have demonstrable carry-over value, facilitating development of skills in self-expression, the use of the Bible, participation in class and department activities, sharing in the corporate worship services of the church. These concomitant values, as well as those directly achieved, put music at the center of the curriculum of religious education.

Knowledge and choices can be secured through music. "Do not be foolish," Paul admonishes, "but understand what the will of the Lord is." In contrast with debauchery, resulting from being "drunk with wine," Paul states the ideal of Christian living as that of being "filled with the Spirit." How does such a life of the Spirit express itself? "Addressing one another in psalms and hymns and spiritual songs, singing and making melody to the Lord with all your heart, always and for everything giving thanks in the name of our Lord Jesus Christ to God the Father" (Eph. 5:19–20). Religious knowledge is both acquired and expressed through music. The Psalms and other musical portions of the Bible are as much inspired truth as its prose. The best of our English hymns and songs are translations of scriptural truths into musical form. Take away the knowledge acquired from the songs we sing, and many of us would be religious illiterates. Much of our Christian faith is built up on the message that comes through music.

Knowledge is incomplete until it has issued in decision and action. Christian teachers seek a verdict. Psychological damage may occur if decision and commitment are not put into action. Music provides a powerful stimulus to choices, leading to overt expression. The determining factor leading to decision for Christ and request for church membership is often the appeal expressed in a song.

Music takes its place alongside teaching and preaching in securing destiny-determining choices.

Conduct and character are shaped by music. Christian education is essentially character education. To *believe* in Jesus Christ requires more than intellectual assent. It is to *live by* his example and teachings. Speaking of the new life in Christ, Paul concludes, "Therefore, if any one is in Christ, he is a new creation; the old has passed away, behold, the new has come" (2 Cor. 5:17). What does this imply for Christian education? Paul replies, "Let the word of Christ dwell in you richly, as you teach and admonish one another in all wisdom, and as you sing psalms and hymns and spiritual songs with thankfulness in your hearts to God." Note the connection between the verbal expression of the new life and its expression in conduct: "And whatever you do, in word or deed, do everything in the name of the Lord Jesus, giving thanks to God the Father through him" (Col. 3:16–17). What is said in song is a challenge to practice in life.

The supreme product of Christianity is regenerate personality. Character represents the impact of personality on others. Effective personality manifesting itself in potent character demands a center of integration. For the Christian this integrating center is Christ and his cross. Few truths have been embodied in Christian hymnody more than this. We cannot think of the truly great hymns of the Christian faith without being reminded of "O Sacred Head, Now Wounded," "When I Survey the Wondrous Cross," "Beneath the Cross of Jesus," "In the Cross of Christ I Glory." From the sincere singing of such hymns as these comes fulfilment of Paul's prayer, "that according to the riches of his glory he may grant you to be strengthened with might through his Spirit in the inner man, and that Christ may dwell in your hearts through faith; that you, being rooted and grounded in love, may have power to comprehend with all the saints what is the breadth and length and height and depth, and to know the love of Christ which surpasses knowledge, that you may be filled with all the fullness of God" (Eph. 3:16–19).

Music for All Through Graded Choirs

The choir as an institution was known in the time of David. David's temple choir consisted of 288 trained musicians, described as "cunning" in their profession; about them were gathered pupils and assistants to the number of four thousand (1 Chron. 23:5; 25:7). An example of antiphonal singing is Psalm 24, in which one choir is answered by another. In Roman Catholic worship, as we have seen, the function of singing was almost wholly monopolized by the choir. In Protestant Christianity, especially in America, the choir developed two main functions—the leadership of the congregation in singing and the provision of choral music. As a rule, the choir was assumed to be made up of adults, although in some churches there was a children's choir.

The system of graded choirs is a relatively late development. Instruction and worship adapted to the needs and capacities of the several age groups inevitably called attention to the wisdom of like gradation in music education and performance. Thus, at length churches developed a graded choirs program, based on the premise that education in music is the right of every church member and that this education must conform to the recognized age levels in other areas of education. The successful operation of the graded choirs plan calls for certain necessary procedures.

The choirs need to be graded and named. The fully graded system of choirs follows closely the departmental age divisions of the church school. There are obvious advantages of such gradation: it simplifies organization; it brings together those who are already in homogeneous groups; it relates music education to Bible school education; it gives easier access both to leadership and to membership. Names of the choirs vary, but certain designations have wide vogue. Children five years of age and under are often known as the "Cherub Choir"; children of Primary age (6–8), "Celestial Choir"; children of Junior age (9–12), "Carol Choir"; Intermediates and seniors (13–18), "Concord Choir"; Young People (19–24), "Chapel Choir"; Adults, "Church Choir." Where constituency and facilities do not afford so many divisions, combinations will, of course, be made.

The choirs need supervision. Unceasing effort is necessary if the graded choirs program is to be maintained at a satisfactory level. Of first importance is the service of a trained, consecrated, enthusiastic, tactful minister or director of music. Not only must his musicianship be unquestioned, but his administrative ability must be of high quality. He must know how to enlist the sympathy and co-operation of pastor and staff, of officers of the church and its several organizations, and of the church membership as a whole. The minister or director of music is far more than a choir leader; he is the responsible head of one of the most important organizations of the church. He should therefore have a well-equipped office, secretarial help, an adequate budget, a studio with sufficient practice rooms and rooms for individual and group instruction. He should be given opportunity to present attractively the church's program of music to the membership and to the community. He should be the consultant of all those in the church who are responsible for services which call for music.

In plans for recruitment and training for leadership, the needs of the music department should be considered. The music minister and the officers of his department should be elected by the church according to the policy followed in securing leaders for other church organizations. The music department should be represented in the making of the budget, with assurance of reasonable financial support. An item in this budget should be a sizable amount for publicity, social events, and special occasions, all in the interest of good public relations.

The choirs need organization. Associated with the minister or director of music will be carefully chosen officers and committeemen, such as president—executive committee chairman; first vice-president—membership chairman; second vice-president—social chairman; third vice-president—program chairman and historian; recording secretary; treasurer; librarian; and custodian of robes, music, instruments. Associated with each of these officers will be appropriate committees selected from the several choirs. Each choir will be organized with officers corresponding to those named, except that the choirs made up of the younger children will have "choir mothers" selected from capable and willing mothers of the children enrolled. If this organization seems too elaborate, it can be simplified to meet the requirements of the local situation. However, authorities insist that the plan will not operate successfully without adequate organization and supervision.

The choirs present problems of scheduling and rehearsing. Ideally, the several choirs will include practically the total church constituency. Actually, of course, there will be limitations due to individual and family circumstances. The purpose of the plan is not primarily to develop performing choirs with superior musical ability but to extend the privileges of music education to all. Obviously, only a few will be included if musical training is confined to those with unusual talent who lead the music on stated occasions of worship.

If education in music is to be extended more widely, a time schedule must be adopted that will be suited to the needs of many. It becomes burdensome for meetings at the church to be multiplied —hence, the advisability of concentration of these meetings as much as possible. Many churches have adopted the "family night" or "church activities night" plan, according to which on Wednesday evening the several younger choirs meet for rehearsal an hour prior to the church family meal; following the fellowship meal, while Sunday school officers and teachers are meeting, the young people's choirs may rehearse. At the close of prayer meeting, rehearsal may be held for the Adult choir. A variation of this plan is to have the choirs come on Sunday evening for an hour of rehearsal preceding the training service, after which they assemble for combined leadership of the evening service. In some instances, there is a rotation of weekday afternoon meetings of the groups who are in school, each choir in turn coming to the church for practice after school dismissal. Care should be taken that no rehearsal is scheduled at a time when any regular service of the church is in session.

"Use us or lose us" applies aptly to the graded choirs. The effects of music training should be felt immediately in the assembly programs of the several church organizations. Instead of desultory and haphazard singing, the music of the assembly programs should be prepared with care and executed with effectiveness. The midweek prayer service may be transformed by the utilization in turn of the several choirs, whose rehearsed singing will add much to attractiveness and attendance. The stated worship services on Sunday afford the best single opportunity for utilization of the choirs, both separately and massed. An otherwise sparsely attended evening service, or no service at all, may be made into a featured occasion with increasing numbers present because of the quality of music furnished by the graded choirs. To the choirs may be added on occasion a well-trained orchestra, which thus utilizes the talents of instrumental musicians. Never is any of this to be thought of as a substitution for preaching but as supplementing the gospel message and giving it added power.

The objectives of music in the church are the same as those of preaching, teaching, worship, evangelism, stewardship, service. Music is not an "extra" but is an instrumentality of the Spirit of God in the service of the church for all the purposes of Jesus Christ. Through music thus conceived and practiced a church under all circumstances may maintain the jubilant and triumphant mood with which the book of Psalms closes:

> Praise the Lord!
> Praise God in his sanctuary;
> > praise him in his mighty firmament!
> Praise him for his mighty deeds;
> > praise him according to his exceeding greatness!
>
> Praise him with trumpet sound;
> > praise him with lute and harp!
> Praise him with timbrel and dance;
> > praise him with strings and pipe!
> Praise him with sounding cymbals;
> > praise him with loud clashing cymbals!
> Let everything that breathes praise the Lord!
> Praise the Lord!

Chapter X

Stewardship Translates Faith into Service

A CHURCH ADOPTED a bylaw forbidding its minister to make an appeal for money from the pulpit. When the necessity arose for such an appeal, it was to be made by the chairman of the finance committee or someone appointed by the deacons.

The regulation dated back to an embarrassment experienced by the church in its early history. The first minister was tireless in his efforts to establish and develop the church. He assumed responsibility for every aspect of its administration, including finances. His idea of raising money was to take frequent special collections. Almost every Sunday he presented a need and asked for an offering. Discriminating people of the church appreciated his zeal but doubted his wisdom. In the interim, between his resignation and the calling of another minister, the church adopted the bylaw referred to.

Whether or not there is such an actual rule of the church, evangelicals generally feel that the minister should not be too prominent in promoting fund raising. This tradition arose in part as revolt against the commercialization of religion by the Roman Catholic hierarchy. The freeness of salvation is a cardinal New Testament doctrine, and anything implying that salvation or security is purchasable touches a sensitive evangelical nerve.

Another objection to ministerial fund raising comes from an interpretation of the New Testament as exalting poverty and decrying wealth. Jesus, although Lord of creation, was completely free from dependence on money. "Foxes have holes, and birds of the air

139

have nests," he declared; "but the Son of man has nowhere to lay his head" (Matt. 8:20). John records that, following a day of intense activity, the disciples "went each to his own house," but that "Jesus went to the Mount of Olives" (John 7:53 to 8:1). Doubtless it was not intentional neglect, but no one remembered to invite Jesus to spend the night with him. Careless of his own comfort, the Lord of life slept on the hillside with the ground for his bed and the sky for his covering.

Paul stands amazed in the presence of this self-forgetfulness: "For you know the grace of our Lord Jesus Christ, that though he was rich, yet for your sake he became poor, so that by his poverty you might become rich" (2 Cor. 8:9). Paul asserted his right to live of the gospel, yet he took pride in the fact that he worked with his hands for his living. To the Thessalonians he wrote: "For you remember our labor and toil, brethren; we worked night and day, that we might not burden any of you, while we preached to you the gospel of God" (1 Thess. 2:9). Jesus said, "Do not lay up for yourselves treasures on earth . . . For where your treasure is, there will your heart be also" (Matt. 6:19-21). Paul applies this teaching to the minister in the prohibition that he be "no lover of money" (1 Tim. 3:3).

Does all this sum up to the conclusion that ministers should be freed from responsibility for church financing? Perhaps so, if church financing is viewed as money raising, especially for his sake. But there is a larger context of which church financing is only a part. This immensely greater matter is the doctrine of Christian steward-ship. The minister has inescapable responsibility for its interpreta-tion and implementation.

Stewardship Begins with the Minister

Yielding to the call to the Christian ministry is frequently referred to as "surrendering." To surrender is to yield one's person and possessions to the power of another. This act of surrender to Christ is an essential element in conversion and is required of every Christian. Surrender to the call of Christ to be his minister in-volves not only this initial yielding but a still further step in com-mitting oneself unreservedly to Christian service as a vocation. The minister thus becomes the church's chief steward.

A stewardship church is well assured if there is full dedication of minister or ministers to the practice of the stewardship of life. Paul did not hesitate to write, "Brethren, join in imitating me, and mark those who so live as you have an example in us" (Phil. 3:17). It is sobering for any man to realize that his example will be followed by others, and especially is this serious in such a significant matter as Christian stewardship.

Stewardship, the continuation of the Christian life, is like conversion, the beginning of the Christian life—both are intensely personal. When Paul was converted, he asked, "What shall I do, Lord?" From that hour forward Paul considered his life as not his own but an entrustment from God to be lived in partnership with Jesus Christ. Confidently he could say: "Indeed I count everything as loss because of the surpassing worth of knowing Christ Jesus my Lord. For his sake I have suffered the loss of all things, and count them as refuse, in order that I may gain Christ" (Phil. 3:8).

The essence of the minister's stewardship is this absorbing sense of partnership with Christ. He repeats with Paul, "For to me to live is Christ, and to die is gain" (Phil. 1:21). Like the partner in a firm the success of which means everything, the minister asks daily, How can I invest my time and energy so as to bring profit to the partnership? This means more than the continual search for texts and sermon materials that will fulfil his responsibility as preacher. It means alertness to take advantage of every occasion "to buy up the opportunities," despite all difficulties. This sense of partnership should pervade the minister's total life—at home, in his study, in his business affairs, on the street, in his social and civic relationships, in his personal and public evangelism, in his teaching and preaching, in his pastoral ministries, in his denominational and interdenominational services.

The minister's awareness of his stewardship may be kept alive in many ways. He should keep abreast of the rich and extensive literature of the subject. He should keep in close contact with denominational headquarters in order to know what plans are being promoted to implement the doctrine of stewardship. He should be thoroughly acquainted with opportunities for investment in Christian enterprises—missions, Christian education, benevolences, evangelism, and similar causes. Just as an investment counselor studies the securities market, so should the minister study the fields of need and opportunity which will yield the best dividends for Christian investment.

The minister's stewardship extends especially to his use of time. The minister is peculiarly tempted to misuse or waste time. Time is not lost that is spent in needful recreation, but the minister should be careful not to spend too much time on the golf course or at the ball park or on fishing trips or reading or watching television for entertainment. Since the minister punches no time clock and is responsible to no one for the way in which he spends his working hours, he may lack system in his activities and develop the habit of dawdling. All the more because he is his own boss the minister should be a faithful steward in the use of time.

The minister must watch his step in financial affairs. His stewardship of influence is at stake when he abuses his credit and becomes known as "slow pay." Debt is sometimes necessary, but it should be kept within the strict limits of ability to meet obligations promptly. In his giving through the church the minister should unostentatiously set a good example. Occasionally a minister indulges in the false reasoning that since he is giving all his time to the church he is exempted from the obligation of tithing. It would be difficult, if not impossible, for a minister to lead his people to do what he neglects to do himself. The fact that he earns his living in church work in no wise exempts him from the duty of regular and systematic giving with the tithe as a minimum. His giving to the church will not relieve him from sharing in support of the community chest, Red Cross, health campaigns, and the like. If such giving places too heavy drain on the minister's financial resources, it is evident that the church is at fault in its stewardship of responsibility for the minister. His compensation should be fixed with a view to enabling him to set a good example of generosity in his gifts both to the causes of the church and the community.

The minister's stewardship compels him to give first consideration to the service of the church which employs him. The minister who spends too much time in other activities, even though good in themselves, may sin against himself and his church. His church may suffer because he gains a reputation as a revivalist, a lecturer, or a writer, if such demands made on his time cause him to neglect his duties to his supporting congregation and field.

The minister's crowning stewardship responsibility is that of growing a stewardship church. To this end he must proclaim a vital stewardship message from the pulpit. He must teach stewardship and gather about himself those who will aid him in this teaching. He must interpret stewardship in private conversation with individuals. He must pray unceasingly that the spirit of stewardship may possess the church, beginning with himself and staff and church-elected leaders. "In all the claims upon the pastor's loyalty to his Christian calling," Paul H. Conrad writes, "the true criterion of his example is the unqualified acceptance of responsibility for fulfilling God's requirements. His gracious acceptance of all the duties, sacrifices, and labors which are inexorable for a good minister furnishes the best recommendation of such virtues to others." [1]

Stewardship Is the Gospel for the Saved

Jesus Christ came with good news—the gospel. This good news was first of all for the lost. Men had always sought salvation but had been told the bad news that only a few could be saved. Salvation, they were taught, was an inheritance of the chosen or an achievement of the near perfect. The Jews claimed salvation on the ground that they were Abraham's seed and confirmed their claim by the righteousness of the law. The Gentiles depended on the occult powers of their priests and priestesses, who through ceremony and sacrifice appeased their deities and thus gained deserved favors. Jesus swept away all these misconceptions and revealed God as Father, with infinite love for all his human creation and compassionate forgiveness for all who would repent and believe. His good news for the lost is summed up in John 3:16.

Correlative with the good news for the lost is Jesus' good news for the saved. The salvation promised by Jews and Gentiles was fundamentally inadequate, at no point more so than in its failure to provide security for the "saved." Salvation by righteousness of the law demanded a near sinlessness that could not be maintained; hence, one might be saved today and lost tomorrow. The salvation promised by the pagan cults depended on the priestly mediation and was subject to the whims of the gods. Devotees might attain high merit but were always in danger of lapsing. Jesus brought the good news of irreversible salvation and unforfeitable security. In the shadow of the cross he said concerning his disciples, "My sheep hear my voice, and I know them, and they follow me; and I give them eternal life, and they shall never perish, and no one shall snatch them out of my hand" (John 10:27–28).

The Christian's life of stewardship does not earn or maintain salvation—it is evidence of it. How may one know that he is saved? Paul replies, "Therefore, if any one is in Christ, he is a new creation; the old has passed away, behold, the new has come" (2 Cor. 5:17). This salvation is by grace, not of oneself; it is the gift of God, not of works. Yet it is not apart from a life of devoted service: "For we are his workmanship, created in Christ Jesus for good works" (Eph. 2:10). The purpose of God in salvation is not fulfilled in the initial experience of conversion: "For we are fellow workmen for God; you are God's field, God's building" (1 Cor. 3:9).

Evangelism is always this twofold proclamation of good news: Christ will both save and keep those who trust him. The security of the believer brings release from anxiety concerning salvation. This has been settled once for all. Energy which would otherwise be wasted in anxious fear is available for unanxious service. Failure to emphasize this gospel for the saved is faulty evangelism and has resulted in vast spiritual wastage. The evangelist who says, "Come to Christ!" but who does not say, "Be Christ's partner!" is preaching a one-sided gospel. A saved soul minus a useful life equals a poor church member. Analysis of a typical church membership roll will indicate that fully five out of ten members fall into this category. The loss to the church and to its kingdom causes is immense, but the loss to these unfruitful church members themselves is incalculable. Perhaps the greatest reformation that could come to today's churches would be the salvaging of this tragic waste. Stewardship should therefore be presented not as a burdensome obligation but as glorious good news.

Every life must have its control. The power of control may be self-interest, family, business, politics, humanitarianism. All of these controls limit personal freedom and satisfactions—they will not outlast time. John M. Versteeg says that this is the "foolishness" of which Paul writes that is in reality "the wisdom of God." Paul includes himself when he writes, "For the love of Christ controls us" (2 Cor. 5:14). "The explanation seemed so natural to him," Versteeg comments,

that he never thought to put an exclamation mark back of that. But for people who have all along missed his point, the exclamation mark may well be added. Christ controls me! he confessed; *Christ* controls me! He likes to recur to the theme: "I am what I am through Christ; if any man be in Christ he is new." What is new about him? This! Christ controls him! It is no longer he, but Christ! Christ lives in him and his! Christ is everywhere and in everything expressed! You look for me? asks Paul. But I am no longer here. This is Christ! This is Christ talking! "It is God which worketh in you." [2]

This glad acceptance of Christ's control of all of one's life is the meaning of Christian stewardship and the reward.

The instinct of acquisition and possession is deeply imbedded in original human nature. According to the Genesis account, when God made man in his own image, he decreed that man should "have dominion over the fish of the sea, and over the birds of the air, and over the cattle, and over all the earth, and over every creeping thing that creeps upon the earth" (Gen. 1:26). This power to possess is therefore one of the marks of the image of God in man. Its proper exercise accounts for much of human progress. Its abuse likewise accounts for much of the disaster that has befallen the human race.

"Property" is an extension of the word "proper," naturally belonging to a person or thing. "Property," therefore, is the right of possessing, enjoying, and disposing of anything. This right may be violated covetously or forcibly. "Thou shalt not covet" and "thou shalt not steal" are Commandments in protection of property rights. Almost all the wars of history have originated in the violation of these two Commandments. Much of the strife among families and neighbors and much of the criminality that crowds the dockets of the courts have stemmed from covetousness and theft or fraud. Back of these national and group and individual disasters lie false interpretations of the doctrine of property.

The pagan doctrine of property is the oldest and still the most prevalent. "Let him get who can and keep who may" is the forthright statement of this doctrine. Why does one nation lift up sword against another nation? In the main, to gain property. The justification is that "might makes right." From the dawn of history until now war has been the biggest single business of the nations. Often disguised, the real motive back of most of these wars was economic. The invading army sought to acquire the property that belonged to another people; the army of defense fought to preserve its property rights. In more recent years the wars over property have been to preserve balance of power in trade or to gain economic advantage, but they have stemmed from the pagan principle that property belongs to him who can get it from another.

The pagan theory of property has never worked successfully. Forcible seizure inevitably results in forcible resistance, thus creating wasteful strife climaxed by the disaster of war. The claim of royalty to ownership of a nation's property became less and less tenable with the rising demands of the people to land ownership. The Magna Charta (the Great Charter of 1215) represents a turning point in Western history when King John of England agreed to certain limitations of the rights of the crown and granted to the people certain basic liberties and protections. On this foundation began to be built the system of free enterprise.

The next three centuries witnessed the development of free city-states, notable among these being Venice, Florence, Genoa, the Germanic cities of the Hanseatic League. All of this brought a revolutionary concept of property, namely, that it could be privately owned and bartered. A new social class emerged—the tradesmen. The invention of steam-driven machinery brought industrial revolution. The old feudal system gave way to an industrial order, with labor bought and sold in the market in the same fashion as goods. This system of free enterprise came to be known as capitalism and from the seventeenth century onward became the dominant economic system of Western civilization. Capitalism represents a vast improvement over paganism in that it replaces acquisition by force with acquisition by voluntary exchange, not only making possible private ownership, but surrounding it with laws intended to safeguard such ownership. Capitalism says, "Let him get who can and keep who may within the limits of the law."

The capitalistic system in its earlier stages produced some bitter fruits. Free enterprise abused its freedom and gave to industrialists frightful power over labor. One reads with horror accounts of revolting working conditions during the latter part of the eighteenth century. Among the most fearful of these abuses was child labor. It is quite evident that capitalism thus practiced was just another form of the pagan doctrine of property. The right of private ownership and unrestricted competition enriched the capitalist but impoverished and enslaved the laborer.

Out of the inequities of perverted capitalism arose social theories of property. Wealth, economic philosophers began to say, is produced primarily by labor. The workers, the producers of wealth, have the right to a fair share in their product. Robert Owen, with his "Villages of Cooperation," laid foundations for the modern co-operatives. Saint-Simon, with his doctrine of the duties and rights of laborers, gave embryonic shape to the modern labor union. Charles Fourier, with his proposal to divide workers into phalanxes according to their aptitudes and abilities, furnished the modern pattern of specialization and trades jurisdictions. Thomas More with his *Utopia* ("Nowhere"), descriptive of a place where everything is perfect, started men dreaming that they might make a near heaven of this world.

These dreams took shape in the nineteenth century as a political–economic movement called socialism. To define socialism is very difficult. In general, it connotes an ideal economic system in which industry is carried on under social direction and for the benefit of society as a whole. Its doctrine of property allows private ownership but would put under government control all property in which men have common rights and the instruments of production of public wealth. Instead of the world's work being carried on under the domination of private ownership, the process would be reversed under socialism. The welfare state is the outcome of socialism in operation.

In socialism, private and public ownership of property are compatible. Yet the effort to maintain their partnership is exceedingly difficult. The question began to be asked, Why cannot all property be publicly owned? Is not inequality inherent in private ownership? Two men—Karl Marx and Friedrich Engels—collaborated in the development of what they called "dialectical materialism"—dialectical because aggressively controversial, materialistic because it assumed that all real value is in matter or substance. They sought to give economic interpretation to all of life and history.

The business of mankind, they said, is to clothe and feed and house themselves. The struggle for possession of material goods brings inevitable conflict, and this conflict results in human misery. Capitalism, they held, contains the seed of its own destruction. Socialism is a compromise and offers no satisfactory solution. What is needed, they argued, is a revolution which will replace both capitalism and socialism with collectivism. The collectivist system is communism.

All wealth and the means of producing wealth are to be owned by the people in common. Labor is the unit of value, since labor is the indispensable element in the production of goods. "From every man according to his ability; to every man according to his need" stated the Communist formula. A classless society was envisioned, with none having advantage over another. The working class, Communist theories predicted, would rise and overthrow their privileged over-lords, destroy capitalism, and institute an economic order according to which none would have too much and none too little.

Communism found its great opportunity in the fertile soil of Russia following the revolution against the czarist regime and its supporting Orthodox Catholic Church. Repudiating religion as "the opiate of the people," the revolutionaries seized control, established a Communist form of government, and with fanatical zeal have pressed their cause until "the Party," under an intolerant dictator-ship, dominates the lives of a majority of the people of the world. The darkest shadow over the human race is that cast by this false doctrine of property.

Stewardship Furnishes a Christian Doctrine of Property

None of the doctrines of property described can claim to be Chris-tian. Christians can more readily operate under capitalism at its best than any other of the economic systems, but they can live and bear their witness no matter how unfavorable may be the economic order. The early Christians carried out Christ's Commission in a predominantly pagan world; Christians today are winning for Christ in spite of atheistic materialism. Obviously, however, Chris-tianity would have a better opportunity to flourish in a society whose economic principles and practices were in accord with New Testament ethics.

Is there a Christian doctrine of property? Both Old and New testaments reply affirmatively. Few matters are given more atten-tion in the Scriptures than man's relation to property. The moral law emphasizes the sanctity of property rights and the sin of viola-tion of these rights. Jesus was clear and explicit in his teaching con-cerning the necessity of acquiring and using property in accordance with the will of God. Over and over Jesus warned against enslave-ment to property and taught that account must be given for its wise use. Throughout its pages the Bible teaches that all persons and things belong to God, the owner, and all that men are and possess is an entrustment to be used under the will of the owner for the purposes of Jesus Christ. The Christian doctrine of property rests on four pillars: (1) God is owner; (2) man is trustee; (3) tithes and offerings should be given in acknowledgment of God's ownership and man's stewardship; (4) what remains should be used for God's glory and man's good.

An economic order built on this foundation would solve many of the world's most difficult problems. It would save the individual from covetousness and rightly relate him to God and his fellow man. It would bring order out of the chaos of labor–management conflicts. It would serve as a corrective of free enterprise and make untenable the fallacies of socialism and communism. It would guarantee a just and enduring peace by removing the basic cause of war. It would abolish predatory wealth and debasing poverty, yet preserve individual initiative and reward superior ability and effort. It would hold out no chimerical promise of utopia, but would give a sound basis for human progress in all fields of legitimate endeavor. The practice of the doctrine of Christian stewardship would bring calm to the world's storm that otherwise may break into indescribable disaster. A church is ministering to human need, individual and universal, when it thus interprets and applies the Christian doctrine of property in terms of Christian stewardship.

Stewardship Is Implemented Through Sound Church Financing

It has been well said that stewardship is not a way of financing a church; financing a church is a way of implementing stewardship. In the several doctrines of property described, the conflict has gathered about ownership. The question concerning which men have fought through the ages is, To whom does property belong and by what right? The Bible settles the dispute by declaring simply, "The earth is the Lord's and the fulness thereof, the world and those who dwell therein" (Psalm 24:1). The Christian steward gladly recognizes that he owns nothing, not even himself—he has been "bought with a price." Believing this as a fundamental of his Christian faith, the Christian may yet prove to be a poor steward in practice because his church does not furnish a satisfactory plan. The making and operation of such a plan is the duty of every church and the leadership responsibility of every minister.

The first step in such a plan of stewardship financing is the commitment of the church to its inclusiveness. No member of the church is any more or less a steward than any other member. There is no more reason for a member to be exempted from his stewardship obligation than from his obligation to be baptized. Stewardship as the gospel for the saved should be preached and taught as clearly and earnestly as the gospel of faith salvation for the lost. That every member will participate in the support of the church and its causes should be a well-established assumption.

A church then becomes a steward of the funds entrusted to it. Its budget should likewise be inclusive, adequately caring for its own needs, for the sharing of the gospel with the unsaved near and far, for the care of the needy at home and abroad, for the education of its youth around the world, for the maintaining of justice and righteousness among all peoples. "At least as much for others as for ourselves" should be its principle of division. Through its denominational agencies it may channel the funds entrusted to it. These agencies in their turn become stewards of the money entrusted to them. The contributor should have the deep satisfaction of knowing that his contribution will be equitably divided so that no proper Christian cause will be neglected.

The inclusive and equitable budget thus devised should be based on the giving possibilities of the church. This calls for regular and faithful analysis of the membership roll to discover contributors and noncontributors and to estimate the total if every available member were reached. All too often budgets have been built on a minimum basis—the least amount members would give in order that necessary expenses be met. A worthy budget would reverse the procedure, seeking the maximum amount that members could give if they accepted their stewardship obligation.

What shall be a practical measure of this stewardship obligation? Again, the Bible gives the indisputable answer: "All the tithe of the land, whether of the seed of the land or the fruit of the trees, is the Lord's; it is holy to the Lord" (Lev. 27:30). If it is objected that tithing was required of the Jews under the law and that Christians are under grace, the reply may well be that to give less under grace than the Jews gave under law would be a disgrace! Tithing, commanded in the Old Testament and approved in the New Testament, is not a legal requirement but a reasonable equitable minimum, below which the Christian may go in an extremity of distress, above which he should go in prosperity. Tithing provides a divinely commended system for giving, the practice of which blesses the giver and the church. A church ministers satisfyingly to its members and to the needs of a lost world when it preaches and teaches tithing.

To implement the Christian ideal of every-member stewardship-tithing requires careful and prayerful planning. Six steps over a period of four weeks call successively for (1) planning—discovering giving possibilities, setting budget goals, adopting campaign schedules, devising attractive publicity, securing co-operation of church organizations; (2) preparing—stewardship preaching and teaching, information mailed to members, invitations to "loyalty dinner" mailed, training of leaders, continued publicity; (3) presenting—stewardship testimonies, budget adopted, budget with explanatory letter mailed to members, further training of leaders, special stewardship lessons taught in Sunday school, canvass teams completed, publicity continued; (4) promoting—continued stewardship teaching, pledge cards with explanatory letter mailed to members, "loyalty dinner," preparations completed for Loyalty Day; (5) pledging—pledge cards signed by all present at Sunday school or worship services; canvass of all those not pledging; continued follow-up until every member is accounted for.[3]

Will all this detailed planning and activity overemphasize money and tend to despiritualize the minister and the church? No, not if it is kept in the perspective of the Christian doctrine of stewardship and is made a means rather than an end. While obviously more money will be obtained by reason of such planning and promotion, even greater spiritual values will accrue because channels will be provided through which Christian devotion may flow and increase with the flowing. Set in the context of the recovery and practice of the doctrine of Christian stewardship, and as a solution to the vexed problem of property, such a "forward program" will yield dividends vastly greater than just an enlarged and more adequate budget.

Stewardship Makes Christians World-Minded

The money-centeredness of life today tends to make Christians worldly-minded. The Christian alternative is that they become world-minded. Church members in America are among the most privileged persons in the world. They need to search their hearts with such questions as these: Why do I have religious liberty when so many others are deprived of it? Why am I well housed, well fed, and well clothed while millions of my fellow men lack these necessities? Why do I enjoy luxuries while half the people of the world live below the level of subsistence? Why do my children possess privileges and opportunities that are denied the majority of other children of the world? Why do I have the light of Christ while a billion of my fellow men sit in darkness and the shadow of death?

Assuredly, the answer cannot be that certain of us are God's favorites. Nor can it be that by our industry and merit we have lifted ourselves to the enjoyment of these deserved blessings. The answer must be in the nature of the call of God to Abram, "I will make of you a great nation, and I will bless you, and make your name great, so that you will be a blessing" (Gen. 12:2). The history of Israel is the record of faithfulness to the divine mission instituted in Abram. Jesus stated this principle with finality: "Every one to whom much is given, of him will much be required; and of him to whom men commit much they will demand the more" (Luke 12:48). Our abundance increases our obligation, and failure to discharge it will bring certain failure to us as individuals and loss to us as a nation.

We believe our American way of religious liberty and free enterprise approaches the Christian ideal, but we must be aware that it is subject to abuse and may degenerate to failure and disaster. The corrective is the sharing of our good fortune with the less fortunate, from our doorsteps to the end of the earth.

Peter writes of Christians who are the recipients of undeserved favors as "stewards of God's varied grace" (1 Peter 4:10). God's crowning gift is the gift of salvation through Christ; hence, the highest form of stewardship is the sharing of the gospel. Partnership in the missionary enterprise is therefore the supreme expression of stewardship. Never since Christ commanded to go and teach all nations have opportunity and necessity so combined to give urgency to the missionary commission as today. We cannot buy the peace of the world with American dollars. Back of all our economic aid to depressed and threatened peoples must be the motive of Christian love. Missions represent Christian stewardship motivated by love. Such love "does not mean a sentimental dispensing of charity," writes John C. Bennett, nor does it mean a disregard for all considerations of self-development or a willingness to sacrifice the welfare of one's family. It does involve a willingness to scale down our living standard; to give to causes and institutions that depend on private support; to welcome the justice that is often embodied in public taxation; to support economic changes that may be costly to us if they are in the public interest; to share and share again wisely and generously.[4]

This description of Christian love is best represented in the missionary enterprise. In daring and successful prosecution of world missions we can confidently stand by Paul's proposal: "This is how one should regard us, as servants of Christ and stewards of the mysteries of God. Moreover it is required of stewards that they be found trustworthy" (1 Cor. 4:1–2).

Chapter XI

Counseling Provides Ministry to the Troubled

PREACHING IS THE ART of persuasive speaking. Counseling is the art of selective listening. How can the minister shift from one role to the other without danger of split personality? Is preaching the antithesis of counseling? Can the minister be at one and the same time an eloquent preacher and an effective counselor?

It is well for the minister to confront and resolve this problem, for he cannot escape the necessity of the dual role. He must preach, and he must counsel. The solution is found not in the neglect of one to the magnifying of the other, but rather in seeing preaching and counseling as two aspects of the same pastoral function. Preaching may be thought of as group counseling—helping a number of people to solve their problems collectively under the guidance of the minister as he explains and applies the Bible. Counseling may be thought of as preaching in reverse—the counselee, as an individual or as a group, presenting the problem to the minister and seeking with him to find the solution based on revelation and reason. In this view the minister does not have two separate tasks—preaching and counseling. He has a single responsibility—to help persons find the supply of their needs through guidance given in the Bible as it leads to Christ, the answer. The heart of the matter is that the minister must be person-minded, whether in the pulpit facing an audience or in the home or the study facing an individual.

After showing that much of the apparent conflict between "theology" and "pastoral theology" is without foundation, Seward Hiltner

154

defines pastoral theology as "an operation-focused branch of theology, which begins with theological questions and concludes with theological answers, in the interim examining all acts and operations of pastor and church to the degree that they involve the perspective of Christian shepherding." [1] The heart of pastoral care is thus seen to be contained in the concept of the minister as shepherd. Shepherding involves the care of the sheep, concerning whom Jesus said, "I am the good shepherd; I know my own and my own know me," and again, "My sheep hear my voice, and I know them, and they follow me" (John 10:14,27). Preaching is at its best when the pastor knows his people and they know him, when they hear his voice and follow him; and counseling is just another aspect of the work of the shepherd, as he identifies himself with those who, in their troubles, need and seek his guidance.

The importance of the ministry of counseling is emphasized by the modern human situation. Many people find it difficult to know the difference between right and wrong or, knowing the difference, to make the right decision. Tensions bring strained relations, and these lead to personal, family, and group disruptions. Much new light has been thrown on the old problem of body-mind relationship, bringing deeper understanding of illness as resulting from emotional upset and spiritual maladjustment. Doctors know that much of the sickness of their patients is due to what they haven't rather than to what they have. The minister has a source of supply of these deep-seated needs which makes him a member of the healing team. Psychiatry, with all its helpfulness, is often helpless in the face of spiritual needs that science cannot supply. "Talk is cheap" and never cheaper than in our age when the turn of a dial surfeits the listener. The longing arises for recognition of the individual as a person in a person-to-person relationship. A mass-minded society needs a person-minded ministry. Science is exploring the universe, in its microcosm and its macrocosm, but much of this leaves the individual bewildered and lonely, often doubtful of his significance and moral responsibility, without theological anchorage. Speakers from platform, radio, television, and picture film cry insistently, "Let me tell you . . ." Overburdened with all this talk, the lone individual wants to say, "Let me ask you . . ." The minister's personal touch gives him unique opportunity for a service that nobody else will perform.

In Roman Catholic polity and practice the parishioner went to the priest; the priest rarely visited the parishioner. Worship, baptism, confirmation, the Mass, ordination, the wedding, the funeral became services of the sanctuary. Confession was to a priest in prescribed place and manner. Clinic baptism and private Mass might be administered in exceptional circumstances, extreme unction was permitted privately, but the work of the priest or bishop was carried on chiefly within the confines of the church property.

The reformers broke with this Catholic tradition and began ministering to the people in their homes. Luther's catechetical instruction was a family affair. Calvin attacked compulsory auricular confession and organized in Geneva a plan of disciplinary care of the church members. The plan included visitation of the sick and of prisoners and the catechizing of children. Calvin wrote letters of advice and comfort and sought personally to minister to the bereaved. In Anglicanism and Presbyterianism, increasing stress was laid on the ministry of care and comfort. Baptist, Congregationalist, and Methodist ministers sought the people where they were and early established the tradition that a call be made by the minister in the home of every parishioner at least once a year.

With the multiplying of denominations in America a competitive spirit arose among many ministers, who often vied with one another as to who could make the most calls. The saying, "A home-going pastor makes a churchgoing people," was accepted uncritically. As churches grew in membership and the community in population, this demand for house-to-house visiting laid on ministers an intolerable burden. They, as well as thoughtful members, began to ask, Why all this visiting? Ministers began to say that they had offices and office hours; why not let the people come to them for counsel and service just as to the doctor or the lawyer? In the privacy of the church office, with a secretary close at hand and with a schedule of appointments, could not the pastor render better service than by a round of visits in homes where conditions are less favorable? Exceptions would, of course, have to be made for emergencies and in cases in which illness prevented the parishioner from visiting the church; but, in the main, said these ministers, would it not be better to dignify pastoral care and counseling by putting it on a professional level?

Granting that there are elements of soundness in this position, it yet breaks down at a number of points. First, there is the New Testament pattern. Then, there is the deeply entrenched tradition that the evangelical pastor should go into the homes of his people. Again, if he does not go to them, many in need will not come to him. Moreover, the pastor who preaches to the human condition of his parishioners must know them with a degree of intimacy that is impossible unless he knows something of their home life, their everyday surroundings, their family relationships, their neighborhood problems, their temptations and sins, their aspirations and ambitions. The home-going pastor may not of necessity make a churchgoing people, but visitation does make the minister life-centered in his preaching and pastoral care and helps the people to find in Christ their Saviour and Friend, whether they attend the church regularly or not.

The question of counseling the people who come to the minister at his office or of his going to them in their homes should not be stated as an alternative. The good physician does both. The physician of souls should do both. Paul found profit and satisfaction in this dual service, calling the Ephesian elders to witness that his was a full-rounded ministry among them, as he taught them "in public and from house to house" (Acts 20:20).

A Systematic Plan of Pastoral Care

Haphazard doorbell ringing is wasteful of the energy of the pastor and the time of those visited. A round of calling on those who live within a given area, just to be able to say that all have been visited, has little more to commend it. An effective plan is needed.

A classified file should be kept of those visited. On the pastor's desk, ready for instant reference, should be the "calling file," indexed somewhat as follows: (1) Emergency cases—those who need immediate attention because of accident or acute illness or bereavement or unusual distress. (2) Chronic cases—invalids, incurables, the aged, shut-ins, the troubled of long standing. (3) Prospective members—children looking toward reception into the church, unreached outsiders to be evangelized, unaffiliated and straying church members to be reclaimed, newcomers to be welcomed and invited. (4) The in-service group—comrades in the service of the church, deacons and their wives, general officers, officers and teachers of the Sunday school, leaders of the several church organizations, helpers in the worship services, chairmen of committees, and the like. (5) Prospective service group—persons with leadership potential who should be interested, instructed, enlisted. (6) Problem persons—the mentally defective, the maladjusted, the defeated, the eccentric, the perverted, the neurotic. (7) The unacquainted— church members and others who are strangers, whom the pastor can come to know through a personal visit.

A policy of calling according to need should be established. Daily, weekly, monthly the pastor will study this classified file, continually revising it. Whom to visit will be determined by urgency of need. Top priority will be claimed, of course, by emergency cases. When accident or acute illness or death or personal tragedy or moral disaster occurs, the pastor should go instantly as representative of Christ and the church to minister to the urgent need. Nothing that the minister is doing should take precedence over this call. He need not wait on notification or request for his services. He should go at once.

Chronic cases call for a schedule of visitation and should not be neglected because of their long standing. Clinging to the minister's hand and trying to prolong his all too short visit, a bedridden old lady pathetically cried, "You do not know what it means to be old and sick and forgotten!" These shut-ins, for whom the death angel is tardy in coming, test the reality of the shepherd heart of the minister. Yet he would do well not to build up an expectation of frequent visits that may eventually make intolerable demands on his time.

Rarely should a week pass in which the pastor has not presented the claims of Christ and the church to those "other sheep" which should be brought into the Good Shepherd's fold. The temptation is to excuse himself from this delicate and often difficult responsibility, but for his own soul's sake as well as for the sake of lost souls the pastor must put this kind of calling high on his list.

With conscientious regularity the pastor should call on his helpers in the work—deacons and general officers, Sunday school officers and teachers, leaders of the several organized activities, committee members. Studying their responsibilities and problems, he may place in their hands or call to their attention an appropriate book or pamphlet; he may inquire into their needs and discouragements; he may suggest ways of improvement; he may invite confidences as to personal problems; he can always express appreciation. Church workers, like wives, do not like to be taken for granted. A sincerely appreciative pastor, who unfailingly shows his gratitude for the services of his fellow servants in the church, will provide incentive that is more than money.

Newcomers to the community appreciate a friendly call by the minister. His motive need not be that of securing their attendance on the church in return for his visit. He may go just to say "Welcome!" and to make friendly inquiry as to how he and the church may serve them. Information casually gleaned may point the way to more direct approach in seeking to help them establish church relations. Always the person-minded minister will be alert to symptoms of abnormality and will make himself available for counseling on a deeper level, in the home or at his office.

Division of responsibility for care and visitation should be made. The enumeration of these to be visited and this bare outline of policy based on need bring to the pastor a baffling sense of inadequacy. No man can render alone all this personal service and at the same time meet the demands made on him for public service. The staff offers some relief but is not the full answer. Pastor and staff must enlist the aid of church members, especially those who constitute the leadership circle.

A workable plan of lay care and visitation may be suggested: (1) Use of key persons for community oversight: division of the church community into convenient districts, with at least one devoted church family in each district charged with specific responsibility to note cases of need and opportunity, to call if possible when the occasion arises, and always to report the situation to pastor or church office. This requires no elaborate organization but appointment and continual reappointment of key persons who are willing to render this simple service. (2) Use of Sunday school officers and teachers: closer than any other lay leaders to the church's total constituency, these men and women are the logical reliance of pastor and staff for systematic and purposeful visitation. An essential aspect of their training should be in this weekday ministry of care and counseling, sometimes more significant and valuable than their Sunday services. (3) Use of men's and women's organizations: the Brotherhood and the Woman's Missionary Society, or their equivalents, are usually made up of dependable and trustworthy men and women to whom the pastor may delegate certain forms of care and visitation demanding maturity, insight, patience, and skill. (4) Use of community resources: information of value may be obtained from the files of public utilities concerning newcomers and changes in residence. "Vital statistics" in the newspapers give information as to births, marriages, deaths. Co-operation may be established with community chest agencies and with physicians and hospitals for similar mutuality of concern and service. (5) Use of visitors' cards: at all regular services of the church and its agencies, cards should be available on which names of visitors may be obtained, together with addresses and checked items indicating type of need which might be met through visit of pastor or someone else representing the church.

The Pastor Must Be a Counselor

There is value in the simplest expression of interest when one person calls on another in the name of Jesus Christ and the church. The value is greatly enhanced, however, when the one calling does so with purpose, insight, and skill. To the art of visiting should be added the art of counseling. Demands for his services will come continually to the pastor who possesses both insight and willingness to serve.

"Pastor, we are planning to be married, and we want you to perform the ceremony. We not only want a pretty wedding; we want our marriage to succeed. Will you help us?"

"Pastor, our marriage is going on the rocks. Maybe we should get a divorce. Will you talk it over with us?"

"Pastor, I'm having in-law trouble. It threatens to wreck my home. What do you think I ought to do about it?"

"Pastor, my husband is drinking heavily. I have scolded and cried and threatened, but nothing seems to do any good. I can't go on this way. You've just got to help me!"

"Pastor, our boy is breaking our hearts. He's been drinking, and now we think he is taking dope. He steals everything he can get his hands on. We are desperate. Isn't there something you can do?"

"Pastor, our daughter has us worried. She is acting strangely, claims that she hears voices, and thinks she has committed the unpardonable sin. She seems to be unbalanced over religion. What ought we to do?"

And so it goes day after day: The pastor confronts one problem after another. This is inescapably true because the lives of many of his people are beset by difficulties and temptations which are beyond their powers to meet. We confidently proclaim that Christ is the answer, but Christ's answer to life's needs must often be sought and found through inquiry and sharing, through struggle and prayer, many times through repentance and tears. The only way of escape from dealing with such human problems is to be like the Scotchman's minister, whom he described as being "six days in the week eenveesible and on the seventh eencompreheensible."

The call is imperative for pastors who are skilled and effective counselors. The question is not whether the pastor will or will not be a counselor. The question is whether he will be skilled or unskilled, a master of the art or a bungler, a helper or a hinderer as he deals with people and their problems. If the minister complains that this type of service takes too much of his time, the answer is twofold: first, there is no other way in which he can spend his time to better advantage; second, he must train others to help him in this task just as he must in other phases of the work of the church.

As in any other difficult art, the burden is lightened and may become a joy with the achievement of a high order of ability. If the older minister shies away, saying, "This was not included in the 'body of divinity' when I was in the seminary," the obvious reply is that few seminaries omit this from their basic studies as they have become more life-centered. The simple fact is that no man can be a good pastor who is not a skilled counselor. The very call to the Christian ministry is a call to compassionate concern for people and their problems—a concern that must express itself in the intelligent effort to help them solve their problems.

The Art of Counseling Can Be Learned

A pastor, after having listened to a heart-rending story of family troubles, said in effect: "I am deeply sorry for you. I advise you to pray constantly, to read your Bible every day, and to attend the preaching and prayer services regularly. 'Rest in the Lord, and wait patiently for him: . . . Cease from anger, and forsake wrath: fret not thyself, in any wise to do evil.' Let us pray." Certainly this was good as far as it went, but did it go far enough? The minister might better have turned to these words of wisdom from the practical James:

Who is wise and understanding among you? By his good life let him show his works in the meekness of wisdom. But if you have bitter jealousy and selfish ambition in your hearts, do not boast and be false to the truth. . . . For where jealousy and selfish ambition exist, there will be disorder and every vile practice. But the wisdom from above is first pure, then peaceable, gentle, open to reason, full of mercy and good fruits, without uncertainty or insincerity. And the harvest of righteousness is sown in peace by those who make peace (James 3:13–18).

Even so, would the specific needs of the individual have been met, or would he still have turned away unsatisfied? God has given us a part in growing the fruits of righteousness and in meeting the conditions of peace. Here, as elsewhere, divine power and human power meet and work together in securing the ends of welfare and happiness. Prayer and Bible reading and churchgoing in themselves do not produce magical results.

Effectual remedies for our diseases may be in the hands of the physician and the druggist, but they are administered only after careful diagnosis following personal examination. So it is with our moral and spiritual troubles; divine resources must be made available by the physician of souls in the light of knowledge of individual needs. The doctor who gives "shotgun doses" for the cure of all ills alike is thought of as a quack. Is not the minister in danger of putting himself in the same category if his prescriptions are not skilfully adapted to the needs of persons whose troubles he has carefully diagnosed?

Counseling requires more than professional skills. It is an art and requires an artist. The first requisite of an artist is that he loves his art. The painter must delight in colors, the musician must be sensitive to sounds, the sculptor must thrill to symmetry. The minister who would be an artist-counselor must love people. His love for people—all sorts of people—must be deep, genuine, and pervasive. His secret is that of Will Rogers, who said, "I never saw a man I didn't like." Perhaps Mr. Rogers exaggerated a bit, and the honest pastor may not be able to go quite that far, but his interest in and concern for people for their own sakes must be unforced and unfeigned. This lesson of love for people, for the unlovely as well as the lovely, he must learn from him who washed his disciples' feet and then said: "You call me Teacher and Lord; and you are right, for so I am. . . . For I have given you an example, that you also should do as I have done to you" (John 13:13–15). No self-seeking pastor will ever make a good counselor. The ministry of the effective counselor will be unheralded, unnoticed, sometimes even unappreciated. His satisfaction will be that of every true artist—the creative results which appear.

Some ministers seem to have a greater aptitude for counseling than others. This is true in other aspects of the minister's work; some excel as preachers, some as administrators, some as teachers, some as evangelists. But just as each man may improve his gifts in any of these fields, so every man can develop his ability as counselor. The way of improvement toward mastery is continual practice based on sound theory following good example. Of course, nothing can take the place of experience. To learn to be a good counselor one must actually work with people, listen to their troubles, take their burdens on his heart, enter into their joys and sorrows, and pay the price of trying to help them out of trouble. There is no royal road. This comes very close to what Jesus meant when he said, "If any man would come after me, let him deny himself and take up his cross and follow me" (Matt. 16:24).

The Heart of the Counseling Process

It is not easy to define the work of the counselor. Certainly, no exact formula can be laid down, for each step is conditioned by what precedes or follows. And the ministry to each individual is different.

Wayne Oates, in *The Christian Pastor*, conceives of counseling as helping people in life crises to find the Christian solution to their problems under the sympathetic and intelligent guidance of a man of God who is accepted as their friend. Seward Hiltner says in *Pastoral Counseling* that pastoral counseling is the endeavor by the minister to help people through mutual discussion of the issues involved in a difficult life situation, leading to a better understanding of the choices involved, and toward the power of making a self-chosen decision which will be as closely bound up to religious reality as the people are capable of under the circumstances. Carroll Wise, in *Pastoral Counseling: Its Theory and Practice*, describes counseling as a form of communication between two people for a special purpose—one trying to communicate a problem to the other for the purpose of getting help; the other intelligently and sympathetically listening with a view to giving help. Otis Rice declares that in pastoral counseling,

the parishioner is permitted to present his problem, to marshal his own resources for solving that problem. He then tries for a solution. But he must always be welcome to return with his failures, his successes, and what insights he has gained from trying out a plan discovered and decided upon by the pastor and the parishioner in consultation. . . . The pastor simply allows himself to be used in the relationship so that resources may become apparent and usable, so that new horizons may appear for the parishioner.[2]

Russell Dicks, in *Pastoral Work and Personal Counseling*, says that pastoral counseling consists of passive listening, active listening, interpretation, reassurance. Paul E. Johnson considers counseling to be "a responsive relationship arising from expressed need to work through difficulties by means of emotional understanding and growing responsibilities."[3]

The counseling process may be thus synthesized: (1) personal, face-to-face relationship, (2) between a person needing help and one skilled in the art of providing help, (3) in which the person needing help is stimulated and guided to self-expression, self-revelation, and self-understanding, (4) in which the one seeking to provide help enters intelligently and sympathetically into the other's difficulty and furnishes a screen upon which it may be freely projected, (5) as a result of which the troubled friend discovers the real root of the difficulty, finds resources for dealing with it, and undertakes constructively a solution of his own choosing, (6) in all of which Christ and the gospel are given maximum opportunity to demonstrate their adequacy for every need in every area of life, (7) with conscious dependence upon the Holy Spirit for illumination and guidance and with quiet confidence in the fulfilment of Christ's prayer promises when the conditions are met.

Carroll Wise rightly insists that insight is the goal in counseling:

The capacity of the human mind to see into and understand itself and its motives, once it is placed in a secure and understanding relationship with another, is one of the gifts of the grace of God to mankind. It is difficult for many to have faith in this capacity. But such faith is essential to the counselor. It is the achievement of insight into the nature of life that in part gives counseling an inherent religious quality.[4]

The Practice of Counseling Will Enrich All Other Ministries

Counseling is not a pastoral specialty. It is a vital element of almost every pastoral function. A pastor does not do certain things and then on stated occasions, in his office and with office hours, perform the duty of counselor. He is always counseling, in one way or another, in nearly everything that he does. The less he advertises himself as a counselor, the better counselor he will be.

The counseling pastor will be a better administrator. The need for administration arises largely out of the problem of interpersonal relations. Even in business and industry the purpose of administration is not primarily production and profits but the welfare of persons and the maintenance of high morale as they live and work together. The good administrator foresees difficulties and seeks to prevent them. When tensions and conflicts arise, he looks for their causes. He utilizes the art of the counselor in almost every aspect of his work. The pastor who is a good administrator will of necessity be a wise counselor.

The pastor-counselor will be a better preacher. Preaching is at its best when there is continuous interaction between the preacher and the congregation, when preacher and people are sharing an experience that results in decision and commitment. In a sense, preaching is group counseling. If the elements that enter into effective counseling are present in preaching, the results will be richly rewarding.

The pastor-counselor will be a better teacher. Teaching is more than transmission of facts and truths. It is stimulation and guidance in the quest for truth that will throw light on life. The teacher may begin with the lesson or with the group, but in the use of the counseling procedure he will always be keenly conscious that he is teaching persons through lessons, never lessons apart from persons. The teacher's fruitfulness may well depend upon whether he considers himself a lecturer or a counselor. Often the teacher's best work is done in a face-to-face relationship with an inquiring learner who needs counsel more than he does instruction.

The minister-counselor will be a better evangelist. Evangelistic counseling seeks self-revelation of the lost man's need so that he sees himself as lost and without hope. The counseling soul-winner induces his lost friend to seek and find Christ for himself and then to make decision and commitment from an inner experience rather than from outward persuasion. The evangelist as counselor does not stop with public confession, baptism, and church membership but guides into a life of fruitful Christian service. Many a lost man or woman who would resist the evangelist's doing all the talking and trying to sell "the plan of salvation" as if it were an insurance policy will co-operate eagerly with the sincere and skilful counselor who is trying to help the troubled soul find answer to the deep heart cry, "What shall I do to be saved?"

In every aspect of pastoral care and counseling stress is laid on the high importance of being a good listener. Even in preaching the minister needs to listen, if not during the sermon, certainly before and after. In the counseling philosophy selective listening is more important than talking. Trained to speak, the minister may talk too much. Every phase of his ministry would be enriched if he could learn to practice the art of listening. Perhaps on occasions the greater part of his service to others will be to listen.

A Counseling Church Will Fulfil Christ's Ideal

A New Testament church is more than building, organization, services. It is essentially a fellowship of baptized believers. The "priesthood of believers" means not only that every believer may go to God as his own priest, but that every Christian has the right and the duty to go to God for his fellow Christian. Luther claimed for every Christian the right, equal with that of the ordained priest, of "binding and loosing." *Seelsorge allen an allen* ("the care of all for the souls of all") was his apt statement of the principle. This is one of the most revolutionary teachings of the New Testament. According to this doctrine, the gifts of the Spirit are for the whole membership of the church, empowering the members individually and collectively to exercise the priestly office. In the ideal of the counseling church, the principle is recovered and implemented. Its recovery calls for abandonment of the harsh punitive church discipline with its unchristian excommunication and puts in its place the teaching of Jesus that repentance of the offender is to be sought with utmost diligence, with forgiveness exercised not "seven times, but seventy times seven" (Matt. 18:22). This counseling ideal calls for the practice of Paul's injunction: "Brethren, if a man is overtaken in any trespass, you who are spiritual should restore him in a spirit of gen-

tleness. Look to yourself, lest you too be tempted. Bear one another's burdens, and so fulfil the law of Christ" (Gal. 6:1–2).

It is in this process of building a counseling church that the pastor
enters fully into his partnership with Jesus Christ. Our Lord's three-
fold test of Peter may well be applied to every pastor. "Do you love
me?" was the searching question, repeated three times. To Peter's
mounting affirmation Jesus replied, "Feed my lambs," "Tend my
sheep," "Feed my sheep." How better can the demands of this
shepherd-flock relationship be met than in the process that has been
described as counseling? Into this service should be drawn an ever
increasing number of shepherd-hearted members, whose self-realization as mature Christians will be achieved as they become competent counselors. The service of lay office bearers will take on new
meaning and power when they learn that their service consists not
primarily in performing routine duties in an organization but in the
fascinating business of finding solutions for the endless variety of
human problems and needs. James states this idea practically when
he says: "Therefore confess your sins to one another, and pray for
one another, that you may be healed. The prayer of a righteous man
has great power in its effects" (James 5:16).

Georgia Harkness thus reflects the spirit of Christ and his New
Testament interpreters:

> Give me, O God, the understanding heart—
>   The quick discernment of the soul to see
> Another's inner wish, the hidden part
>   Of him who, wordless, speaks for sympathy.
> I would be kind, but kindness is not all:
>   In arid places may I find the wells,
> The deeps within my neighbor's soul that call
>   To me, and lead me where his spirit dwells.
> When Jesus lifted Mary Magdalene
>   And Mary came with alabaster cruse,
> A deed was wrought—but more; there was seen
>   The bond of holy love of which I muse.
> Give me, O God, the understanding heart,
> Lit with the quickening flame Thou dost impart.[5]

Chapter XII

Love Motivates All Ministries

A BAPTIST DEACON IN Calcutta, India, holding an executive position with an international airline, was being questioned about his conversion to Christianity. His family, he related, was high caste Hindu, and he was brought up in the best Hindu tradition. While in the university he became interested in Christianity, but rejected it on philosophical grounds. Then he came in contact with Christian missionaries and began to observe them and their activities.

The missionaries fascinated and puzzled him. Men and women of superior ability, they did not hesitate to give themselves in sacrificial service to the lowliest outcasts. Why did they do it? There was but one answer: They loved persons as persons, without distinctions and without expectation of reward. Why this sacrificial love? They worshiped and served a God of love who had incarnated himself in Jesus Christ, the embodiment of love. "I became a Christian," he said, "because the missionaries won me to Jesus Christ through their demonstration of love in action."

Kagawa, the noted Japanese Christian evangelist, bears a similar testimony. He became captive to the love of God in Christ and then gave himself in utter abandonment to the preaching and practice of this gospel of love. In his *Love, the Law of Life* he exclaims: "Ah, this famine of love! How it saddens my soul! In city and country, in hospital and factory, in shop and on street, everywhere this dreadful drought of love! Not a drop of love anywhere: the loveliest land is more dreary than Sahara and more terrible than Gobi." [1] These words, written ten years before Japan's attack on the United States, fulfils his prediction of world conflict with men "armed with guns, swords, spears, and even ancient maces, hating and suspecting one another!" The basic hunger of human beings is for love; the most fatal starvation is the violation of love; the deepest satisfaction is the supply of love.

Christianity's claim to universality needs no stronger support than this: It is the religion of love. Jesus declared that the law of love to God and man sums up "all the law and the prophets" (Matt. 22:40). His coming was the gift of God's love; his great commandment was that his disciples love one another. When John the beloved disciple sought to equate God in the simplest and yet most profound way possible, he said, "God is love" (1 John 4:8). The surest evidence of being a Christian is just this: "We know that we have passed out of death into life, because we love the brethren" (1 John 3:14). A minister without love directing the ministries of a loveless church is as "a noisy gong or a clanging cymbal" amounting to nothing (1 Cor. 13:1–2).

Christian Love Is the Supreme Imperative

When the minister begins to get restless, when he feels frustrated and ineffective, when distant pastures seem greener, he may soliloquize: "What's the matter with me? I love the Lord, I love the Bible, I love the church; yet I seem to be getting nowhere. What's the matter?" Notice that he did not say, "I love people, especially the people of this community." If he could honestly say that, the chances are that his discouragement, if it came at all, would soon vanish.

The word "love" needs to be re-examined. It is one of the most abused words in the language. "Love" may be used to describe sensual satisfactions, aesthetic appreciation, romantic infatuation, personal affection, intellectual exploration, abstract devotion, self-realization, ego-inflation. Anders Nygren distinguishes between *agape* and *eros,* both of which are translated from the Greek in the New Testament as "love." *Agape* is God's spontaneous love bestowed upon persons without respect to their merit. It is that impartial love of God according to which "he makes his sun rise on the evil and on the good, and sends rain on the just and on the unjust" (Matt. 5:45). It is the love that God commends toward us, "in that while we were yet sinners Christ died for us" (Rom. 5:8). Christian *agape* is that attitude which men have toward one another that resembles

God's attitude. In this sense, to love another is to feel and act toward him as God feels and acts.

Eros denotes sensuous love—love that has in it an element of self-seeking and self-gratification. It is love that seeks to get more than to give, to enjoy more than to give enjoyment, to be happy more than to make another happy. Such love, Nygren holds, is essentially self-love and cannot be recognized as Christian. "Self-love separates men from God; it blocks the channels of self-spending and self-offering, both toward God and toward man." [2] Even ministers may confuse *agape* and *eros*, thus deceiving themselves that they are manifesting Christian love when in reality it is a species of self-love.

Dr. Smiley Blanton, physician of long experience and keen insight, states the alternative: Love or perish! "Whatever you do in life," he advises, "do with love! We have no alternative save to act from motives of hate—yet how doleful to make this our choice! For hate is the destroyer of life, where love is its guardian. Hate blinds our vision and warps our talents; but love releases our energies for the creative action that sustains mankind." [3] Dr. Karl Menninger takes much the same position as he shows that hate, the alternative to love, produces most of mankind's ills, individually and collectively. He confronts humanity's most desperate problem: "How can we encourage love and diminish hate? How can we promote their fruitful fusion? Is it possible to dispose of our aggressions more expediently than by killing ourselves and one another, and to foster and cultivate that tremendous power which draws men and men, and men and women together, that sovereign remedy which stills the hate that forces men apart?" [4] When we say that "Christ is the answer," what do we mean? Are we not saying that Christ has the power to replace hate with love?

Why do men hate? There is profound insight in the words of John: "There is no fear in love, but perfect love casts out fear. For fear has to do with punishment, and he who fears is not perfected in love" (1 John 4:18). Fear is the spring of dislike, animosity, hostility, hate. Fear and anxiety are two aspects of the same thing. Fear is an emotional response to the threat of immediate danger; anxiety is chronic fear of the future. Those persons of whom we are afraid or who induce in us a sense of anxiety we find reasons for disliking, and the consequent withdrawal of love builds up to hate.

Not all hatred is acknowledged as such. In fact, few people will admit that they hate another. It is exceedingly difficult to maintain a strictly neutral attitude—either we like or we dislike, we trust or we fear, we love or we hate.

Ministers, being human, face this struggle of the soul. How can they love some of their unlovely members? How can they avoid a feeling of hostility toward those who criticize, who object and hinder and otherwise threaten the minister's prestige and success? How can members of the church avoid feeling antagonistic toward fellow members who "rub them the wrong way"? It is unrealistic to hold that a Christian, born again and thus a new creature, is thereby rid of the normal human reaction toward those who threaten his pride or sense of importance or successful achievement.

Obviously, lack of love and its obverse sense of dislike block the pathway to service. People will not work long together in Christian activity if there is no bond of love but, conversely, a sense of antipathy. The fact that this is unadmitted makes it all the more difficult to cope with. Ministers may be dealing with symptoms, in themselves and in their parishioners, when they concern themselves with nonattendance, unenlistment, even backsliding. The basic cause is lovelessness, and until the cause is removed the symptoms will continue to appear. "Thou shalt love" is an imperative, divinely demanded and humanly indispensable.

Christian Love Must Be Taught and Learned

How does one come to possess and express Christian love? Is such love an enduement which accompanies the new birth and finds expression naturally and involuntarily? Assuredly, a part of the conversion experience is a change of attitude, not only toward God but toward fellow men. It would be a mistake, however, to assume that the new born Christian attains immediately to maturity in the matter of Christian love, even as in other aspects of Christian character. The conversion experience gives rise to Christian impulses, but these must be nurtured and given direction. The spiritual life, as the physical and mental, may be arrested and never get beyond the childhood level.

It is assumed that the Christian must grow intellectually, hence the elaborate program of teaching and training provided by the church. Similar guidance of emotional growth has in the main been neglected. Indeed, the question may be raised as to whether or not there can be education of the emotions. Love, by its definition, is primarily an emotional response. Is it subject to the discipline which we think of as teaching and training?

Erich Fromm makes loving the finest of the fine arts. To love is not just to experience a pleasant sensation; it is not something that one "falls" into; it is not a flower that grows wild. The problem of love is not just to find a suitable object but the development of a latent faculty. To love another is more than to find a nice package of qualities in another which one then seeks for oneself on the personality market. According to this superficial view, we love those who appeal to us and are loved by those to whom we have appeal. In this view, love is simply a matter of mutual attraction. It is, therefore, not subject to the educative process.

Love that is self-regarding is not truly Christian. Jesus teaches love that includes even enemies. "Love your enemies," he commanded, "and pray for those who persecute you" (Matt. 5:44). Such height of love can be obtained only through discipline that results in emotional maturity. This attainment is an art, to be mastered as any other art through continuous practice based on sound theory under the guidance of a competent teacher.

The art of loving is not taught and learned directly. The teacher might define love, and the students might respond with assent and understanding; yet no one might actually learn to love. Ministers and teachers have often made this mistake, to think that preaching and teaching about love would result in loving. Bitter quarrels have developed among church members who could readily repeat the thirteenth chapter of 1 Corinthians. Hatred in the heart has expressed itself in violence among people committed to the teaching of Jesus about love. Clearly, something else is needed besides verbalization if church members are to practice the art of loving.

The clue is found, according to Fromm, in the realization that "love is an activity, not a passive effect; it is a 'standing in,' not a 'falling for.' In the most general way, the active character of love can be described by stating that love is primarily *giving*, not receiving." In further explanation he says,

Giving is the highest expression of potency. In the very act of giving, I experience my strength, my wealth, my power. This experience of heightened vitality and potency fills me with joy. I experience myself as overflowing, spending, alive, hence as joyous. Giving is more joyous than receiving, not because it is a deprivation, but because in the act of giving lies the expression of my aliveness.[5]

Here giving is not primarily the giving of money—it is the giving of self in service. Self-giving bridges the gap that separates us from others. In serving together for Christ's sake we not only realize our best selves; we come to understand and to appreciate those with whom we serve. Devotion to a common cause overcomes fear and anxiety, since the success of another is no longer a threat to our success, and differences of viewpoint are merged in the unity created by the lordship of Christ.

Membership in activity groups vitally related to the church and the kingdom of God as a whole is thus seen to be the way in which Christians mature in love. Jesus probably had this principle in mind when he sent the disciples out two by two. The principle was demonstrated in the close-knit fellowship of the twelve and later the seventy and in the community of goods following Pentecost. When criticism is leveled against a church because of "activism"—its many busy groups engaged in service activities—it should be recalled that this is essentially the way church members learn to love. Ministers with insight know that preaching and teaching, which set forth the beauty and the duty of love, are not enough. Theory must be put into practice if the art of loving is to be learned. "We come to worship—we leave to serve" represents the cycle of learning in the school of love.

Jesus provided two beautiful and meaningful ceremonials that represent love in action—baptism and the Memorial Supper. Baptism seals the covenant of love between Christ and the believer. It is a public repudiation of the mastery of self and commitment to the control of Christ. Going into the water symbolizes the leaving of the old self behind; submersion beneath the water symbolizes burial with Christ; emergence from the water symbolizes commitment henceforth to walk in a newness of life. The attachment of any mysterious saving power to baptism wholly misses the mark. It is a transaction between the saved and the Saviour, an evidence of a love relationship made public, a pledge that "we might no longer be enslaved to sin" (Rom. 6:6). Every service of baptism should bear this testimony on the part of the one being baptized, on the part of the church into whose family the new member is being received, and on the part of the triune God approving this act of obedient love. Baptism should thus mark the beginning of a life of Christian service.

The Supper marks the continuance of the love relationship. Jesus knew how easily we forget and how quickly our love grows cold. The Supper is symbol, but it is more than mere symbol. It is a reminder of God's love in Christ seeking men and of that love going to the utmost limit of suffering and death to prove God's love. When we observe the Supper aright, we are teaching our souls to respond to the love of God. "We cannot force our own souls to love or to be grateful towards God any more than we can force anybody else to feel love or gratitude toward us," says J. B. Phillips,

but we can at least put ourselves in the way of responding to God's love. We can meditate on it, upon the nature and character of God as revealed by Christ, and we can deliberately associate in our minds with God all those lovely and heart-warming things which, despite the evil, adorn our common life. It is only love that can beget love, and self-giving that can stimulate self-giving. We cannot force the pace here but we can quietly look upon what sort of person our God really is.[6]

Every observance of the Supper, in preparation and administration, should serve as an unforgettable lesson in the school of Christian love. Unless the observance sends us out with renewed purpose and zeal to serve for Christ's sake, it will have been in vain.

Christian Love Cements the Bonds of Marriage

Marriage is the fulfilment of *eros,* love on the human level. While the New Testament contains no hint that marriage is a sacrament in the Roman Catholic sense, it gives to the union of man and woman religious sanction and significance. There is profound meaning in the ancient words, "Therefore a man leaves his father and his mother and cleaves to his wife, and they become one flesh" (Gen. 2:24). Jesus, confirming the Genesis statement, added, "What therefore God has joined together, let no man put asunder" (Matt. 19:6). There is no ground for the doctrine that the married estate is less holy than the celibate. There is entire justification for making a wedding a religious affair.

Marriage in civilized lands is regarded as a legal contract given civil sanction. Until the Reformation, marriage in Christendom was under ecclesiastical law and was numbered among the seven sacraments. Where there is separation of church and state, marriage is governed by ordinary civil law. Some form of license is required, and the marriage is recorded. The ceremony may be performed by a qualified civil officer.

Reminiscent of ancient practice and in recognition of the peculiar sacredness of the contract, qualified ministers are legally authorized to officiate at weddings. At this point the state overlooks its separation from the church in recognition of marriage as the basic human contract and in concern for its permanence. Ministers are, of course, under no obligation to perform the ceremony and are always at liberty to decline to do so.

Obviously, the minister does not act as a private person but as a representative of the church when he performs the wedding ceremony. He is therefore under sacred obligation to officiate only on occasions which the church would approve. The minister should lead the church to adopt a policy for his guidance, thus saving him from the embarrassment or personal offense should he decline to officiate. When Jesus said, "What therefore God has joined together," he evidently meant that a marriage should be such as to have divine approval. What is basically necessary if God is to approve the union? Clearly, the basic requisite is love. Love alone can guarantee permanence of the union. Adultery is a rupture of love or a disclosure that it never existed, hence is ground for separation or divorce. Should divorced persons ever remarry? Love once solemnly pledged to a mate cannot be transferred to another in its virginity; it has been adulterated. There is, therefore, strong presumptive evidence that the remarriage will lack permanence. If the evidence is positively to the contrary, a second marriage may be justified. Conscientious ministers, thus convinced, are sometimes willing to perform the ceremony, with approval of the church. Others feel that to make exceptions would involve increasing difficulty and so lead the church to support them in declining to officiate.

The wedding ceremony, performed in the home or in the church, should be a service of love. It should be preceded by thoughtful counseling of the contracting parties, to the end that they and the minister may be quite convinced of divine approval of the union and its permanency "until death shall part." The ceremony to be used should be read aloud beforehand and its meaning explained.

The wedding itself should be marked by simplicity and in accordance with the good taste prescribed by correct social usage. Following the wedding, the church should surround the couple with loving concern, seeking to win them to Christ if not already Christian and engaging them in Christian service as one of the surest guarantees of a happy, unbroken home.

Paul E. Johnson likens the aisle of the church to the course of life. It is, he says beautifully, like an hourglass,

broad at the top to represent the many friends and influences that socialize the learning of love in the growing child and young person. At the center the stem is narrow to indicate the time when two persons arrive at mate love and devote themselves exclusively to each other. At the bottom is the broadening dimension of expanding love as the couple have children and turn outward to share their love in unselfish social ways with even larger circles of the human family. Pouring through the hourglass is the unfailing purpose of the heavenly Father, who gives time and impetus to develop love in persons and groups with dynamic overflowing generosity.[7]

Blessed is the church and blessed are the young people where love flowers in the soil of Christian service and where it finds its fruition in activities that cement the bonds of love into such permanence that neither life nor death can disrupt!

Christian Love Comforts in Trouble

"Comfort ye, comfort ye my people," (Isa. 40:1, AV). God commanded the prophet at a time when disaster was about to strike. This commission to comfort is still the divine requirement of the minister. It is related that a group of ministers visited J. H. Jowett, perhaps the greatest English-speaking preacher of his generation, near the close of his ministry. They asked him, "If you had your life to live over, what would you emphasize?" Quickly he replied, "I would major on compassion and comfort." To comfort is more than to assuage grief. Basically, it is to strengthen. The strong and the weak alike are beset by troubles which they cannot bear alone. To help them find in God the source of courage and confidence is the minister's high privilege in public discourse and in private conversation.

Trouble often comes in the form of accident or illness. The visit of the minister to the sick room or the hospital bed is not just a perfunctory fulfilment of duty. The presence of the man of God, representing the church, brings comfort to the suffering, not by relief of pain as the doctor may bring through hypodermic needle, but by supplying strength to endure the pain with Christian fortitude. The warm handclasp, the appropriate verse of Scripture, the reassurance of divine care, the brief prayer of faith and intercession may at times be worth more than medicine or surgery. The faithful minister, alert to this need of comfort on the part of many, will gather about him some of his members who are sensitive to suffering and will train them to share with him in this ministry of comfort.

The terminus of life is death. It is as truly God's gift as birth. Its approach calls for strength to wrest victory from defeat. The minister may be called on to prepare the dying person for the experience. Always this should be done with the approval of the doctor and the consent of near relatives. Here indeed is a ministry of comfort, as the minister clasps the hand of one approaching death and quietly leads him in repeating the Shepherd's Psalm or the familiar first verses of John 14 or the closing verses of Romans 8, followed by the Lord's Prayer. Seldom will there be needed any statement that the end is near; the dying man, if still sensibly conscious, will understand and open the way for conversation concerning his readiness to go.

"And he died." This closes the earthly story and affords opportunity for the final service, the funeral. Funeral customs vary widely, but almost always a religious burial is desired. Here again, the minister officiating at the funeral does not act in private capacity but as representing Christ and the church. As in the solemnizing of marriage, the minister should lead his church to adopt a policy concerning funerals. Such a policy might well include the use of the church building and its facilities, distinction between the responsibility of the church for a member and a nonmember, for whom flowers should be provided by the church, the furnishing of music, responsibility for pallbearers, expenses of the minister when such are incurred. Again, as in weddings, the matter of a fee should be clarified by the church. In general, it is better that the minister receive no fee personally for either of these services. If a gift is made, it should of course be graciously received but put into a fund to be used at the minister's discretion for gifts appropriate to such occasions—a book of counsel and inspiration for the newlyweds and of comfort and consolation for the bereaved.

The funeral service should be carefully planned, simple, brief. Most funeral directors are skilled and helpful and will give proper guidance to details. The minister will of course co-operate with the mortician, taking care not to be officious, yet seeking to make the service truly Christian. The service honors the memory of the dead but is for the sake of the living. Words of censure or of undue praises are out of place. A brief sermon usually is expected and in some communities is almost obligatory. There are sources of help for the busy minister in the form of the funeral service and in the content of the message, such as *The Funeral,* by A. W. Blackwood, and *The Funeral Encyclopedia,* compiled by Charles L. Wallis.

The funeral, as a religious event, is primarily a service of comfort. To serve this purpose it must always present a Christian view of death. Such a view interprets death for the Christian as victory, not defeat; as a new beginning, not the end of life. If the deceased was not a Christian, the opportunity to present the Christian view of death is no less, for the message does not concern the fate of the one presumed unsaved. That is left with God. The message of hope in Christ is for the living, for whom there is still an opportunity to receive God's gift of eternal life through Christ.

Grief at parting is not to be suppressed. Indeed, we read that Jesus wept. His tears at the tomb of Lazarus were not for the loss of this dear one nor just in sympathy with Mary and Martha. Rather, he grieved at the wrong view of death evidenced by the unseemly mourning of the neighbors and the hopeless grief of the sisters. A service of inestimable worth is performed by the minister who takes occasion at the funeral to rid minds of morbidity concerning death and to present the Christian view of transference for the believer to a new and eternal life.

Christian Love Welcomes the Coming of Children

Adam . . . became the father of a son in his own likeness, after his image" (Gen. 5:3). God, it is recorded, made the first man in his own image. Thereafter men have begotten children in their image. Children, begotten of men and born of women, are God's means of renewing his human family. The ultimate disaster would not be the physical wreck occasioned by atomic explosion but the sterilization of men so that no more children would be born. Marriages are made meaningful by the coming of another generation.

There is deep religious significance in the birth of a child. Even pagans recognize an element of the supernatural in such an event. A young mother, looking down into the face of her newborn baby, exclaimed, "How could one be a mother and not believe in God!" Not all children are born of believing parents, nor are they all the fruit of love. Yet every child has the right to God and to love. Ministers and churches who default on their obligation to welcome children into life and into their Christian care and concern are guilty of inexcusable neglect.

Christ gives full warrant for a church's loving interest in children. His coming marks a new era in the history of childhood. Until he came, children in much of the world were considered the property of their parents, to be disposed of if unwanted and to be abused without legal protection. The fact that God in Christ came as a baby is of enormous significance. His birth and childhood are a part of the redemptive plan. His example and teaching glorify childhood. His anger flared out against those who would have kept the children from coming to him. He made the child, innocent and trusting, an example for his followers and a type of citizen of the kingdom. He had no illusions about the inherited tendency of the child to sin, but he poured out his bitter woe upon those who caused a child to stumble. One of the most remarkable statements ever to fall from his lips was: "See that you do not despise one of these little ones. . . . So it is not the will of my Father who is in heaven that one of these little ones should perish" (Matt. 18:10–14). He made it clear that a church's most irreparable loss is that of its children and that its most disastrous sin is to cause children to stumble and to perish spiritually.

Concern for children led early to a perversion that took the form of infant baptism. Since every child is born with an inherited tendency to sin and into a sinful environment, how can the child's salvation be assured before it is old enough to believe? The answer was found in the rite of baptism, which mysteriously removed the guilt of original sin and made the infant a child of God. This error has persisted even until now, and where rejected in the light of the clear teaching of the Scriptures, it is clung to as a ceremonial of commitment of parents and church to the religious upbringing of the child.

Many thoughtful Christians feel deeply that the use of baptism, even as a means of influencing parents and the church to recognize their responsibility for children, is contrary to New Testament teaching and a spiritually dangerous practice. No one would assert that the infant exercises saving faith, and few would rationally argue that the child can be saved by proxy faith. The child may be led to believe that through baptism he is made a member of the kingdom and need never know a time when he is not consciously a Christian. He is thus made to feel that he does not need to undergo a saving experience, leading to a decisive commitment. It is easily possible for such a person to be lost and yet to be deluded into believing that he is saved. Of course, it is possible to be saved in spite of this practice, for many baptized in infancy have come later to personal faith and commitment, but the risk remains.

Those who reject infant baptism and sacramental salvation may be guilty of an equally great error—the neglect of children. "Let the child alone," they may say, "until he is old enough to make up his mind for himself." How old shall this be? Traditionally, those who hold this view have considered twelve the minimum. In some circles an even more advanced age is required. Others would set the "age of accountability" as the requisite, regardless of chronological age.

What shall be done to influence the child religiously during the intervening years? Falling back on the doctrine of election, some would say that nothing can be done—the "elect" child will eventually and inevitably confess his faith and ask for baptism. Others, not so rigidly Calvinistic, hold that the gospel should be presented with urgency but without persuasion. In any case, there is grave danger of fatal neglect.

The trend in Christian education is away from either extreme of sacramental salvation or neglectful predestinarianism. Understanding of child life and the importance of the early years calls for the leading of the child toward Christ from birth. Teachers and parents will seek then to lead the child to Christ in personal and decisive commitment and then into Christ with maturing knowledge and devotion.

The name of the newborn baby will be placed on the Cradle Roll of the church at once. Christian concern will thus be expressed for both child and parents. An attractive nursery will be provided where the child can be made aware of the church's love and parents be given opportunity to attend the teaching and worship services. Grade by grade the child will be advanced through Beginner and Primary departments, with increasing knowledge of the Bible, appreciation of the church, and understanding of the need of faith in Jesus Christ as friend and Saviour.

Sometimes clear and intelligent decision will be made before the Junior years, but during these four years and the four Intermediate years that follow the church will surround its growing boys and girls with such teaching and training that they will make intelligent decisions and commitments and thus come into the church on New Testament terms. Special occasions may well be provided, such as Dedication Day for the babies—not that the babies are dedicated, but that church and parents dedicate themselves to the welfare and religious upbringing of the little ones; and Declaration Day, when the older children, having been led to saving faith through teaching and personal conversation, will publicly declare their allegiance to Christ and ask for baptism at the hands of the church.

Let it never be forgotten that a church that loses its children eventually loses its life. Every activity of the church may well be tested by the question, What effect will this have on the children? A place should be made for the boys and girls of the church in all of its services on the level of their characteristic interest and needs. The minister whose sermons are listened to by adults only should re-examine his preaching. There is something seriously wrong with the worship service if it holds little or no attraction for children. Jesus was speaking to his disciples—and to us—when he said, "Whoever receives one such child in my name receives me; but whoever causes one of these little ones who believe in me to sin, it would be better for him to have a great millstone fastened round his neck and to be drowned in the depth of the sea" (Matt. 18:5-6).

Christian Love Gives Meaning to Ministries

Sometimes the charge made against church services is that they are just busy activities. There may be many meetings, many sermons, many lessons, many programs, many visits, many money-raising efforts, many enlargement campaigns, many revivals, yet apparently without much meaning. The complaint lodged against these multiplied activities would disappear if they were motivated by love.

If we agree that love gives meaning to service—or to any other worthwhile activity—the question arises: What kind of meaning? Is meaning to be found in knowledge, in intellectual comprehension? Is meaning to be found in emotional satisfactions? Does meaning flow from the making of right choices? Is meaning discovered through positive thinking that leads to successful achievement? Is meaning found in the attainment of nirvana, the absorption of self into the soul of the universe? The search goes on for the meaning of meaning.

The unique revelation of Jesus Christ is that meaning derives from relationship—the relationship of God to man and man to God and man to his fellow man. This relationship very simply is one of love, as a consequence of which the promise of Christ can be claimed: "Peace I leave with you; my peace I give to you; not as the world gives do I give to you. Let not your hearts be troubled, neither let them be afraid" (John 14:27).

In vain do loveless preachers preach loveless sermons exhorting people to do their loveless duty. In vain do unloving church members devote their money and energies to unloving service in the church. In vain do we measure results that mount ever so high statistically but lack the quality of love. If there be genuine love, visible results may not be impressive; yet the ingredient is present that gives to all service its Christian meaning, without which any service is ultimately meaningless.

The creative spring of service, as of all living, is found in love, because love is of God.

> Beloved, let us love: love is of God;
> In God alone hath love its true abode.
>
> Beloved, let us love: for they who love,
> They only, are His sons, born from above.
>
> Beloved, let us love: for love is rest,
> And he who loveth not abides unblest.
>
> Beloved, let us love: for love is light,
> And he who loveth not dwelleth in night.
>
> Beloved, let us love; for only thus
> Shall we behold that God Who loveth us.
>
> HORATIUS BONAR

Chapter XIII

Evangelism Is the Supreme Ministry

EVANGELISM IS ONE OF the noblest words in the Christian vocabulary. George E. Sweazey says: "Evangelism is every possible way of reaching outside the Church to bring people to faith in Christ and membership in His Church." [1] Literally, evangelism is the practice of the proclamation of the Christian gospel, the sharing of the glad tidings that salvation through Christ is available on terms which anyone can meet. Jesus came preaching, "Repent!"—that is, change your mind and your course of action. To this first demand he added the second, "Believe!"—that is, trust and obey him as Lord and Saviour. "Unless you repent," he declared, "you will all likewise perish" (Luke 13:3). Categorically he said, "For this is the will of my Father, that every one who sees the Son and believes in him should have eternal life; and I will raise him up at the last day" (John 6:40). This is great good news for the lost.

Evangelism is more than winning those without; it is also making the good news or gospel known to and believed by those within the church. The glad tidings to those who have repented and believed is that Christ can keep that which he has saved. The gospel for the believer is as prominent in the words of Jesus and of his interpreters as the gospel for the unbeliever. Consistently we find such statements as these: "My sheep hear my voice, and I know them, and they follow me; and I give them eternal life, and they shall never perish, and no one shall snatch them out of my hand" (John 10:27-28). "I am the resurrection and the life; he who believes in

183

me, though he die, yet shall he live, and whoever lives and believes in me shall never die" (John 11:25-26). "Peace I leave with you; my peace I give to you; not as the world gives do I give to you. Let not your hearts be troubled, neither let them be afraid" (John 14:27). Paul triumphantly claimed this good news when he declared, "I know whom I have believed and I am sure that he is able to guard until that Day what has been entrusted to me" (2 Tim. 1:12). Always there are these two aspects of the gospel—the good news that Christ saves and the good news that he keeps whom he has saved.

The Loss and Recovery of Evangelism

Evangelism lost its primacy in the long period of Roman Catholic domination of Western Europe from the sixth through the sixteenth centuries. The Protestant Reformation, usually identified with Martin Luther and John Calvin, witnessed the revival of preaching intended to convert the listeners, if not to Christ then certainly to anti-Catholic views. The vogue of predestinarianism, which made human effort of no avail, and of deism, which sought proof of the existence of God from reason and nature rather than from revelation, laid their blight on evangelicalism through much of the seventeenth and into the first half of the eighteenth centuries in England and on the Continent.

The Wesleyan movement, which had its beginning about 1740, brought a swing of the pendulum back toward zeal for the salvation of souls with emphasis on human effort and experience. Shut out of the churches, the Wesleys and Whitefield took to the fields and the market places. The revival that swept over England made history and is credited with having saved the land from the bloody excesses which characterized the French Revolution. Whitefield's intermittent visits to America, from 1744 to 1770, stirred the fires of evangelism and aided in producing the Great Awakening.

Many factors combined to set the revivalistic pattern of American evangelism. The level of Colonial morality was low, the growth of population was rapid, scattered families were lonely and welcomed an occasion to come together. Spiritual hunger had well-nigh reached the stage of starvation, the established churches were in disfavor, the doctrine of the worth of the individual and his right to immediate access to God had taken deep root. Inhibitions of the old-world culture were largely removed.

Into this situation came the American revivalists of the eighteenth century. Among names of revivalists not to be forgotten are Tennent, Frelinghuysen, Roland, Blair, Davies, Dickinson, Edwards, Jarratt, Ireland, Webb, Gatch. There were many others of lesser note, some educated, some uneducated, but all preached the doctrines of sin and salvation, of repentance and faith, of hell for the lost and heaven for the saved. Sometimes the revival meetings or camp meetings were marked by violent emotional excesses. While the preaching was usually deeply personal, and converted individuals sought out their unconverted relatives and friends, the preacher addressed himself to an assembled crowd. Hence, the pattern came to be known as "mass evangelism." The results were far reaching in American life, both religious and civic.

The organizational genius of America influenced evangelism in the nineteenth century. Dwight L. Moody, an untutored lay evangelist, and his singer, Ira D. Sankey, were the first to organize the revival on a grand scale and to invade the growing city centers. The intense earnestness and homely sense and humor of Mr. Moody, together with the contagiousness of the spirit of Mr. Sankey as he led great choirs and congregations in the singing of gospel songs, caught the attention and commanded the respect of the multitudes. The pattern of the highly organized union meeting, held in a tabernacle and appealing to the masses, was further advanced by Billy Sunday and Gipsy Smith. Then came World War I with its vast disruptions and its aftermath of rampant secularism. The financial depression and World War II augmented the difficulties of revivalism. For three decades there was no successor to such revivalists as Torrey, Chapman, Mills, Sam Jones, George Stuart, Biederwolf, Billy Sunday, Gipsy Smith. The American historian, W. W. Sweet, concluded in 1945 that revivalism had run its course in America.

The history of evangelism follows the pattern of the up-and-down graph. More than once the conclusion might have been reached that evangelism was dying or dead. During the first three centuries evangelism was at a high level. Then, during the next thousand years, although from time to time there were upward spurts, the general direction was downward. With Wycliffe and Huss in the fourteenth century the graph starts upward. Notwithstanding many sharp declines, the trend of direction has been upward during the past five centuries. The pendulum has never swung backward that it did not again swing forward. The time lapse between evangelistic deadness and evangelistic aliveness has grown steadily shorter. Each era of evangelistic fruitfulness has had its own characteristics and leaders. It remains to be seen what distinctive pattern the evangelism of the latter half of the twentieth century will take, but in the light of history and of the relative failures of the first half of the twentieth century there is reason to believe that the latter half may witness a recovery of evangelism on a broad scale.

Evangelism Meeting the Challenge of Unbelief

In general, two plans of salvation are proposed by the two major Christian divisions. On the one hand is the Roman Catholic system of sacramental salvation. On the other hand is the nonsacramental system, which admits individual freedom and calls for decision. In the sacramental system every child of Catholic parents is brought into the Church and thus saved. Union of church and state identifies membership in the one with membership in the other. Of necessity, if every infant is baptized into the Church and thus made a Christian, the whole population will be saved. Historically, the result was that while the state was "Christianized," the Church was paganized. The nerve of evangelism was cut, its function being replaced by nurture leading to confirmation and a sacramental system guaranteeing eternal benefits.

The repudiation of sacramentalism presents difficulties. One of the most notable aspects of American Christianity was its rejection of the establishment of religion. An obvious consequence of the separation of church and state was the complete freedom of the individual or the family to belong to a church or not. Another consequence was the competition of churches for members. Still another consequence was the number of persons who grew up outside the church or left it on reaching maturity, making inevitable an increasing number of adults without church affiliation. A community religious census ordinarily will disclose 25 to 50 per cent or even more of the population of adult age who are not actively related to any church. Not many of these are opposed to religion or the church, but are indifferent. Many hold nominal church membership but have become unconcerned and have lost their sense of value of the church as being significant for their lives.

The line of least resistance is for a church to retain its faithful families and bring their children into its membership. In the main, American churches have followed this line with good success. However, the policy largely misses the mark of true evangelism. Even for the children of the church it may overlook the necessity for decisive commitment. In a world in which Christianity is on trial before its aggressive enemies, this lack of commitment may prove to be a fatal weakness in the years ahead. Thus, evangelism becomes more than ever an urgent necessity.

Elmer Homrighausen insists that decision regarding Jesus Christ is unique.

It cleaves life in twain; it severs the ties that bind us with death and sinful history. . . . It changes one's situation in time. It dethrones man and puts Christ in command of life. The individual thereby empties himself of his old humanity and becomes unified in God's purpose and love. That is why a decision for Christ Jesus is unlike other decisions, however moving they may be. This decision points two ways. It is negative; it says "No," to the old; it is repentance and sorrow. It is also positive; it says, "Yes," to the new. It means "to cast in one's lot" with Jesus Christ. Such a decision has racial and cosmic significance and implications.[2]

This requirement of decision and commitment does not ignore family influence, early training, education in religion, and the processes of growth. Nevertheless, in the confrontation of the self with Jesus Christ and his claim, choice must be made of him and his way of life. No man today can be brought up in isolation. Very early he faces the claims of self, of the world, of an anti-Christian society. Repentance for the child will not ordinarily mean the giving up of repulsive sins, for he has not committed them; but it does mean a radical change of attitude, an alignment with Christ where alternatives are offered, a facing in the direction in which Christ and his followers are going. There is no escaping the necessity for such decision and commitment if life is to be more than nominally Christian. And if it is only nominally Christian, it is not Christian. Time will almost certainly move the uncommitted person into the ranks of the "good for nothing" church members about whom Jesus trenchantly speaks.

Decision Day for children would better not be at a time of emotional upset during a revival, unless care is taken that the occasion provides opportunity for declaration of that inward decision which has already taken place. Indeed, if the end result is that the child comes into the church without an experience of response to Christ who has sought and met him, and without intelligent personal commitment to him as Lord and Saviour, it matters little whether the error be that of sacramentalism or of emotionalism. The most tragic case of any person is to be in a church, with a sense of false security, unsaved without realizing it.

If evangelism is successfully to meet today's challenge, it must aggressively attack adult unbelief. If our only hope of recruitment is to bring in the children before they are old enough to resist our inducements, are we not practicing "the art of taking advantage of the helpless"? It is notable that every case of conversion specifically described in the New Testament is that of an adult. Jesus sought to win such mature persons as Andrew and John, Peter and James, Philip and Nathanael, Matthew and Zacchaeus, Nicodemus and the Samaritan woman, the nobleman and the beggar, the Pharisees and the publicans. He took little children in his arms and blessed them and declared that to such his kingdom belongs, but he would never have inaugurated a successful program of spiritual world conquest if laying his hand of blessing on little children had been his total strategy. From the first century until now no period of spiritual awakening has come except as Christ's evangelists have sought boldly to win unbelieving adults. A hesitant and apologetic evangelism will never win these adults. Evangelism for our day, as for any day, must seize the offensive and boldly confront the masses of unchristian and nominally Christian adults with the life-changing demands of Jesus Christ.

Types of Evangelistic Method

Mr. Charles Spurgeon, the noted English pastor-evangelist, is quoted as having often said, "There is no wrong way to win persons to Christ." Doubtless he meant that if the outcome is a saving experience with Christ resulting in the new life no means used to bring this about is to be despised. Becoming a Christian is a vital experience, and the experience is as varied as persons are different. Certainly there is no stereotyped evangelistic method. There are, however, types of method which may be grouped together. Some of the most useful of these may be described.

The method of personal interview deserves to be placed at the head of the list. It is the method most used by Jesus and his immediate followers. In his last recorded words to his disciples Jesus said, "But you shall receive power when the Holy Spirit has come upon you; and you shall be my witnesses in Jerusalem and in all Judea and Samaria and to the end of the earth" (Acts 1:8). The heart of the matter is contained in the word "witnesses." A witness is one who knows by experience and whose testimony is valid because of something done or undergone. Personal Christian witnessing must meet this requirement. The witness must have done something and undergone something. What occurred has taken place within his experience. The experience is too precious to be retained for oneself —hence the desire to share it with another. In this process of sharing, the other meets the conditions and undergoes the experience. The impulse to share the experience with another, if obeyed, makes the new Christian a witness. Thus the circle of believers grows, according to the sublimely simple plan of Jesus, until it includes those at "the end of the earth."

The method of public proclamation has from the beginning produced fruitful results. Jesus dealt with individuals, but he also appealed to the multitude. Matthew records that near the beginning of his Galilean ministry Jesus went about "teaching in their synagogues and preaching the gospel of the kingdom and healing every disease and every infirmity among the people. . . . And great crowds followed him from Galilee and the Decapolis and Jerusalem and Judea and from beyond the Jordan" (Matt. 4:23–25). It seems that past the inner circle of the disciples were the listening crowds when he delivered the Sermon on the Mount (Matt. 5:1). "When he came down from the mountain," it is recorded, "great crowds followed him" (Matt. 8:1).

We sense the intense concern of Jesus for the multitudes in the statement that "when he saw the crowds, he had compassion for them, because they were harassed and helpless, like sheep without a shepherd" (Matt. 9:36). He poured out his heart to the multitude to accept him when he stood in their midst and pleaded, "Come to me, all who labor and are heavyladen, and I will give you rest" (Matt. 11:28). When he entered the region of Judea, "large crowds followed him, and he healed them there" (Matt. 19:2). After recording the public teaching of Jesus, Mark comments that "the great throng heard him gladly" (Mark 12:37). Paul made the case for

Christ both in personal conversation and in public proclamation. Mass evangelism has an honorable history when dissociated from the abuses which sometimes gathered about it. The effective communication of the Christian gospel by an earnest and persuasive preacher remains one of the most fruitful ways of winning others to Christ.

The method of visitation evangelism offers remarkable opportunity. It is distinguished from the method of personal conversation in that interviews are carefully planned and sought in organized fashion. The plan calls for the securing of large numbers of names and addresses of unchurched and unsaved people. This information, as we have seen, may be had through a concerted religious census. The resultant information having been correctly tabulated on cards, selected church members are carefully trained in "the art of doorbell ringing." Under the leadership of skilled persons, who often have had previous experience in guiding such an enterprise, the visitors are sent forth to present the claims of Christ and the church to these prospects in their homes or places of business. Going two by two, they do not just invite those whom they visit to attend the church and listen to a preacher; they tell their experience, they present the way of salvation through Christ, they pray and urge immediate commitment. Frequently this type of visitation evangelism is accompanied or followed by special services in the church, as personal commitments are made public through reception into the church. Techniques vary, but the main matter is to organize visitation in such a way as to guarantee that none will be overlooked who should be sought for Christ.

There is the method of educational evangelism. The Sunday school is a logical and effective agency of evangelism. Its officers and teachers usually represent the best intelligence and highest devotion of the church. Its classes and departments constitute units already available for purposes of discovery and visitation. These "cells" within the church afford opportunity for fellowship evangelism, that is, the bringing of outsiders into the fellowship of a group as a first step toward bringing them to Christ and into the church. It has been shown that many persons can be reached for attendance on a class who would be reluctant to attend the formal services of the church. Many difficulties are removed when, in a congenial class, non-Christians are taught the way of life in an uninhibited situation where personal needs can be met and where the influence of others of similar age may be effectually brought to bear. Where the Sunday school is thus used as an evangelistic agency, it is notable that the percentage of additions to the church steadily rises and that the majority of those won become useful members.

The method of mass media especially commends itself as meeting modern conditions of opportunity and need. The gospel message may be communicated by personal letter, by the printed page, and through the air by way of radio and television. In this age of concentration of persons into congested areas the face-to-face presentation of the claims of Christ needs to be supplemented through the use of nonpersonal means. Is it not strange that the example of Paul and of other early Christians should have been so generally neglected? Paul was an inveterate letter writer. He wrote to individuals, to churches, to groups of churches. In every letter he was pleading the cause of Christ.

From the discovery of printing until now, the printed page has been effectively used for evangelism. The attractive, brief tract can lodge the truth about sin and salvation where the spoken word might never reach. The traditional bulletin type announcement of Sunday services may give way to a brief and convincing word about the central message of the church—Christ and his salvation. Newspapers and magazines welcome human interest stories that tell of changed lives, changed homes, changed communities, brought about through the influence of the Christian gospel.

A blind man hit on the idea of calling at random over the telephone each day. He inquired of the one who answered the call, with quiet and earnest concern, about church affiliation, the need of a vital relation to Jesus Christ, the willingness of the respondent to chat for a few minutes about spiritual things. This often led to a letter with the enclosure of a tract, or a visit by a Christian witness, or attendance on a church service. Rarely, he said, was he rebuffed. He found many persons hungry for an opportunity to talk to an intelligent listener about their moral and religious problems.

Radio and television have opened up almost limitless opportunities to communicate the gospel message to countless listeners and viewers. Here again the most successful technique has not been that of the formal sermon but of the sharing of Christian experience, the inviting and answering of questions, the dramatization of the meaning of the conversion experience, the explanation in simple human terms of the way to be saved.

With the population increasing at unprecedented rate, the growth of church membership in America has difficulty keeping pace with population increase. While nothing can take the place of individual work with individuals, the need is imperative for means of making an impact on multitudes of unreached people who must first be interested through these new media of mass communication. To neglect this use while secular and evil forces powerfully avail themselves of it would be to fail Christ at this point of unparalleled opportunity.

The Need of a Program of Graded Evangelism

Near the turn of the present century the need of graded lessons was felt and provided for. The weakness of the earlier uniform lessons was that they ignored changes of interest, capacity, and need at successive stages of growth. Along with this development came the provision of graded worship. Concepts and practice of worship vary with little children, older children, boys and girls, young people, adults. Recognition of this principle of adaptation of instruction and worship to the several age levels has gone far toward vitalizing today's churches. The same principle of gradation applies in evangelism. The good news of Christ's love and redemption is communicated more effectually when account is taken of changing levels of maturation on the part of growing persons.

The gospel may be communicated to little children. It was good news to the children present on that day and to the children of all later generations when Jesus indignantly rebuked the disciples who interfered with the bringing of little children to him. Again, when a quarrel broke out among the twelve, Jesus dealt with it by setting a child in their midst and making of him an object lesson. Their example of selfish ambition was causing the child to stumble. Upon these mistaken men Jesus poured out bitter woe, declaring that no misfortune could befall them greater than that of losing the children. He then concluded, "It is not the will of my Father who is in heaven that one of these little ones should perish" (Matt. 18:14). Thus children early may gain the picture of the loving Jesus, of whom Mark says that "he took them in his arms and blessed them, laying his hands upon them" (Mark 10:16).

Here again is a supremely important and delicate and difficult responsibility—to lead the child from birth toward Christ, to lead the child to definite personal decision and commitment to Christ, and to nurture the child in Christ's way of life. A church should lay this obligation upon all concerned, in the home, in the nursery, in the children's organizations of the church, in all the older church groups, to the end that God's purpose in Christ may be achieved for every child.

The gospel may be communicated to older children. Earlier than perhaps we realize, today's child comes into a personal experience of sin. How could it be otherwise, when he is continually exposed to the allurements of the world, the flesh, and the devil? Later childhood offers to evangelism its greatest single opportunity. "Tell me about God!" "Tell me about Jesus!" "Tell me about the Bible!" "Tell me about myself!" "Tell me about death!" These are clamorous demands made by all normal children.[3] Two dangers are to be avoided: overpersuasion and neglect. We must not violate the child's right of choice by religious forcing, nor should we carelessly wait until this season of inquiry and plasticity is past. The child should be led to see the beauty of Jesus in contrast with the ugliness of sin, the love of Jesus in contrast with the hatred of men, the courage of Jesus over against the cowardice of many, the power of Jesus to make life worthy and abundant against the background of weakness and failure without him.

It is not enough to win the child to oneself, to church membership, to assent to the truths of the Bible. The glorious privilege of parents, teachers, pastors, and others who deal with the child's religious life is to win the child to a deep personal commitment to Christ as Lord and Saviour and from this experience to a lifetime of Christian service.

The gospel may be communicated to youth. The picture of Jesus visualized by many teen-agers and young people is a distorted one. They may perceive him as vaguely ethereal, "out of this world"; or as a sad-eyed "man of sorrows," allegiance to whom takes all the joy out of life; or as a stern critic and judge, with standards so high that "What's the use?" is often the cynical response. Such ideas of Jesus are untrue to the New Testament portraiture. In the eyes of his contemporaries he was a religious and social radical. He proposed the greatest ideal—the kingdom of God on earth as it is in heaven. No hero of history or fiction can be compared with him in courage and heroism. He set in motion influences that changed the course of history.

Christ's is the most challenging program and the most potent force in today's world. Himself a young man, he called about him a group of young men and women, and together they began to change the human race. He came to save the world, and while he has not yet saved it, he has laid hold on it savingly. He is even now calling young people to an enterprise daring beyond imagination—the elimination of ignorance and poverty, the overthrow of injustice and wrong, the bringing in of an era of true blessedness. He proposed all this in the only way that it can conceivably be accomplished —the regeneration of the individual who, combined with other regenerate individuals, will constitute the good society.

Paul was a young man when the risen Christ mastered him. He was an old man when he said, "I have fought the good fight, I have finished the race, I have kept the faith" (2 Tim. 4:7). In between, Christ took Paul's surrendered life and made it a creative force in history. He is seeking to do that for Christian youth today. The good news for every young man or woman willing to accept Christ's mastery is that life can be made tremendously worthwhile, no matter what the odds. Personality cannot attain its fulness and humanity cannot achieve its destiny apart from Christ. Standing in the midst of the world's confusion, Christ's clear voice calls to today's youth, "Follow me, and I will make you to become . . ."

The gospel must be communicated to adults. There is no other word but "must" as time runs out. Adulthood is the last chance for the determination of eternal destiny with or without Christ. These men and women nearing the end of life are forever lost if the end overtakes them before they have found salvation. Sin is an eternal guilt. There is no possibility that an unforgiven sinner, dying apart from Christ's atonement, can be accepted in a holy heaven. Should one such sinner be admitted, heaven would lose its character and become hell. The choice having been made and the gulf having been fixed, there is nothing in revelation or reason to indicate that the course of guilt and its punishment may be reversed.

This conviction of the lostness of men, and of the urgency of bringing them to Christ before it was too late, characterized the great evangelists of the period of the Great Awakening. It is said that

Whitefield seldom got through a sermon without weeping. Criticized, he replied, "You blame me for weeping, but how can I help it when you will not weep for yourselves, though your souls are upon the verge of destruction and, for all I know, you are hearing your last sermon!"

The gospel message for adults is so simple and forthright that we are liable to miss it. Two mighty words comprise the requirement: "Repent!" and "Believe!" The implications of these twin experiences are far reaching and of course need explication, but they should not be cluttered up with theological extras and sectarian arguments. W. E. Sangster sums up the offer of new life in Christ in the five "universals" which constitute the heart of the saving message: "(1) All men need this life. (2) All men may have this life. (3) All men who have this life know that they have it. (4) All men must witness to its possession. (5) All men must press on to perfection." [4] Supporting these universals with the Scriptures, the witness to the unsaved adult must press for assent and then for decision and commitment. Justifying the urgency of the appeal is the realization that the time is short!

Evangelism is an art, and the effective practice of evangelism calls for artists. We dare not be blunderers and bunglers as we deal with the most precious of all stuff—life now and forever. Commonplace exhortations to accept "the plan of salvation," ignoring individual differences, would be unworthy of us as disciples of the supreme Artist, Jesus Christ.

Effective Preparation for Evangelism

Evangelism is a divinely given and divinely led enterprise. It represents the initiative of God in Christ seeking man. Yet God uses human instrumentality in the quest. As in all other activities where God and man are in partnership, on the human side preparation is required. God supplies the conditions for the growing of a crop, but the farmer must prepare and till the soil. Homrighausen well says that the Word and Spirit of God are sovereign, and the evangelist, whether parent, teacher, preacher, or friend, is only a witness and a servant. A part of God's electing grace is his choice of men to "prepare the way of the Lord" by grading up the low places and grading down the high places, by straightening the crooked and smoothing the rough ways, so that Christ may come into human experience, as a consequence of which "all flesh shall see the salvation of God" (Luke 3:4–6). The results of evangelism are more abundant when thorough preparation has been made.

The pastor should prepare himself. Alexander Maclaren, prince of preachers, was fond of saying, "It is equally as important for the preacher to prepare himself as his sermon." A pastor to whom evangelism is perfunctory will be a roadblock on the highway. He should read and reread the Gospels. He should meditate on the lostness of men without Christ. His should be the compassion of his Lord when he saw the crowds, "harassed and helpless, like sheep without a shepherd." Not often will a church rise above the compassion and concern of its pastor. Preparation must begin with him.

The church should be prepared. When Jesus saw the unreached multitude and wept over their spiritual destitution, he announced his plan. Initially, when the disciples gathered about him, he commanded them to pray "the Lord of the harvest to send out laborers into his harvest." Then he called the little group closer to him and prepared them to go first to the "lost sheep of the house of Israel." As they went, they were to preach, saying, "The kingdom of heaven is at hand!" Observe with what meticulous care Jesus instructed these men whom he sent out as his witnesses (Matt. 9 and 10). Later, with the same thoroughness, he prepared and sent out seventy others, two by two, to prepare for his coming after them "into every town and place" (Luke 10).

A prepared church is one in which there are devoted members who are willing to be instructed that they may go both to those within and without the church with the message of Christ. The pastor may make a beginning by going with a member; this member, having learned the simple secret of witnessing, may then be paired with another member. Each of these in turn may find a teammate until the number grows to "seventy also" and beyond.

Those to be reached should be prepared. Is it necessary that the sower's seeds be wasted because of falling on the beaten pathway, or on rocky ground, or among thorns? Why not prepare the soil so that all the seeds will bring forth fruitfully? There are many ways in which the soil of the community may be prepared for sowing of the gospel seeds. Publicity may be wisely and skilfully employed. Andrew W. Blackwood makes much of the use of the midweek prayer meetings for the inspiration and instruction of these "personal workers." Jasper N. Barnette shows with simplicity and clarity how a church may use a well-organized Sunday school to prepare the community for perennial evangelism.[6] Much space is devoted by George E. Sweazey to explicit directions for the enlistment of the church organizations in creating community good will toward evangelism.[7]

Harry C. Munro insists that the most effective preparation of those to be reached for the purposes of evangelism is through the establishment of friendly contacts by members of the church who constitute its organized groups, particularly Sunday school classes and departments. "The surest way to open the life of an unchurched person to those divine forces which actually bring about the life-changing commitment experience is to surround him with loving, congenial, concerned Christian fellowship. The church's evangelistic potential is the vast resources of Christian fellowship that exists, primarily, in these groups." [8]

Thorough preparation should be made for special evangelistic meetings. The announcement of a "revival," with a sign in front of the church, will not necessarily bring revival. Special seasons of evangelistic effort continue to be blessed of God. As a rule, however, this blessing is contingent upon preparation. Months in advance the date should be fixed. Experience indicates that two weeks of continuous preaching and personal witnessing bring the richest fruitage. If assistance to the pastor is needed in the person of an evangelist and leader of the music, such assistance should be engaged long in advance.

Committees should be appointed somewhat as follows: (1) publicity committee, to provide for widespread and attractive announcement of the meeting through all available media; (2) visitation committee, to enlist and train those who will visit in the homes and do personal work; (3) prospects committee, to supervise the taking of a religious census and in other ways obtain the names of unsaved and unchurched persons; (4) committee on home prayer meetings, to arrange for a meeting to be held in every neighborhood for prayer and Bible study; (6) music committee, to seek to provide attractive and appropriate music for the occasion; (7) age-group committees, to be especially responsible to work with the several departments and agencies of the church, enlisting their interest and services; (8) hospitality committee, to be careful to see that visitors are greeted and the congregation made comfortable; (9) finance committee, to look after the payment of all expenses without incurring the suspicion of commercialism. Not every church will need all of these committees, but in most situations each will perform a useful function.

The union evangelistic meeting, held in a tabernacle or civic auditorium and sponsored jointly by all the denominations, tends to overlook the local churches and often fails to make a transfer of loyalty from the big meeting to the churches of the community. The values of co-operation and of local church loyalty are better combined in the simultaneous evangelistic crusade, according to which co-operating churches join in preparing for and conducting a campaign to awaken and revive Christians and win to Christ and the churches the unsaved of the total community.

Conserving the Fruits of Evangelism

An objection sometimes made to evangelism as practiced in America is that it seeks quick and spectacular results that are not lasting. That there is a measure of truth in the charge cannot be denied. The answer is that evangelism should be preceded and followed by Christian education. Evangelism assumes that something more than Christian nurture is needed in the confrontation of the individual with Christ and his claims. Christian education assumes that something more than an appeal for decision and commitment is needed if evangelism is to be according to Christ. Further, a counselor-counselee relation is sought between the Christian witness and the person sought for Christ. Difficulties are brought out into the open, problems are shared, and barriers are removed through the process of uninhibited discussion.

Following reception into the church, new members need special attention. Many churches operate continually a new members' class, into which are brought for instruction and discussion all who have been admitted to membership. In this class their difficulties may be cleared up, their understanding of the church and its program clarified, their place of usefulness as active members determined. Thus they are assimilated into the church body, with a happy sense of belonging and with adequate resources made available for the practice of the Christianity which they have professed. Like the man in the parable of Jesus, they build their house on the rock, so that when the rain falls and the floods come and the winds blow and beat upon that house, it will not fall, because it has been founded on the rock (Matt. 7:24–27).

Chapter **XIV**

Ministries Are Extended
Co-operatively

$\mathbf{A}$T THE BEGINNING of human existence, according to the Genesis record, the Lord said, "It is not good that man should be alone." If it was not good then, it is impossible now. Whereas in the nineteenth century the value of the individual in his solitariness was stressed, in the twentieth century the emphasis is on groups. We are now being told that the group shapes the individual rather than the other way around. The disasters of our century largely have been group-caused. Our advances likewise have been made together, not by lonely leaders.

In our American culture persons are so linked with persons, families with families, communities with communities, states with states, and nations with nations that Paul's word is especially applicable: "None of us lives to himself, and none of us dies to himself" (Rom. 14:7). The group provides the hospital in which most of us are born. The group furnishes the school in which we are educated. The group makes possible the basic necessities of life. The group surrounds us with tangible and intangible means of security. The group protects us in illness and in the declining years. At length we are buried from an undertaker's establishment in a community cemetery.

Our troubles likewise are largely group-made. Forces of organized evil prey upon our children. Political cliques threaten our liberties. Crime may not pay the individual, but when it is organized and powerful, it may yield rich profits. Murder is wrong when committed privately, but mass murder in the form of war may be glorified. A single religious fanatic may be institutionalized, but a whole body of religious fanatics may form a denomination. Displaced persons and dislocated families grasp at opportunities to recover the sense of belonging. As L. C. Marsh has aptly phrased it, "By the crowd they have been broken; by the crowd shall they be healed."

The movement toward group-mindedness constitutes a new threat to the Christian view of the primacy of the individual. In a penetrating article entitled "This Belonging World," Frederick Wyatt, head of the psychological clinic of the University of Michigan, writes:

One could say that the individual in the modern mass society is loosely a part of many groups, but belongs to no one in particular. For just that reason he has pursued the founding and joining of voluntary groups as nobody else before him in history: groups with all kinds of goals, spirituality and recreation, learning and economic protection. . . . A common motive seems to underlie all these efforts at belonging: the loneliness and the isolation of the individual. If he was compelled in the past to belong, and nobody asked him whether he really wanted to belong to this or that, he is now troubled by *not* belonging anywhere in particular and by the basic fact that nobody will tell him precisely what he should be and do.[1]

Some Difficulties Involved in Working Together

Granting that people in today's world must co-operate, since complete isolation is impossible, many questions arise as to how independence and interdependence are to be maintained. Distinctives of polity and practice are deep rooted in the older religious bodies. Some distinctives are fundamental, some are incidental, but because they are religious they are invested with sacredness. Most of the younger bodies have been formed about a leader or leaders who have taken a part of truth and given it significance as if it were the whole. Sometimes the center of the system is a recovered biblical doctrine or practice that has been neglected; sometimes the center takes the form of an alleged new revelation, claimed through prophetic disclosure or psychic insight.

It is often a question as to whether doctrines produce practices or practices are justified by the formulation of supporting doctrines. Obviously, the processes are closely related. At any rate, it is seldom easy to distinguish between basic doctrines and their practical implementation. Thus almost all efforts at amalgamation of religious bodies—even though they possess close kinship—run into the difficulty as to what shall be retained as fundamental and what shall be given up as incidental.

Difficulties of co-operation may be observed on the intrachurch level. Within a local church body there may be those who represent different family backgrounds, different social and cultural standards, different political and economic loyalties. Separateness may be stronger than togetherness. When decisions must be made, groups within the church may be found cohering, not about the principle involved, but about common interests. Unless this tendency to fragmentation is overcome by the power of a higher interest and loyalty, the church becomes divided. The same problem of "splintering" often is found among churches of the same persuasion. Denominations that have split into fragments usually have not done so because certain churches were orthodox while others were heretical, but because family patterns of behavior brought cleavage that was justified, usually after the fact, by resort to proof texts and creedal statement. Conversely, denominational groups have been more closely knit together because polity and practice gave them a secure sense of belonging. It seems to be a matter of what is important in the persons' beliefs.

On the interchurch level, efforts looking toward unity run into even greater difficulties. No matter how convincing the arguments of the leaders that there should be one flock, one Shepherd, the stubborn fact remains that many prefer to stay in the flock where they have always belonged and where they feel at home. This "at-homeness" may be grounded in intelligent commitment to New Testament truth, or it may be due in large measure to the sense of security which comes from familiarity. "Be it ever so humble, there's no place like home." Abandoning one's church home for another like church involves a more painful wrench than many are willing to endure. Within the separate body there may also be a feeling of significance which is threatened when the family becomes too large. Unity of spirit must precede organic unity if it is to be satisfying and lasting. Ecumenicity may be the goal, but harmonious and effective working together, without compulsion, must be practiced first.

The Dynamics of Shared Agreements

The group psychotherapy movement provides a successful approach to unity through shared interests. Dr. Edward Trudeau, a New York physician, contracted tuberculosis and decided to go to the Adirondack Mountains for rest and quiet. His experience led him to found a sanitarium for the open-air treatment of the disease. In 1894 Trudeau opened the Saranac Laboratory, to which he invited victims of the white plague, principally from the working classes. Much of the amazing curative result of this treatment was attributed to the happy atmosphere of the place, where patients with common problems and interests shared with and encouraged one another.

Dr. J. H. Pratt, of Boston, extended the theory and practice of group therapy to the treatment of various chronic diseases. A clinic in Boston took up the idea and employed it in the treatment of undernourished children, establishing the fact that malnutrition was often psychically rather than physically conditioned. A variation of group psychotherapy was developed by Dr. J. L. Merino, a Viennese physician, which he labeled "psychodrama." Problem children were led to act out their problems spontaneously, as a consequence of which both they and their counselors achieved insights which led to solutions. Dr. L. C. Marsh, a psychiatrist working with mental patients, experimented successfully with the technique of the religious revival in the treatment of patients in a large mental hospital. The principle has had wide and successful application by Alcoholics Anonymous, an organization through which victims of alcohol share their experiences and give to one another mutual support.

The unity and healing power of shared interests characterized the New Testament churches. We see this reflected in the account of the Christian community at Jerusalem as recorded by Luke: "And day by day, attending the temple together and breaking bread in their homes, they partook of food with glad and generous hearts, praising God and having favor with all the people. And the Lord added to their number day by day those who were being saved" (Acts 2:46–47). They shared their goods because they shared their agreements, and in the sharing of their goods and their agreements they found health and happiness. Making specific these shared agreements, Paul declared that "there is one body and one Spirit, just as you were called to the one hope that belongs to your call, one Lord, one faith, one baptism, one God and Father of us all, who is above all and through all and in all" (Eph. 4:4–6). Here is an unsurpassed statement of the ideal of vital Christian unity. Consciously and unconsciously, deliberately and incidentally, the members of a church or of a church body or of differing church bodies should make much of their shared agreements. In this kind of sharing true unity grows. In such an atmosphere the unbeliever is more easily led to saving faith, the immature grows in spiritual stature, moral illnesses are prevented and cured, and social and physical health is promoted. Visitors and members alike sense the warm spiritual atmosphere.

The Dynamics of Shared Differences

Unity results from shared agreements; it no less derives from shared differences. Psychiatry and the art of counseling illustrate this correlative approach. The physician and the counselor assume that the difficulty of the upset or distressed person probably arises from some form of repression. Unacceptable impulses, hidden desires, inhibited emotions, feelings of animosity and guilt, unable to find a channel of expression, go underground, so to speak, and emerge as aberrations and perversions. Much of the art of the psychiatrist or counselor lies in his ability to get these hidden and often unconscious impulses and emotions out into the open. The very process of verbalizing and sharing differences often has an amazingly therapeutic value.

In working with others, we sometimes have mistakenly assumed that full agreement is essential. A hush-hush policy may be adopted concerning any ideas or feelings that may not be acceptable to all. Often we have been surprised and even shocked when, in spite of all efforts to keep the peace through continual insistence on agreement, disagreement explodes into conflict. Suppression often makes the explosion all the more violent, and even among Christian people its forms may be almost unbelievably vindictive and unreasonable. Sins against fellow Christians, in the name of religion, have been committed that brought shame even to non-Christians. Historic evidence is found in the Roman Catholic inquisition of the fifteenth and sixteenth centuries, especially the tortures of Christians charged with heresy. Even this ruthless crushing of dissent did not bring about uniformity but rather spread dissension until it reached the proportion of revolution.

A basic principle of co-operation is respect for contrary opinion. That dissent is irritating need not be denied. The temptation to crush it is human. Sometimes its elimination is sought by disregarding it, by ridiculing it, by ruling it out of order, or penalizing it, or disposing of it through majority vote. If the differences are real and are held with honest conviction, no matter how mistaken, they would better be recognized and dealt with respectfully. Historically, minorities have been right as often as majorities. Those with dissenting opinions may make an even more valuable contribution to a church or to church groups than traditional yes men. The sharing of differences should not mean the encouragement of contention but should be a procedure in Christian spirit that teaches persons to reconcile honest differences and work together for the best interests of the church and for the advancement of the cause of Christ.

The Study of the Community as a Joint Enterprise

A church may view the community as means and itself as end, or it may view itself as means and the community as end. Both viewpoints are legitimate. A community can exist without a church, but it is obvious that a church cannot exist without a community. Jesus recognized that at least two or three must be gathered together in his name if they are to be identified with him as his body. A church itself is a community, and its business is to create community. Christian community is characterized by like-minded service of people seeking the common weal in the name and for the sake of Christ. After vital unity has been achieved, the next step is the systematic study of the community. Here is something that can be done together that would scarcely be possible if attempted by one church alone.

There is a difference between a geographical area where people live and a community. Community demands interlinkages, activities or institutions which bring people together because of common concern—the city hall or courthouse, the public school, the trading center, the place of amusement or recreation, the business or industrial enterprise, the church or synagogue, and the like. The more there are of such interlinkages, voluntarily and satisfyingly formed, the greater is the sense of community. Community is hindered by lines of cleavage, such as racial segregation, social exclusiveness, economic class distinctions, political prejudices, religious antagonisms. Community may be all but destroyed by exploitation of the weak by the strong, by delinquency and criminality, by the failure of law enforcement, and by the degeneracy of public institution.

The good community is developed and sustained through informed public opinion in the service of a constructive plan of needed improvement. Seeking this objective, a group of public-spirited men and women representing the several churches may come together and plan the community survey. Committees will form and elect for study such areas as (1) community history and spirit; (2) church affiliation and possibilities; (3) physical boundaries and subdivisions; (4) population facts and figures; (5) social and family conditions; (6) economic factors; (7) constructive and destructive forces. Each group will prepare a survey schedule, consisting of a number of definite items concerning which information is to be sought, together with a list of sources from which the information may be secured. Care should be taken that data secured be definite, objective, accurate, adequate, valuable. Hearsay should be ruled out and subjective opinion carefully tested. The returns should have sufficient spread to give them validity. Facts should be tabulated, classified, criticized, interpreted. Such questions as these should be answered: What have we learned about the community? What have we discovered that is satisfying and commendable? What have we discovered that needs changing? How can we conserve what is right and change what is wrong?

Working Together for Institutional Betterment

The life of a community is conditioned in large measure by its public institutions. A third form of united action is found in seeking to know and to improve the institutions of the community. How may the churches serve the community in this area of united effort? An answer is found in the plan operated for many years at Louisville, Kentucky, under the guidance and inspiration of a devoted citizen and churchman, Mr. George Stoll. A businessman with large interests and heavy responsibilities, this layman early in life committed himself to the ideal of Christian stewardship, not just of money, but of time and talent and influence. Becoming concerned about the institutions of the city and county, he secured the inclusion of the Committee on Institutions as one of the standing committees of the Louisville Council of Churches. Bringing together a group of carefully selected pastors and laymen, he proposed a study of the institutions of the area as a first step. One inviolable rule was agreed upon: no unfavorable public criticism of management of institutions. Four objectives were set up: (1) awareness—that this is a needed, worthwhile, and continuous undertaking; (2) support—of good men doing good things; (3) service—to persons in institutions; (4) prevention—as forestalling need and better than cure. Soon there were some two hundred churchmen serving on the several subcommittees and quietly but effectively bringing about improvements in the institutions of the community.

As a result, such needs as these were discovered and supplied in just one institution: (1) the need for a balanced diet of appetizing food: the committee obtained the service of a prominent cafeteria manager; (2) the need for increased farm production: the committee obtained the advice of a successful farmer; (3) the need for greater appeal and significance of the institution's paper: the committee supported a survey by an Associated Press writer; (4) the need for inmate education evaluation: the committee secured suggestions from a college professor of adult education; (5) the need for religious counseling and services: the committee obtained a fulltime, clinically trained chaplain.

In this plan, survey studies to secure the facts are followed by discussion and interpretation. Books are read and reviewed, bringing to the problem light from reliable literature. Panel discussions are arranged, with informed resource persons called on to answer questions and to express expert opinion. Heads of institutions or other public officials are invited to tell of their purposes and problems and to indicate how Christian citizens can help them do a better job. Careful planning is of course necessary on the part of a steering committee. A competent secretary is needed to keep minutes, send out notices, and record history as it is made. Since some expense is involved, there is a treasurer to handle funds and to serve as business manager. Essential publicity is handled by a competent committee, which are careful to see that it is always constructive and never negative or sensational. With the growth of the project, a general secretary was employed to give full time to stimulation, supervision, promotion.

Communities vary so widely that no one plan of community service can be followed in detail. Yet there is scarcely a community, large or small, simple or complex, in which the broad outlines of the pattern suggested cannot be followed if the churches have a mind to work together.

Working Together for the Improvement of Community Morals

Community conditions make for morality or immorality. Back of juvenile delinquency and crime are causes, and for many of these causes there is community responsibility. True, the remedy for sin lies not in creating a social utopia. But temptation and exploitation can be minimized, positive inducements to right living can be provided, and a community can be made a fit place in which to live and rear children. What is sought for the privileged is equally desirable for the underprivileged. Churches working together may bring about moral improvement.

Abject poverty and mendicancy can be eliminated. There is no longer good reason why any segment of the population should live below the level of decent subsistence. It is not enough to provide first aid for the down-and-out, although this is an important immediate expedient. Causes of grinding poverty can be sought and found in ignorance, which may be corrected through education. Chronic unemployment may be overcome by organized effort of business and industry. Physical handicaps may be alleviated by such enterprises as Good Will Industries. Overcompetition, creating sweatshop conditions, may be effectively dealt with by conscientious labor unions and by Christian appeal to the conscience of employers. Attitudes of helplessness and hopelessness may be transformed by vital Christian experience and hope sustained through Christian friendship. Mendicancy, once sanctioned by the church as a mark of holiness but now recognized as a social disease, may be eliminated as beggars are restored to self-respect and given a chance to earn their living.

Housing conditions may be improved. Slums were long taken for granted as a necessary evil in the city. In the latter part of the nineteenth and the early part of the twentieth centuries conditions in these blighted areas were indescribably bad. Men like Walter Rauschenbush began to prod the Christian conscience, and this conscience began to assert itself in protest against the inhuman conditions under which great numbers were compelled to live. Slum clearance projects were undertaken, first on a small scale and then as a vast government undertaking. Results have been little less than amazing, as evidenced by the low-rent housing areas which have sprung up in almost every town and city of the United States. Much remains to be done, and churches working together can continue to promote the elimination of slums and the provision of decent housing for families in low-income brackets.

Another aspect of the movement for better housing is the unprecedented spread of home ownership. Until fairly recently it was assumed as a matter of course that the majority of working people would rent their places of residence. In most communities this has become the exception, the majority of such families now living in houses which they are paying for rather than renting. The fact of home ownership makes for family stability and should be given every possible encouragement by the churches. A house, however, does not necessarily make a home. The encouragement and promotion of Christian family life thus becomes another major opportunity and responsibility of the churches. Working together, they may seek to realize the ideal of "every child in a Christian home."

Delinquency and crime may be abated. The juvenile court was a step far in advance of the traditional treatment of the youthful offender as a criminal. Yet such a court, at its best, can only seek to repair the damage after it has been done. Far more important is intelligent prevention of delinquency. Disturbed by the increase of youthful misbehavior, vandalism, criminality, communities have instituted research to get at the causes. Blame has been laid on the movies, comic books, taverns, dance halls, and a variety of questionable sources from which juveniles get their ideas and the lowering of their ideals. With due allowance for the bad influence of such sources, competent opinion focuses on two main causes of delinquency—unwholesome family conditions and lack of wholesome outlets for youthful impulses and energies. Churches working together can find the answer to both of these needs.

Crime in America is so commonplace that it has almost ceased to be news. From delinquency to crime is but a step which is often taken swiftly and all but inevitably. Crime is the end product of sin, and sin is a condition of the inner life. Prisons are not the answer to crime. The rehabilitation of the criminal should be the objective of the penal institution, but practical wardens know that they get most of their prisoners too late. Preachers preach against sin and crime, teachers teach that sin and crime do not pay, churches take their stand against sin and crime, but not often is there an aggressive effort made to reach and convert the sinner and thus prevent his criminality.

Churches working together can go boldly to those who operate such crime-producing businesses as distilleries and breweries, gambling houses, stores selling unwholesome literature, places of immorality, with the Christian appeal to cease, but even more earnestly with the appeal to repent of sin and believe on the Lord Jesus Christ. To those whose sins have found them out and who are suffering even the loss of liberty, the churches may go with the Christian message of hope. Such united expression of Christian concern would do much to prevent and cure delinquency and crime.

Community consciousness may be elevated. "Chicago," a sociologist once remarked, "is a state of mind." According to psychosomatics, one's state of mind is a highly important factor in one's bodily functioning. This truth about a person holds good for a community. What is its state of mind? How did it get that way? What difference does it make? Can anything be done about it?

The state of mind of a community, whether it be that of a neighborhood, a nation, or the world, may be one of suspicion, jealousy, fear, antagonism, self-seeking; or it may be one of confidence, courage, tolerance, peace, generosity. A community as well as an individual may be sick-minded or healthy-minded. Between the extreme may be all shades of mental attitudes, taking first one and then the other direction. Many factors influence the soundness or unsoundness of the community's consciousness. History plays a part, for good and bad attitudes have a way of perpetuating themselves. Leadership plays a part, for the community's mind reflects the personality of dominating figures in its past and present. The schools play a part, for they pass on the inheritance, for weal or woe. The media of communication play a part, for what the people read, listen to, and view largely determines how they think and feel and who they are.

The intangible called "community consciousness" makes momentous difference in the conduct and character of the people. It makes a difference as to whether the people are static or progressive, narrow or broad in their sympathies, provincial or ecumenical in their outlook, stingy or generous in their giving, egocentric or altruistic with their possessions, individualistic or co-operative in their relations, pagan or Christian in their religious beliefs and prac- tices. If one institution above another were singled out as being chiefly responsible for the character of community consciousness, it probably would be organized religion as represented by the churches. If in the main the churches have represented the spirit of suspicion, jealousy, contention, narrowness, unco-operativeness, the chances are that the community will reflect this spirit. If, on the other hand, the churches reflect the spirit of confidence, considerate- ness, charity, conviction, co-operation, with the golden cord of love binding all these together, community consciousness will likely partake of this spirit.

Working Together for the Improvement of Education

In the race between education and disaster, education may prove to be on disaster's side. It is significant that the educated, not the uneducated, have brought to the world its greatest disasters and now present its most serious threat. At the beginning of the twentieth century Germany was the best educated nation on the globe. Yet within the space of half a century Germany precipitated the two most devastating wars of history. The inventions that possess potentiality for the wiping out of civilization are the products, not of savages, but of highly educated scientists. The leadership of men like Hitler, Mussolini, and Stalin was made possible not by mass ignorance, but mass miseducation. From the family through the community to the nation and the world, the kind of education to which the multitudes are exposed will determine human destiny.

About three hundred years ago a tremendous shift was made in Western education—from the church to the state. This has been called the greatest revolution of modern times. In the early period of the democratic revolution the shift was made and accepted with en- thusiasm. It seemed to the founding fathers of the United States of America a guarantee of the safety and perpetuity of democracy. Subsequent events have not justified their fond hope. Schools wholly apart from the church, education separated from religion, have produced a secularism that has weakened both the national and the social structure. Thoughtful citizens and professional educators join in their concern for some arrangement that will preserve the principle of separation of church and state, yet provide for the inculcation of moral and spiritual values.

Several courses are open to the churches as they work together on this problem. They may establish competing parochial school systems, bidding frankly for the patronage of their communicants. While such schools no doubt render a service, carried to a logical conclusion they would weaken the public school system to its probable decay and collapse and divide communities into rival camps by religious bodies seeking support for their schools. Viewed in the large, this is not the democratic way.

Another approach is that of co-operation of the public school authorities with the churches in a parallel program of weekday religious education. Since by Supreme Court ruling this kind of church-centered instruction cannot be given in tax-supported school buildings, the resort is to released time, when students are assembled in churches of their choice or in a community building and instructed by teachers satisfactory both to the school board and to the church committee. If this plan is not practicable, individual churches or church groups may provide for weekday religious instruction during the free time of the students—recess, after school hours, on Saturdays, or during vacation.

Another approach is that of frank demand by the community that faculty and staff of the public schools be chosen from Christian men and women whose contagious Christian personality and vital Christian living will serve to infuse the classrooms with a religious spirit even though the Bible or related religious subjects are not taught formally. The assumption is that the community which supports its public schools has the right to make requirements of those whom it employs as its teachers and that this right may well include satisfactory evidence of Christian attitudes and character. Religious tests, in the sectarian sense, would of course be avoided, but the quality of the teacher's Christian life would be considered as significant for success in meeting the community's needs.

A final approach may be considered—that of informal co-operation between the public schools and the church schools. According to this plan, regular conferences will be held between representatives of the public schools and representatives of the churches who are seeking to teach the same children. Realizing that they have many interests in common, they will discuss ways and means of mutual reinforcement, not organically but informally. The public schools, for instance, could encourage attendance on the Sunday schools; those responsible for the Sunday schools could magnify the work and importance of their fellow teachers in the public schools. Public school teachers could aid in lifting the educational level of the church schools; church school teachers could aid in the religious motivation of public school education. "Go to Sunday School Week" may be featured regularly in the public school; "Teacher Appreciation Week" likewise may be featured in the church schools. Working thus together, the school and the church can break down the sharp line between secular and religious education, to the enrichment of both.

In no one of the approaches suggested, nor others which may be developed, will be found all the answers to this supremely important problem of so combining education and religion as to secure all the values of each. Perhaps a combination superior to any one plan can be worked out. Obviously, a matter of such vast importance and significance as this challenges the churches to work together to find a plan that will best meet the community's need.

Working Together for World Community

Wendell Willkie wrote of "one world." Statesmanlike scientists are saying, "One world or none." John Wesley said, "The world is my parish." Jesus Christ said, "The field is the world." No church or group of churches today dare think of community in less than world terms. If Christianity is not adequate for the whole world, it is not adequate for any part of it. Our plans and projects demand a world vision and possible application.

Transportation has made the world a neighborhood, and communication has made it a whispering gallery. Barriers of space and time have been all but annihilated. Yet the paradox is that with the removal of these physical barriers intangible barriers have been erected that separate men from one another as never before. The iron curtain of Russia has proved less penetrable than the ancient Chinese wall or the more recent Maginot Line. The commission of Christ to go into all the world and preach the gospel to the whole creation was never physically easier nor psychologically more difficult than now. No church singlehanded can hope to obey fully

Christ's marching orders. So tremendous is the undertaking that it calls for the most effective possible co-operation.

Churches can work together in the study of missions. No longer may we think of "home missions" and "foreign missions" as if they were in separate categories. Every local church field is a mission field. Its field of missions extends in ever enlarging concentric circles from its immediate community through its regional community to its national community and then into "regions beyond." Through tracts, books, pictures, the needs and opportunities of these fields may be made appealing and real. A school of missions may bring the whole constituency, by age groups, to the church for a fascinating study of missions. Ignorance of the missionary enterprise is inexcusable. The churches together may launch and conduct a vast campaign of missionary education.

Churches can establish missions. Almost every church of any considerable size can establish and maintain a mission in its own territory. Much has been said of overchurched communities, but too little has been said of communities that are underchurched. Wherever there is a group of people who are not within reach of a church or whom social or other barriers prevent attending the church within reach, a branch Sunday school or mission is indicated. Its operation should be largely the responsibility of lay people of the church. Distance should not hinder the establishment of such missions. A church anywhere in the United States may be responsible for a mission in South America, or the Orient, or Africa, or Europe, or an island of the sea. Mission boards will gladly arrange for the establishment and support of such missions under satisfactory guarantees of continued support.

Churches can give to missions. Too long the missionary enterprise has received the leftovers of the churches' giving. Between the financial support of missions and of the military establishment, the former is vastly more important for world peace and security. We might have been spared the waste of billions spent for war had we given a fraction of this amount for missions. Working together, the churches can arouse their members to a realization of the urgency of the missionary crisis and the necessity of large-scale giving of money with which to meet it. No investment will yield richer returns, now and forever, than money invested in the missionary enterprise.

Churches can pray for missions. The missionary undertaking, to make of the whole world a Christian community, is so overwhelmingly great and difficult that its only hope of success lies in the linking of human effort with divine power. The connection is made through prayer. Over and over Jesus made this clear. Even of himself he said, "The Son can do nothing of his own accord, but only what he sees the Father doing" (John 5:19). To his disciples he said, "He who believes in me will also do the works that I do; and greater works than these will he do, because I go to the Father." Then he added this tremendous promise: "Whatever you ask in my name, I will do it, that the Father may be glorified in the Son" (John 14:12–13). The claiming of this promise is the surest guarantee of missionary success. Paul states the heart of the matter when he says, "For we are fellow workmen for God" (1 Cor. 3:9).

Notes

Grateful acknowledgement is made to publishers for permission to use quotations from the following sources:

Chapter I

1. Alexander Roberts and James Donaldson (eds.), revised and arranged by A. Cleveland Cox, *The Ante-Nicene Fathers* (New York: Charles Scribner's Sons, 1925), V, 374–75.

2. James Bryce, *The American Commonwealth* (New York: The Macmillan Company, 1906), II, 570–73.

3. E. Y. Mullins, *The Axioms of Religion* (Philadelphia: Judson Press, 1908), p. 185.

4. S. L. Greenslade, *The Church and the Social Order* (London: S.C.M. Press, Ltd., 1948), p. 121.

5. George Laird Hunt, *Rediscovering the Church* (New York: Association Press, 1956), p. 16.

6. Emil Brunner, *The Misunderstanding of the Church* (Philadelphia: Westminster Press, 1953), p. 113.

Chapter II

1. Alexander Roberts and James Donaldson (eds.), revised and arranged by A. Cleveland Cox, *The Ante-Nicene Fathers* (New York: Charles Scribner's Sons, 1925), V, 374–75.

2. *Ibid.*, p. 381.

3. John F. Sullivan, *The Visible Church* (New York: Kennedy & Sons, 1920), pp. 59–70.

Chapter III

1. Richard Baxter, *The Reformed Pastor* (Grand Rapids, Mich.: Zondervan Publishing House, 1955), p. 162.

2. *Ibid.*, pp. 169–70.

3. Theodore L. Cuyler, *How to Be a Pastor* (New York: Baker and Taylor Company, 1890), p. 20.

4. A. W. Blackwood, *Pastoral Work* (Philadelphia: Westminster Press, 1945), p. 13.

5. J. H. Jowett, *The Preacher, His Life and Work* (Garden City, N. Y.: Doubleday, Doran & Company, Inc., 1928), p. 193.

6. Arthur W. Hewitt, *Highland Shepherds* (Chicago: Willett, Clark & Company, 1939), p. 183.

7. Ordway Tead, *The Art of Administration* (New York: McGraw-Hill Book Company, Inc., 1951), p. 6.

8. *Ibid.*

9. *Ibid.*, p. 208.

10. Karen Horney, *Our Inner Conflicts* (New York: W. W. Norton & Company, Inc., 1945), p. 42.

11. Henry Clay Lindgren, *The Art of Human Relations* (New York: Hermitage House, Inc., 1953).

12. Robert C. Walton, *The Gathered Community* (London: Carey Press, 1944), p. 33.

13. Paul E. Johnson, *Personality and Religion* (New York: Abingdon Press, 1957), p. 108.

Chapter IV

1. W. E. Martin, N. Gross, and J. D. Darley, "Leaders, Followers, and Isolates in Small Groups," *Journal of Abnormal Psychology*, pp. 838–42.

2. C. A. Gibb, "The Principles and Traits of Leadership," *Journal of Abnormal Social Psychology*, pp. 267–84. Quoted by Thomas Gordon, *Group-Centered Leadership* (New York: Houghton Mifflin Company, 1955), p. 49.

3. Ordway Tead, *The Art of Leadership* (New York: McGraw-Hill Book Company, Inc., 1935), pp. 82–114.

4. Supervisor's Manual, State Farm Insurance Company, Birmingham, Alabama, Office.

5. *Ibid.*

6. Paul F. Douglass, *The Group Workshop Way in the Church* (New York: Association Press, 1956), p. 7.

7. Wesley Shrader, "Our Troubled Sunday Schools," *Life*, XLII (Feb. 11, 1957), 100–114.

8. Douglass, *op. cit.*, pp. 14–15.

9. Henry Clay Lindgren, *The Art of Human Relations* (New York: Hermitage House, Inc., 1953), p. 135.

Chapter V

1. Willard A. Pleuthner, *Building Up Your Congregation* (New York: Wilcox & Elliott Company, 1950).

2. Ordway Tead, *The Art of Administration* (New York: McGraw-Hill Book Company, Inc., 1951), p. 166.

Chapter VI

1. William H. Whyte, Jr., *The Organization Man,* (New York: Simon and Schuster, 1956), p. 13.

2. Charles Ellwood, *The Social Problem* (New York: The Macmillan Company, 1915), pp. 13–14.

Chapter VIII

1. W. R. McNutt, *Worship in the Churches* (Philadelphia: Judson Press, 1941), p. 29.

Chapter IX

1. Joseph N. Ashton, *Music in Worship* (Boston: Pilgrim Press, 1943), p. 6.

2. Karl Pomeroy Harrington, *Education in Church Music* (New York: The Century Company).

3. Cassie Burk, Virginia Meierhoffer, and Claude A. Phillips, *America's Musical Heritage* (Chicago: Laidlaw Brothers, Publishers, 1942), p. 17.

4. Carl Emil Seashore, *The Psychology of Musical Talent* (Boston: Silver, Burdett and Co., 1919).

Chapter X

1. Paul H. Conrad, *The Chief Steward in the Local Church,* a pamphlet published by the Department of Stewardship of the Council on Finance and Promotion of the American Baptist Convention.

2. John M. Versteeg, *When Christ Controls* (New York: Abingdon-Cokesbury Press, 1943), p. 35.

3. "The Forward Program of Church Finance of Southern Baptists," Executive Committee, Southern Baptist Convention, Nashville, Tennessee.

4. John C. Bennett, *Christian Values and Economic Life* (New York: Harper & Brothers, 1954), p. 256.

Chapter XI

1. Seward Hiltner, *Preface to Pastoral Theology* (New York: Abingdon-Cokesbury Press, 1958), p. 25.

2. Otis Rice, "Pastor-Parishioner," *Pastoral Psychology,* June, 1952.

3. Paul E. Johnson, *Psychology of Pastoral Care* (New York: Abingdon-Cokesbury Press, 1953), p. 73.

4. Carroll A. Wise, *Pastoral Counseling: Its Theory and Practice* (New York: Harper & Brothers, 1951), p. 141.

5. Georgia Harkness, *Be Still and Know* (New York: Abingdon Press, 1953), p. 15.

Chapter XII

1. Toyohiko Kagawa, *Love, the Law of Life* (St. Paul, Minn.: Macalester Park Publishing Company, 1951).

2. Anders Nygren, *Agape and Eros* (Philadelphia: Westminster Press, 1953), p. 170.

3. Smiley Blanton, *Love or Perish* (New York: Simon and Schuster, 1956), p. 12.

4. Karl Menninger, *Love Against Hate* (New York: Harcourt, Brace and Company, 1942), pp. 5–6.

5. Erick Fromm, *The Art of Loving* (New York: Harper & Brothers, 1956), pp. 22–23.

6. J. B. Phillips, *Appointment with God* (New York: The Macmillan Company, 1954), pp. 72–73.

7. Paul E. Johnson, *Christian Love* (New York: Abingdon-Cokesbury Press, 1951), pp. 149–50.

Chapter XIII

1. George E. Sweazey, *Effective Evangelism* (New York: Harper & Brothers, 1953), p. 19.

2. Elmer G. Homrighausen, *Choose Ye This Day* (Philadelphia: Westminster Press, 1943), p. 59.

3. See Mary Alice Jones' "Tell Me" Series.

4. W. E. Sangster, *Let Me Commend* (New York: Abingdon-Cokesbury Press, 1948), p. 37.

5. Andrew W. Blackwood, *Evangelism in the Home Church* (New York: Abingdon-Cokesbury Press, 1942).

6. J. N. Barnette, *The Pull of the People* (Nashville: Convention Press, 1956).

7. George E. Sweazey, *op. cit.*

8. Harry C. Munro, *Fellowship Evangelism* (St. Louis: Bethany Press, 1951).

Chapter XIV

1. Frederick Wyatt, "This Belonging World," *Adult Leadership*, III, No. 2, 9.

For Further Reading

Chapter I

ABELL, A. I. *The Urban Impact upon American Protestantism.* Cambridge: Harvard University Press, 1943.

BRUNNER, EMIL. *The Misunderstanding of the Church.* Philadelphia: Westminster Press, 1953.

DOBBINS, G. S. *Building Better Churches.* Nashville: Broadman Press, 1947.

———. *The Churchbook.* Nashville: Broadman Press, 1951.

FLEW, R. NEWTON. *Jesus and His Church.* Nashville: Abingdon Press, 1938.

GREENSLADE, S. L. *The Church and the Social Order.* London: S.C.M. Press, Ltd., 1948.

HERSHBERGER, GUY F. (ed.). *The Recovery of the Anabaptist Vision.* Scottdale, Penn.: Herald Press, 1957.

HUDSON, WINTHROP S. *The Great Tradition of the American Churches.* New York: Harper & Brothers, 1953.

HUNT, GEORGE LAIRD. *Rediscovering the Church.* New York: Association Press, 1956.

LAVIK, JOHN R. *The Christian Church in a Secularized World.* Minneapolis: Augsburg Publishing House, 1952.

MANSON, T. W. *The Church's Ministry.* London: Carter and Stone, Ltd., 1948.

MILLER, PARK HAYES. *The New Testament Church.* Philadelphia: Westminster Press, 1926.

MULLINS, E. Y. *The Axioms of Religion.* Philadelphia: Judson Press, 1908.

NICHOLS, J. H. *Democracy and the Churches.* New York: Association Press, 1951.

SPERRY, W. L. *Religion in America.* New York: The Macmillan Company, 1946.

SWEET, W. W. *Story of Religion in America.* New York: Harper & Brothers, 1950.

WALTON, ROBERT C. *The Gathered Community.* London: Carey Press, 1944.

Chapter II

BEVAN, EDWYN ROBERT, and SINGER, CHARLES (eds.). *The Legacy of Israel.* London: Clarendon Press, 1927.

220

HEWITT, A. W. *Highland Shepherds*. Chicago: Willet, Clark and Co., 1939.

LUCKHARDT, MILDRED CORELL. *The Church Through the Ages*. New York: Association Press, 1951.

MCNEILL, JOHN T. *A History of the Cure of Souls*. New York: Harper & Brothers, 1951.

MOORE, GEORGE FOOT. *Judaism in the First Century of the Christian Era*. Cambridge: Harvard University Press, 1930.

NIEBUHR, H. RICHARD, and WILLIAMS, DANIEL D., *The Ministry in Historical Perspectives*. New York: Harper & Brothers, 1956.

OATES, WAYNE E. *The Christian Pastor*. Philadelphia: Westminster Press, 1951.

STREETER, B. H. *The Primitive Church*. New York: The Macmillan Company, 1929.

Chapter III

BURSK, E. C. *How to Increase Executive Effectiveness*. Boston: Harvard University Press, 1954.

HORNEY, KAREN. *Our Inner Conflicts*. New York: W. W. Horton & Co., Inc., 1945.

JOHNSON, PAUL E. *Personality and Religion*. New York: Abingdon Press, 1957.

LANDIS, JAMES M. *The Administrative Process*. New Haven: Yale University Press, 1938.

LINDGREN, HENRY CLAY. *The Art of Human Relations*. New York: Hermitage House, Inc., 1953.

OSBORN, A. F. *Applied Imagination*. New York: Charles Scribner's Sons, 1953.

SHELTON, ORMAN L. *The Church Functioning Effectively*. St. Louis: Christian Board of Publications, 1946.

SIMON, HERBERT A. *Administrative Behavior*. New York: The Macmillan Company, 1947.

SMITH, HOWARD. *Developing Your Executive Ability*. New York: McGraw-Hill Book Co., 1946.

TEAD, ORDWAY. *Democratic Administration*. New York: Association Press, 1945.

———. *The Art of Administration*. New York: Association Press, 1935.

WHITE, LEONARD D. *New Horizons in Public Administration*. University of Alabama Press, 1946.

Chapter IV

BLACKWOOD, ANDREW W. *Pastoral Leadership*. New York: Abingdon-Cokesbury Press, 1949.

BUSCH, HENRY M. *Leadership in Group Work*. New York: Association Press, 1934.

222 A MINISTERING CHURCH

DOUGLASS, PAUL F. *The Group Workshop Way in the Church.* New York: Association Press, 1956.

FRANK, LAWRENCE K. *How to Be a Modern Leader.* New York: Association Press, 1954.

GORDON, THOMAS. *Group-Centered Leadership.* New York: Houghton-Mifflin Co., 1955.

GWYNN, PRICE H., JR. *Leadership Education in the Local Church.* Philadelphia: Westminster Press, 1952.

HARAL, STEWARD. *Public Relations for Churches.* New York: Abingdon-Cokesbury Press, 1945.

HUTCHINSON, ELLIOT. *How to Think Creatively.* New York: Abingdon-Cokesbury Press, 1941.

JENNINGS, H. H. *Leadership and Isolation.* New York: Longmans, Green and Co., 1950.

KNOWLES, MALCOLM S., and ULDA F. *How to Develop Better Leaders.* New York: Association Press, 1955.

MILHOUSE, PAUL W. *Enlisting and Developing Church Leaders.* Anderson, Ind.: Warner Brothers, 1946.

PRESTON, MARY FRANCES. *Christian Leadership.* Nashville: Sunday School Board of the Southern Baptist Convention, 1934.

TEAD, ORDWAY. *The Art of Leadership.* New York: McGraw-Hill Book Co., 1935.

WOLSELEY, R. E. *Interpreting the Church Through Press and Radio.* Philadelphia: Muhlenburg Press, 1951.

Chapter V

CROSSLAND, WELDON. *A Planned Program for the Church Year.* New York: Abingdon-Cokesbury Press, 1951.

DOBBINS, GAINES S. *Can a Religious Democracy Survive?* New York: Fleming H. Revell Co., 1941.

HUSS, JOHN. *Ideas for a Successful Pastorate.* Grand Rapids, Mich.: Zondervan Publishing House, 1953.

LAVIK, JOHN R. *The Christian Church in a Secularized World.* Minneapolis: Augsburg Publishing House, 1952.

LEIFFER, MURRAY H. *The Effective City Church.* New York: Abingdon-Cokesbury Press, 1956.

LUCKHARDT, MILDRED CORNELL. *The Church Through the Ages.* New York: Association Press, 1951.

McNEILL, JOHN T. *A History of the Cure of Souls.* New York: Harper & Brothers, 1951.

MEIBURG, ALBERT L. (ed.). *Laymen at Work.* New York: Abingdon-Cokesbury Press, 1956.

NELSON, J. ROBERT. *The Realm of Redemption.* Chicago: Wilcox & Follett Co., 1951.

NISBET, ROBERT A. *The Quest for Community.* New York: Oxford University Press, 1953.

OXNAM, G. BROMLEY. *The Church and Contemporary Change.* New York: The Macmillan Company, 1950.

PLEUTHNER, WILLARD A. *Building up Your Congregation.* Chicago: Wilcox & Follett Co., 1953.

POWELL, SIDNEY W. *Where Are the People?* New York: Abingdon-Cokesbury Press, 1942.

————. *Where Are the Converts?* Nashville: Broadman Press, 1958.

Chapter VI

BLACKWOOD, CAROLYN P. *The Pastor's Wife.* Philadelphia: Westminster Press, 1951.

LEIFFER, MURRAY H. *City and Church in Transition.* Chicago: Willet, Clark and Co., 1938.

SCHUETTE, WALTER E. *The Minister's Personal Guide.* New York: Harper & Brothers, 1953.

SMITH, ROCKWELL C. *Rural Church Administration.* New York: Abingdon-Cokesbury Press, 1953.

STEWARD, GEORGE. *The Church.* New York: Association Press, 1938.

WHYTE, WILLIAM H., JR. *The Organization Man.* Garden City, N. Y.: Doubleday & Co., Inc., 1956.

Chapter VII

BRUBACHER, JOHN S. *A History of the Problems of Education.* New York: McGraw-Hill Book Co., 1947.

CARRIER, BLANCHE. *Free to Grow.* New York: Harper & Brothers, 1951.

DOBBINS, GAINES S. *Building a Better Sunday School Through the Officers and Teachers' Meeting.* Nashville: Convention Press, 1957.

EAVEY, C. B. *The Art of Effective Teaching.* Grand Rapids, Mich.: Zondervan Publishing House, 1953.

FLAKE, ARTHUR. *Building a Standard Sunday School.* Nashville: Sunday School Board of the Southern Baptist Convention, 1954.

EDGE, FINDLEY. *Teaching for Results.* Nashville: Broadman Press, 1956.

HIGHET, GILBERT. *The Art of Teaching.* New York: Alfred A. Knopf, 1950.

LIGON, ERNEST M. *Dimensions of Character.* New York: The Macmillan Company, 1956.

LAMBDIN, J. E. *Building a Church Training Program.* Nashville: Sunday School Board of the Southern Baptist Convention, 1946.

MCKIBBON, FRANK M. *Christian Education Through the Church.* New York: Abingdon-Cokesbury Press, 1947.

MURSELL, JAMES L. *Successful Teaching.* New York: McGraw-Hill Book Co., 1954.

SMART, JAMES D. *The Teaching Ministry of the Church.* Philadelphia: Westminster Press, 1954.

SULLIVAN, JAMES L. *Your Life and Your Church.* Nashville: Broadman Press, 1951.

VIETH, PAUL H. *How to Teach in the Church School.* Philadelphia: Westminster Press, 1935.
————. *The Church and Christian Education.* St. Louis: Bethany Press, 1947.

Chapter VIII

BLACKWOOD, A. W. *The Fine Art of Public Worship.* New York: Abingdon-Cokesbury Press, 1929.
BOWMAN, CLARICE. *Restoring Worship.* New York: Abingdon-Cokesbury Press, 1951.
COFFIN, HENRY SLOAN. *The Public Worship of God.* Philadelphia: Western Press, 1946.
DOBBINS, GAINES S. *Deepening the Spiritual Life.* Nashville: Sunday School Board of the Southern Baptist Convention, 1954.
HARKNESS, GEORGIA E. *The Religious Life.* New York: Association Press, 1957.
HEIMSATH, CHARLES H. *The Genius of Public Worship.* New York: Charles Scribner's Sons, 1944.
McDORMAND, THOMAS B. *The Art of Building Worship Services.* Nashville: Broadman Press, 1946.
PLEUTHNER, WILLARD A. *More Power for Your Church.* New York: Farrar, Straws, and Young, 1952.
SMITH, ROBERT S. *The Art of Group Worship.* New York: Abingdon Press, 1938.
SPERRY, W. L. *Reality in Worship.* New York: The Macmillan Company, 1925.
UNDERHILL, EVELYN. *Worship.* New York: Harper & Brothers, 1937.
VOGT, VAN OGDEN. *Art and Religion.* New Haven: Yale University Press, 1921.

Chapter IX

ASHTON, JOSEPH H. *Music in Worship.* Boston: Pilgrim Press, 1943.
BOWMAN, CLARICE. *Restoring Worship.* New York: Abingdon-Cokesbury Press, 1951.
FERGUSON, DONALD N. *A History of Musical Thought.* London: Routledge & Kegan, 1948.
MININGER, RUTH. *Growing a Musical Church.* Nashville: Broadman Press, 1947.
THOMAS, EDITH LOVELL. *Music in Christian Education.* New York: Abingdon-Cokesbury Press, 1953.

Chapter X

BENNETT, JOHN C., BOWEN, HOWARD R., BROWN, WILLIAM A., JR., and OXNAM, G. BROMLEY. *Christian Values and Economic Life.* New York: Harper & Brothers, 1954.
COX, OLIVER C. *The Foundations of Capitalism.* New York: Philosophical Library, 1959.

ELLIS, H. W. *Christian Stewardship and Church Finance*. Grand Rapids, Mich.: Zondervan Publishing House, 1953.

HARWOOD, E. C. *Useful Economics*. Great Barrington, Mass.: American Institute of Economic Research, 1956.

HEILBRONER, ROBERT L. *The Worldly Philosophers*. New York: Simon and Schuster, 1953.

KAUFMAN, MILO. *The Challenge of Christian Stewardship*. Scottdale, Penn.: Herald Press, 1955.

KNIGHT, FRANK H., and MERRIAM, THORNTON W. *The Economic Order and Religion*. New York: Harper & Brothers, 1945.

LONG, ROSWELL C. *Stewardship Parables of Jesus*. New York: Abingdon-Cokesbury Press, 1947.

McCALL, DUKE K. *God's Hurry*. Nashville: Broadman Press, 1949.

MUNCY, W. L., JR. *Fellowship with God Through Christian Stewardship*. Kansas City: Central Seminary Press, 1949.

ROLSTON, HOLMES. *Stewardship in the New Testament*. Richmond: John Knox Press, 1946.

VERSTEEG, JOHN M. *When Christ Controls*. New York: Abingdon-Cokesbury Press, 1943.

Chapter XI

BONNELL, JOHN S. *Psychology for Pastor and People*. New York: Harper & Brothers, 1948.

BUBER, MARTIN. *I and Thou*. Edinburgh: T. & T. Clark, 1937.

———. *Between Man and Man*. New York: The Macmillan Company, 1954.

HILTNER, SEWARD. *Pastoral Counseling*. New York: Abingdon-Cokesbury Press, 1949.

———. *Preface to Pastoral Theology*. New York: Abingdon-Cokesbury Press, 1958.

HORNEY, KAREN. *Our Inner Conflicts*. New York: W. W. Horton & Co., 1945.

———. *Psychology of Pastoral Care*. New York: Abingdon-Cokesbury Press, 1953.

KLAPMAN, J. W. *Group Psychotherapy*. New York: Greene & Stratton, 1947.

MENNINGER, KARL. *Love Against Hate*. New York: Harcourt, Brace & Co., 1942.

MUDD, EMILY HARTSHORNE. *The Practice of Marriage Counseling*. New York: Association Press, 1951.

MURPHY, GARDNER. *Personality*. New York: Harper & Brothers, 1947.

OATES, WAYNE E. *The Bible in Pastoral Care*. Philadelphia: Westminster Press, 1953.

ROGERS, CARL R. *Counseling and Psychotherapy*. New York: Houghton Mifflin Co., 1942.

SHERILL, LEWIS JOSEPH. *The Struggle of the Soul*. New York: The Macmillan Company, 1954.

SLAVSON, S. R. *The Practice of Group Therapy.* New York: International Universities Press, 1947.

SULLIVAN, DOROTHEA F. *Readings in Group Work.* New York: Association Press, 1952.

WALLIS, CHARLES L. *The Funeral Encyclopedia.* New York: Harper & Brothers, 1953.

Chapter XII

BLANTON, SMILEY. *Love or Perish.* New York: Simon and Schuster, 1956.

DOBBINS, GAINES S. *Winning the Children.* Nashville: Broadman Press, 1953.

FROMM, ERICH. *The Art of Loving.* New York: Harper & Brothers, 1956.

GOULOOZE, WILLIAM. *Victory Over Suffering.* Grand Rapids, Mich.: Baker Book House, 1949.

JENKINS, GLADYS G., SCHACTER, HELEN, and BAUER, WILLIAM W. *These are Your Children.* Chicago: Scott, Foresman and Co., 1953.

JOHNSON, PAUL E. *Christian Love.* New York: Abingdon-Cokesbury Press, 1957.

JONES, MARY ALICE. *The Faith of Our Children.* New York: Abingdon-Cokesbury Press, 1943.

————. *Guiding Children in Christian Growth.* New York: Abingdon-Cokesbury Press, 1949.

MORRISON, JAMES D. *Minister's Service Book.* New York: Willet, Clark & Co., 1937.

NYGREN, ANDERS. *Agape and Eros.* New York: The Macmillan Company, 1953.

PHILLIPS, J. B. *Appointment with God.* London: Epworth Press, 1954.

TRENT, ROBBIE. *Your Child and God.* New York: Harper & Brothers, 1941.

Chapter XIII

BARLOW, WALTER. *God So Loved.* New York: Fleming H. Revell, 1952.

BARNETTE, J. N. *The Place of the Sunday School in Evangelism.* Nashville: Sunday School Board of the Southern Baptist Convention, 1945.

BLACKWOOD, ANDREW W. *Evangelism in the Home Church.* New York: Abingdon-Cokesbury Press, 1942.

CALKINS, RAYMOND. *How Jesus Dealt with Men.* New York: Abingdon-Cokesbury Press, 1942.

CHASTAIN, THERON. *We Can Win Others.* Philadelphia: Judson Press, 1953.

DOBBINS, GAINES S. *Evangelism According to Christ.* Nashville: Broadman Press, 1949.

————. *Winning the Children.* Nashville: Broadman Press, 1953.

LEAVELL, ROLAND Q. *Evangelism: Christ's Imperative Commission.* Nashville: Broadman Press, 1951.

MATTHEWS, C. E. *Every Christian's Job.* Nashville: Convention Press, 1951.

MORGAN, G. CAMPBELL. *The Great Physician.* New York: Fleming H. Revell, 1937.

MUNRO, HARRY C. *Fellowship Evangelism Through Church Groups.* St. Louis: Bethany Press, 1951.

PHILLIPS, J. B. *Making Men Whole.* New York: The Macmillan Company, 1953.

POWELL, SIDNEY W. *Toward the Great Awakening.* New York: Abingdon-Cokesbury Press, 1949.

SWEAZEY, GEORGE E. *Effective Evangelism.* New York: Fleming H. Revell, 1948.

SWEET, W. W. *Revivalism in America.* New York: Charles Scribner's Sons, 1945.

WHITESELL, FARIS D. *Basic New Testament Evangelism.* Grand Rapids, Mich.: Zondervan Publishing House, 1949.

Chapter XIV

BRUNNER, EMIL. *The Misunderstanding of the Church.* Philadelphia: Westminster Press, 1953.

DOBBINS, GAINES S. *Can a Spiritual Democracy Survive?* New York: Fleming H. Revell Co., 1941.

KLAPMAN, J. W. *Group Psychotherapy.* New York: Grune & Stratton, 1947.

JONES, MAXWELL. *The Therapeutic Community.* New York: Basic Books, Inc., 1953.

LEIGH, ROBERT D. *Group Leadership.* New York: W. W. Norton & Co., 1936.

NEVE, J. F. *Churches and Sects of Christendom.* Blair, Neb.: Lutheran Publishing House, 1944.

NEWBIGEN, JAMES E. L. *That All May Be One.* New York: Association Press, 1952.

SCHAVER, J. L. *The Polity of the Churches.* Grand Rapids, Mich.: Kregel, 1947.

SLAVSON, S. R. *The Practice of Group Therapy.* New York: International Universities Press, 1947.

STUBER, S. I. *How We Got Our Denominations.* New York: Association Press, 1948.

SULLIVAN, DOROTHEA F. *Readings in Group Work.* New York: Association Press, 1952.

VAN DUSEN, HENRY P. *World Christianity.* New York: Abingdon-Cokesbury Press, 1947.

Index

Date Due

STRICT RESERVE	10/15 10:00	5/5 9am	SEP 5 '72
OCT 23	10-29-9am	5/16 9am	JAN 9 '73
2 00	10-30-9am		NOV 29 '73
10 00	11-11-9am	5-18-9am	APR 9 '74
10:00	11-17 9AM	5/9 9am	DEC 5 '75
7:00	11-24-9am	5/23 9AM	OCT 16 '78
10:00	12-2 9am	5/24 9AM	JAN 5 '77
8:30 10/30	NOV 3 '65	1/18 9AM	MAR 11 '80
8:30 11/5	3/13 9am	2/9 9am	
8:30 1/7	3/3 9am	2/13 9am	
3 00	3/7 9am	2/14 9am	
10:30	3/9 9AM	2/27 9am	
9:00 9/23	3/15 9AM	AUG 2 '68	
9 am 9-29	3/16 9am	FEB 3 '69	
9AM 9/30	4/6 9am	JAN 20 '69	
11:00	4/7 9am	APR 22 '70	
10-7 9am	4/20 9AM	APR 30 '70	
10-14 9am	4/27 9AM	JUN 2 '72	

PRINTED IN U. S. A.